Praise for *A Widower's Lament*

"Ronald Rittgers has given us access to a remarkable early Lutheran document of Christian piety as a new widower copes with loss and grief and looks for consolation. This sensitive and deeply personal book will enrich any reader, whether an interested non-specialist or, thanks to the superb introduction and copious annotations, a professional historian."

—Kenneth G. Appold, James Hastings Nichols Professor of Reformation History, Princeton Theological Seminary, and author of *The Reformation: A Brief History*

"This edition will be of great interest to scholars working on the history of religion, gender, and the emotions and to general readers alike. Ron Rittgers introduces and translates a unique and hitherto unknown source on spousal grief in the early modern period, in which Johann Christoph Oelhafen sought to come to terms with his overwhelming emotions in an outpouring of poetry and prayers preserved for his children and posterity in a beautiful manuscript. His sense of bereavement and desperate search for consolation in his faith still resonate today."

—Jill Bepler, Herzog August Bibliothek, Wolfenbüttel, Germany

"Rittgers brings the religious and emotional world of a seventeenth-century Lutheran layman to life in unparalleled depth through his eloquent translation and illuminating introduction and annotations. We see how the widowed Johann Christoph Oelhafen poured out his deep grief after the death of his beloved wife, Anna Maria, and how he wove together prayers and hymns, scripture and sacraments to strengthen his faith and find consolation. Rittgers's presentation will challenge and enlighten historians of the late Reformation even as Oelhafen's meditations may still inspire twenty-first-century believers."

—Christopher Boyd Brown, Boston University

"It is a truly extraordinary and rare moment when a scholar uncovers a source that opens a window onto the inner lives of those who experienced the convulsive religious changes and daily vicissitudes of the early modern world. Ron Rittgers expertly and sensitively guides us through the pain and joy of a grieving husband and father who sought and found comfort in a resilient faith expressed in deeply moving prayer and poetry. It is one of those precious moments when a vanished culture reappears in all its harsh and redemptive realities."

—Bruce Gordon, Yale University

"Prof. Rittgers has discovered and brought to light evidence of profound lay Lutheran piety from the late Reformation. In this deft translation, Oelhafen's laments echo across the centuries, reminding us that sorrow and lament are deeply human and deeply Christian. Rittgers provides comprehensive introductory comments that situate this piece in its personal, religious, social, and cultural context. Extensive explanatory notes deepen understanding of the text. He also considers how this document relates to today's scholarly discussions of the late Reformation. Rittgers has provided remarkable insight into how a Lutheran layman understood and practiced his faith in the early seventeenth century."

—Mary Jane Haemig, professor emerita of church history, Luther Seminary

"Ron Rittgers brings Oelhafen's grief and tenacious faith to life with his dexterous translation and insightful notes. In this four-hundred-year-old book of meditations, we travel with a new widower through his first year of widowhood. Amid the agony of loss, he turns to God to seek comfort for his distress, drawing both on the religious resources of his Lutheran faith and on his own creativity. Rittgers is a trustworthy guide to Oelhafen's world and heart."

—Anna M. Johnson, Garrett-Evangelical Theological Seminary

"Ronald Rittgers's discovery, editing, and interpretation of this devotional diary of Johann Christoph Oelhafen open exciting new vistas into the practice of piety in the wake of Luther's Reformation. The volume provides unique, multifaceted insights into the religious life of laity in the early modern period. Rittgers's careful, perceptive reading of the text draws readers into the devout mindset of the seventeenth century through his sensitive engagement with Oelhafen's devotional meditations. Rittgers's firm editorial eye and hand enhance readers' ability to glean a rich harvest of historical context and theological significance of this singular ego-document."

—Robert Kolb, professor of systematic theology emeritus,
Concordia Seminary, Saint Louis, Missouri

"In his superb introduction and translation, Ronald Rittgers makes an uncommon record of early modern emotional response available to a general audience. The work provides an important source for those exploring the history of emotions and the way that an early modern layman sought consolation in scriptural texts, prayers, songs, and even contemporary religious works. It also provides a fascinating exploration of the universality of grief for the spouse left behind.

"Widower Johann Christoph Oelhafen, a Lutheran lawyer in Nuremberg, spent a year writing out daily meditations on his often-personalized responses to scriptural texts, prayers, songs, and even contemporary religious works as he navigated work and family life. The text itself is particularly poignant when Oelhafen expresses his loss and suffering and seeks consolation as he faces difficult moments such as giving away his deceased wife's clothes and marking his first wedding anniversary after her death."

—Marjorie Elizabeth Plummer, University of Arizona

"Ron Rittgers's elegant translation of this moving lament offers a rare glimpse into the emotional life and loss of an early modern Christian layman. *A Widower's Lament* explores grief and the timeless search for meaning in the face of the devastating loss of a loved one. A work of poetry, prayer, and poignant emotional reflection, it will make fresh and welcome reading for courses on early modern Europe, the history of Christianity, family history, and indeed any and all seeking consolation in the face of death, grief, and loss."

—Tom Robisheaux, professor of history
and Bass Fellow at Duke University

"'You have torn away a piece of my heart.' With these words addressed to God, Johann Christoph Oelhafen begins his personal meditations in the wake of the death of his dear wife. This astounding manuscript of a seventeenth-century widower from Nuremberg, here turned into fine English prose with useful annotations, represents Prof. Rittgers's splendid gift not only to students of late-Reformation studies but also to those interested in Christian lament and grief as experienced by a Christian layperson and expressed in a Lutheran key. As one who was widowed, I can vouch for just how moving this evangelical voice from the past is and how contemporary are the feelings he expresses. Providing proper historical and theological perspective through the kind of erudite introduction we have come to expect from him, Prof. Rittgers offers the reader a remarkable slice of early modern life, very much in the tradition of his mentor Steven Ozment's *Magdalena and Balthasar*. This book is a must-read for all those interested in the Reformation and its continuing history, for those looking for insight into the spiritual life of lay Christians, and for those who today confront deep loss and sorrow."

—Timothy J. Wengert, Emeritus Ministerium of Pennsylvania
Professor of Reformation History and the Lutheran Confessions,
United Lutheran Seminary, Philadelphia

"Not only does Ron Rittgers's labor of love provide a window into the theology and piety of early Reformation society; it may also be a mirror by which we meditate on our own experiences of loss, grief, and lament.

Do we hold God responsible when death takes our beloved ones? If we do, can we count on any blessings for the future? How do we describe our participation in a creation marked by death and other tragedies? Are we willing to offer full expression of our own losses, or do we imagine that such expressions threaten to uncover a failure of faithful hope or the threat of the onset of debilitating depression?

"Anyone who has sought to console someone who is grieving knows how precarious life can seem. We hope that our friend will not be lost to grief, so we are tempted to counter their lament with a platitudinous gospel.

"Rittgers's translation of the *Pious Meditations* of Johann Christoph Oelhafen provides us an example of one who fully gives himself over to his grief as a way of doing theology that both acknowledges the gravity of the loss and prepares him for continuing life."

—Jim Wetzstein, university pastor, Valparaiso University

"In a work deeply reminiscent of Lewis's *A Grief Observed*, we gain here a glimpse into early modern piety, the family, indeed love, refracted through the lens of loss, pain, and grief. Rittgers has done scholars of early modernity, cultural history, the history of the family, and emotions a great service in finding, then translating this deeply personal story of one man's loss."

—David Whitford, Baylor University

"The *Pious Meditations* of Johann Christoph Oelhafen are an extraordinary find and an invaluable contribution to late-Reformation studies. Yet this collection of a widower's prayers and meditations is even more tremendous as a witness to deep marital love and still deeper Christian faith, a witness that spans the centuries. Rittgers has introduced us not just to an object of study, but to a long-lost friend and saint."

—Rev. Dr. Sarah Hinlicky Wilson,
Tokyo Lutheran Church, Tokyo, Japan;
Institute for Ecumenical Research, Strasbourg, France

A Widower's Lament

A Widower's Lament

The *Pious Meditations* of Johann Christoph Oelhafen

Translated with an Introduction, Notes, and Epilogue
by

Ronald K. Rittgers

Fortress Press
Minneapolis

A WIDOWER'S LAMENT

The *Pious Meditations* of Johann Christoph Oelhafen

Front, back, and inside flap images: *Gebetbuch des Hans Christoph Oelhafen*, GNM-HA, Familienarchiv von Oelhafen, Rep. II/80, Nr. 32 (no page or folio numbers). Translation of inscription on front cover: "AMICO, beloved darling, where have you gone?"

Cover design by Laurie Ingram

Print ISBN: 978-1-5064-2480-4
eBook ISBN: 978-1-5064-2481-1

For John B. Toews, mentor and friend

Contents

Figures

Acknowledgments

This project has been a labor of love. I can still remember being absolutely astonished by the extraordinary richness of Johann Christoph Oelhafen's *Pious Meditations* when I first discovered the source in the Historical Archive of the German National Museum in Nürnberg a number of years ago. I could not wait to get to the archive each day to read further in this remarkable work. I had never had a source captivate me the way this one did (and still does). After some investigation, I learned that no scholar had ever worked on it, or perhaps even seen it, and this certainly added to my excitement—I had made an original find! But the work's novelty was not its primary appeal for me; its admirable artistry, haunting candor, and inspiring faith were what drew me to the archive afresh each day. As with all research projects, my own life context also shaped my early engagement with this source. There I was, a husband of fifteen years and a father with three young sons, reading the *Pious Meditations* of a man whose beloved wife of eighteen years had died, leaving him a devastated widower with eight surviving children. Scholarly objectivity eluded me at times. Oelhafen's tragedy struck very close to home, forcing me to confront my own vulnerability to a similar misfortune, as unthinkable as it was (and is) for me. (Thankfully, I have never suffered this misfortune.) In time, some semblance of a scholarly perspective returned, but my own life context has continued to influence my relationship with the *Pious Meditations*, something I trust has enriched this book rather than somehow compromised it.

So many people have helped bring this project to fruition, and I owe many debts of gratitude. I wish to thank the following staff members of the Historical Archive of the German National Museum for their assistance during my visits to the archive and their prompt replies to requests for digital copies of sources essential to my research: Evelyn Bujnoch-Zink, Melanie Haase, Susanne Irmer, Kati Kohl, Laura Metz, Dr. Matthias

Nuding, and Frederike Uhl. For additional research assistance, I am grateful to Dr. Peter Fleischmann and Elke Löffler of the Nürnberg Staatsarchiv, Carolin Gillich of the Nürnberg Stadtbibliothek, Sigrid Kohlmann of the manuscript library of the Friedrich-Alexander Universität Erlangen-Nürnberg, and Elfi Heider of the Johannisfriedhof in Nürnberg. A host of scholars have provided helpful advice on matters historical, theological, linguistic, musical, artistic, poetic, and psychological: Jacob Baum, Christopher Close, Mary Jane Haemig, Joseph Herl, Allannah Karas, Konrad Klek, Craig Koslofsky, Robin Leaver, Anna Linton, Benjamin Mayes, Mitchell Merback, Cornelia Niekus Moore, James Nelson, Dennis Ngien, Anselm Schubert, Jeffrey Smith, Jonathan Strom, Anne Thayer, Maura Wade, Mark and Chelsea Wagenaar, and Thomas Gerhard Wilhelmi. The research support I have received from holding the Erich Markel Chair in German Reformation Studies at Valparaiso University has been essential in enabling me to complete this project. It has been an honor holding this chair, and I remain grateful for it, even as I now look forward to taking up a new chair at Duke Divinity School.

I am grateful to Fortress Press for taking on this project. I have wanted it to reach both scholarly and church audiences, and Fortress has been an ideal publisher for it. Thanks go to Michael Gibson for first showing interest in the project and to Will Bergkamp for expertly shepherding me along the way to its completion. Laurie Ingram took great care in creating the cover design. The staff at Scribe Inc. have been prompt, professional, and responsive—everything one could ask of a book production crew.

Three scholars deserve special acknowledgment: Jill Bepler, Bob Kolb, and Wolfgang Mährle. They each read a draft of the work in full; offered helpful commentary on the introduction and epilogue, including many bibliographical suggestions; and most important, provided absolutely invaluable help with the translation of the *Pious Meditations*. I am deeply grateful to them for their sacrifice of time and talent on my behalf. Their considerable expertise, generosity, and patience have enriched this project immeasurably and have saved it from many false steps. The ones that undoubtedly remain are entirely my own.

My dear friends in Nürnberg, Norbert (Nobbi) and Kristina (Didda) Knöll, invited my family into their home a number of times as I worked on this project, on one occasion offering up their own living space to us for nearly three months as they retreated to the basement. I owe them an immense debt of gratitude for their generosity and hospitality.

Alec, Blake, and Owen, my three sons, have been part of this project from the beginning. As they have grown older, they have frequently asked, "How's the Oelhafen book coming along, Dad? When will it be finished?" I am delighted that I can finally respond, "Jungs, es ist endlich fertig!" As on no other project, my wife, Jana, has been on my mind and in my heart through every hour of this one. Working on this widower's lament has made me all the more grateful for our life together and for the true treasure I have in her. This project simply would not have been possible without her love, support, and sacrifice—without her.

My dissertation adviser, the late Steven Ozment, introduced me to archival research and provided me with the necessary paleographical and detective skills to carry it out. I remain grateful to him for these gifts along with many others he imparted to me. His own work on autobiographical sources, many of them from Nürnberg, has motivated and informed this project in numerous ways.

I have dedicated this book to John B. Toews, my mentor at Regent College in Vancouver, British Columbia, where I completed my master's degree. John taught me always to look for the human in the past, to try to engage human experience—especially individual human experience—as fully as I am able in my work as a historian. He taught me that the study of humanity—of what it means to be human—is the proper purview of the historian. He also taught me to bring my own humanity to bear on this important task, mostly by the way he did so in his teaching, research, and life. I hope this book reflects at least something of what I learned from my mentor and friend so many years ago.

Ronald K. Rittgers
Eastertide 2021
Valparaiso, Indiana

Abbreviations

ADB *Allgemeine Deutsche Biographie* (accessible via DB).

BC Robert Kolb and Timothy J. Wengert, eds. *The Book of Concord: The Confessions of the Evangelical Lutheran Church*. Minneapolis: Fortress Press, 2000.

Biedermann Johann Gottfried Biedermann. *Geschlechtsregister des Hochadelichen Patriciats zu Nürnberg*. Bayreuth, 1748.

DB *Deutsche Biographie*. Available online at https://www.deutsche-biographie.de.

Diarium Johann Christoph Oelhafen. *Diarium Familiare et Domesticum Generale*, GNM-HA, Familienarchiv von Oelhafen, Rep. II/80, Nr. 36.

EKO *Die evangelischen Kirchenordnungen des XVI Jahrhunderts*, 24 vols. (vols. 1–4 edited by Emil Sehling; vols. 5/1–7/2[1], 8, and 11–15 edited by the Institut für evangelisches Kirchenrecht der Evangelischen Kirche in Deutschland; vols. 7/2[2], 9–10, and 16–24 edited by Gottfried Seebaß and Eike Wolgast on behalf of the Heidelberger Akademie der Wissenschaften). Leipzig: O. R. Riesland, 1902–1913 (vols. 1–4); Tübingen: J. C. B. Mohr (Paul Siebeck), 1955 (vols. 6/1–24).

ELW *Evangelical Lutheran Worship*. Minneapolis: Augsburg Fortress Press, 2006.

FWB *Frühneuhochdeutsches Wörterbuch*. Available online at https://fwb-online.de.

GNM-HA Germanisches Nationalmuseum, Historisches Archiv (Nürnberg, Germany).

Grimm *Deutsches Wörterbuch von Jacob und Wilhelm Grimm*. 16 vols. in 32 fascicles. Leipzig: Verlag von S Hirzel, 1854–1961. Quellenverzeichnis, 1971. Available online at https://tinyurl.com/4jzy3k7c.

HAB Herzog August Bibliothek, Wolfenbüttel, Germany.

LSB *Lutheran Service Book*. St. Louis, MO: Concordia, 2006.

LW *Luther's Works*, American ed. Edited by J. Pelikan and H. T. Lehmann. 55 vols. St. Louis, MO: Concordia; Philadelphia: Fortress Press, 1955–. (Concordia is currently expanding this collection. The general editors for vols. 56–82 are Christopher Boyd Brown and Benjamin T. G. Mayes. Vols. 56–60, 67–69, 73, and 75–79 have been published.)

MRM Robert Lippe, ed. *Missale Romanum Mediolani, 1474*, vol. 1, Text. London: Harrison & Sons, 1899. Available at https://tinyurl.com/48z47xey.

NDB *Neue Deutsche Biographie* (accessible via DB).

NStaatsA Nürnberg Staatsarchiv.

NStadtA Nürnberg Stadtarchiv.

Pious Meditations Johann Christoph Oelhafen. *Piae Meditationes Vidvitatis, Ehev, Moestissimae* (*Pious Meditations on the, Alas, Most Sorrowful Bereavement*). Archive title: *Gebetbuch des Hans Christoph Oelhafen*, GNM-HA, Familienarchiv von Oelhafen, Rep. II/80, Nr. 32.

SM *Speciale missarum secundum chorum Bambergensum*. Bamberg, 1506 (VD16 5557). Available at https://tinyurl.com/yuxeyutc.

SN *Stadtlexikon Nürnberg* (accessible via https://www.nuernberg.de/internet/stadtarchiv/ [Online-Recherche])

TRE Gerhard Krause and Gerhard Müller, eds. *Theologische Realenzyklopädie, Studienausgabe*. 36 vols. Berlin and New York: Walter de Gruyter, 1993–2006.

UEN Universitätsbibliothek Erlangen-Nürnberg (the library of the Friedrich-Alexander-University Erlangen-Nürnberg). Online catalog: https://ub.fau.de.

VD16 *Verzeichnis der im deutschen Sprachbereich erschienenen Drucke des 16. Jahrhunderts*. Edited by the Bayerische Staatsbibliothek in Munich in partnership with the HAB. 25 vols. Stuttgart: Anton Hiersemann, 1983–2000. Available online at https://tinyurl.com/4sbnc5v8.

VD17 *Das Verzeichnis der im deutschen Sprachraum erschienenen Drucke des 17. Jahrhunderts*. Edited by the HAB, the Bayerische Staatsbibliothek in Munich, and the Staatsbibliothek in Berlin, Preußischer Kulturbesitz, 1996. Available online at https://tinyurl.com/2ckhpxea.

WA *D. Martin Luthers Werke, Kritische Gesamtausgabe, Schriften*. 73 vols. Weimar: Böhlau, 1883.

Wackernagel Philipp Wackernagel, ed. *Das deutsche Kirchenlied von der ältesten Zeit bis zu Anfang des 17. Jahrhunderts*. 5 vols. Hildesheim: G. Olms, 1964 (reproduction of original version: Leipzig: Teubner, 1864–1877).

Introduction

Lament is essential to human thriving. It allows us to cope with significant loss, an inescapable feature of our mortal existence. Lament is the passionate outpouring of deep sorrow and grief over such loss, which helps us avoid being completely overcome by the strong emotions that attend it. Lament is cathartic and also constructive. It is a necessary step in coming to terms with loss and in moving forward in life. Not to lament is not to live—or at least not to live very fully, deeply, or well.

Lament is also essential to Christian faith. There is a rich tradition of lament in Scripture that gives eloquent voice to the pain and bewilderment of both personal and corporate loss, including the perceived loss of God's presence and blessing. In Scripture, lament is directed primarily to God and frequently involves protest or complaint to God.[1] The traditional Christian doctrine of the divine inspiration of Scripture suggests that God both allows and welcomes lament, at least in some cases. In the midst of his suffering, Job exclaims, "I cry out to you and you do not answer me; I stand, and you merely look at me" (Job 30:20). The psalmist similarly laments, "I am weary with my mourning; every night I flood my bed with tears; I drench my couch with my weeping" (Ps 6:6). The psalmist also asks, "O God, why do you cast us off forever? Why does your anger smoke against the sheep of your pasture?" (Ps 74:1) and "Will the Lord spurn forever, and never again be favorable? Has his steadfast love ceased forever? Are his promises at an end for all time? Has God forgotten to be gracious? Has he in anger shut up his compassion?" (Ps 77:7–9). Or simply, "How long, O Lord?" (Ps 79:5). On the cross, drawing on Psalm 22:1, Christ himself utters the most famous lament in the Christian tradition: "My God, my God, why have you forsaken me?" (Matt 27:46; Mark 15:34). While the biblical tradition of lament has suffered neglect in Western Christianity, it has never been completely lost.[2]

This book deals with one instance of Christian lament in the late Reformation. It does so by exploring the efforts of a talented yet little known layman to cope with the death of his beloved wife. It provides full access for the first time to the remarkable work of private devotion that he authored to express his lament, *Pious Meditations on the, Alas, Most Sorrowful Bereavement* (*Piae Meditationes Vidvitatis, Ehev, Moestissimae*, 1619). A work of haunting candor, impressive artistry, and searching faith, the *Pious Meditations* is an extraordinarily rare and valuable source that has received very little scholarly attention.[3] It furnishes fresh insight into life in the past as well as important resources for life in the present. Written in a period that knew no radical separation between the academy and the church, it was informed by the author's experience in both and can continue to speak to both today.

The Loss of AMICO

Johann Christoph Oelhafen (1574–1631) was a well-educated and widely traveled jurist and legal advisor to the council of patricians that governed Nürnberg, one of the most prominent cities of the day.[4] He was also a devout and sensitive soul.[5] On May 25, 1601, he married Anna Maria Harsdörffer (1582–1619), a young woman who, in terms of family standing, was every bit his social equal—in fact, she was his social better.[6] The couple seems to have enjoyed an especially rich life together—certainly Johann Christoph thought so, as did later Oelhafens. The Oelhafen Family Book (*Familienbuch*) records that they had a "most loving and blessed marriage" (*gantz liebreiche und gesegnete ehe*).[7] The couple also experienced the blessings and woes of family life in the early modern period. Their first child, a daughter, died at eighteen months, while their second child, a son, died shortly after his birth.[8] But in Anna Maria's next nine pregnancies, just one of their children died prematurely, providing the couple with eight living offspring, four sons and four daughters. This must have made for quite a bustling household.

Johann Christoph cared a great deal about the formation of his children in the Lutheran faith, a concern that Anna Maria certainly shared.[9] The two served as *Hausvatter* and *Hausmutter* of their own *Hauskirche*—the latter term is one contemporaries used to refer to the central place of the home in the devotional life of families, especially those of the upper classes. The house church included parents, children, and servants and could convene in the morning, in the evening, at mealtimes, and before and after religious services in a local church, which it sought to complement.[10] As was true of house-church devotion in general, religious formation in the Oelhafen *Hauskirche* must have included plenty of music and hymn-singing, as Johann Christoph was well versed in Christian hymnody, especially of the Lutheran sort.[11] He even composed his own hymns,[12] and it seems that Anna Maria enjoyed singing them while accompanied by her husband on the lute.[13] Johann Christoph was a theologically informed person who, according to one source, began and ended each day by reading Scripture; he also authored his own prayers.[14] Thus, catechesis, Bible study, and prayer must have also been common features of the family's religious life, along with regular church attendance, including participation in the Lord's Supper and private confession.[15] (Anna Maria may well have shared her husband's love not only for hymnody but also for other sources of devotion, including Scripture, but aside from his repeated praise for her Christian piety,[16] we have no other sources to document her life of faith.)

Bodily illness and fear of the same were likewise notable aspects of the family's life, especially where Anna Maria was concerned.[17] The cumulative effects of thirteen total pregnancies over the course of her married life certainly took their toll,[18] along with whatever other vicissitudes of early modern existence might have afflicted her. According to Johann Christoph's diary (*Diarium*), not long after giving birth to their twelfth child on September 4, 1617, Anna Maria suffered from severe intestinal pain, almost dying in late October and remaining bedridden until mid-November. The child died on November 12; Anna Maria composed her last will and testament the next day.[19] She recovered but might well have been in a weakened condition when she gave birth to their thirteenth and final child on November 23, 1618. The child died shortly thereafter. The loss of five of their thirteen children at an early age, although certainly difficult for Johann Christoph and Anna Maria, was by no means unusual for their time; in fact, they fared better than many parents. In the early modern period, roughly one out of every four or five children died in their first year of life, and only half reached the age of ten.[20]

Anna Maria was still bedridden in early January 1619, with her condition worsening. On January 30, she spent the whole night vomiting bile (*gallen*); the same happened on February 1 and 10.[21] On February 11, Johann Christoph asked Anna Maria if she thought she would improve. She replied, "Ah, dear heart, how I wish I could say yes, but God knows that I am only growing weaker."[22] She asked him to distribute her things evenly among their children. Johann Christoph summoned his two oldest sons, Christoph and Johann Jacob, home from the nearby Altdorf Academy, where they were enrolled. He also called for a pastor to attend to Anna Maria. On February 12, she again threw up a great deal of bile for much of the day. As her two oldest sons approached her bed, she exhorted them to obey their father and then exclaimed, "Alas! Alas! I now see both of you one more time before my end in this world."[23] As the day wore on into the night, her remaining strength left her. Her pulse gradually faded, and she began to grow cold and slip away. Still, she was able to speak to her husband one last time: "Oh darling, help me just once more out of this torment!"[24] Thirty minutes later, she suffered a stroke. Johann Christoph records that Anna Maria died peacefully in his arms, as she had wished, at 12:45 a.m. on February 13; she was thirty-six years old.[25]

Johann Christoph was shattered by the loss of his AMICO—this was his pet name for Anna Maria, an acrostic of their joint initials intended to convey his sense of the union between them: Anna Maria Iohann Christoph Oelhafen. In order to contend with his grief, later the same day the forty-four-year-old widower began his *Pious Meditations*, his yearlong lament.

ICO and His City

Johann Christoph Oelhafen was born in the imperial city of Nürnberg,[26] a fact that certainly shaped his religious and intellectual training and convictions and also helped determine his vocational opportunities and pursuits. As with other imperial cities in the German lands of the Holy

Roman Empire, Nürnberg enjoyed a privileged status with the emperor that provided it with a high degree of religious and political autonomy. Prior to the Reformation, it was technically under the spiritual authority of the nearby bishop of Bamberg, but already in the later Middle Ages, the body of patricians who governed Nürnberg—the Smaller Council (*der kleinere Rat*)—exercised considerable sway in religious matters. Although Nürnberg could experience tension with neighboring nobility, no prince, duke, or margrave held authority over it, so complete was the Smaller Council's control of the city's affairs. Nürnberg was among the largest and wealthiest of the imperial cities, having around forty thousand inhabitants in the sixteenth century. Since the mid-fourteenth century, it had also enjoyed the special honor of having all new emperors crowned in its fortress, which was a favorite temporary residence for them. Additionally, Nürnberg was an important center of higher learning and the arts. Home to the likes of Hartmann Schedel (1440–1514), Willibald Pirckheimer (1470–1530), and Albrecht Dürer (1471–1528), the imperial city played a key role in the northern Renaissance. In 1526, with the help of Philip Melanchthon (1497–1560), the city established a school to provide its elite (male) youth with a humanistic education, the first of its kind in Germany.[27] Johann Christoph would benefit directly from such education.

His parents were Johann (Hans) Oelhafen (1520–1580) and Susanna Harsdörffer (1549–1621). Both the Oelhafens and the Harsdörffers were prominent families,[28] but only the latter were considered *ratsfähig*—that is, worthy of serving on Nürnberg's Smaller Council and thus part of the imperial city's patrician class. The Oelhafens did not receive this honor until 1729,[29] most likely because they first came to the imperial city in the late fifteenth century. (The Oelhafens were from Nördlingen, having moved there in the fourteenth century from Zurich by way of Lauingen.)[30] Still, the Oelhafens were highly respected in Nürnberg, owing especially to the efforts of Sixtus I (1466–1539),[31] the paternal grandfather of our Johann Christoph. Born in Nördlingen, he had been educated in Nürnberg and moved to the imperial city in 1501. Sixtus worked as chief secretary (*oberster Sekretär/Secretarius*) and legal advisor (*Hof*

Rath) at the imperial courts of Frederick III, Maximilian I, and Charles V. He was also a member (*Genannte*) of Nürnberg's Great Council (*der Grosse Rat*), which was occasionally convened by the Smaller Council to approve new taxes, declare war, and discuss matters relating to the city's safety.[32] In 1489, Emperor Frederick III had raised the Oelhafens to the imperial nobility and presented Sixtus and his brother with an official coat of arms.[33] Sixtus also had the opportunity to meet Martin Luther at the Diet of Worms (1521) and was favorably impressed by his person and teaching, although he was circumspect (at least initially) in his support of the reformer, likely for fear of imperial reprisal.[34] Sixtus married twice, in both cases proving himself worthy of a wife from a *ratsfähig* family, the Pfinzings and Rieters, respectively.[35] The father of our Johann Christoph was born to Sixtus and his second wife, Barbara Rieter.

Hans Oelhafen left Nürnberg at the age of fourteen to study at the University of Wittenberg, where he was a table companion of Luther and Melanchthon.[36] His father had apparently overcome his initial hesitation about declaring his support for Luther publicly, no doubt because in the interim, Nürnberg had embraced the evangelical faith and emerged as one of the leading cities of the Lutheran Reformation.[37] The first imperial city to adopt the evangelical faith—it did so in 1525—Nürnberg soon came to play a central role in the promotion and institutionalization of the Lutheran Reformation, especially in southern Germany. In the late 1510s, Luther's spiritual mentor and the head of his monastic order, Johann von Staupitz (1460–1524), had visited Nürnberg, where he found a warm reception for his strongly Augustinian preaching, especially among a circle of humanists in the imperial city. This circle, which adopted the name *Sodalitas Staupitziana* to signal its solidarity with the prominent guest, included some of Nürnberg's most noteworthy citizens: the Smaller Council secretary Lazarus Spengler (1479–1534), the lawyer Christoph Scheurl (1481–1542), Albrecht Dürer, and several members of the Smaller Council. Scheurl obtained a copy of Luther's *95 Theses*, and another member of both the Smaller Council and the *Sodalitas*, Kaspar Nützel (1471–1529), translated the work into German. Luther visited the imperial city in 1518 to much acclaim and was also warmly received by the *Sodalitas*. (There is no evidence of a meeting between Sixtus and Luther on this occasion.)

Lazarus Spengler wrote the first lay defense for the Wittenberg friar-professor, the popular *Apology for Luther's Teaching* (1519), which caused him to be named on the papal bull that threatened Luther with excommunication.[38] (His name was later removed.) In the 1520s and early 1530s, the Smaller Council appointed important evangelical preachers to the city's two leading churches: Andreas Osiander (1498–1552) in the St. Lorenz Church and Veit Dietrich (1506–1549) in the St. Sebald Church. Evangelical liturgies soon replaced the Catholic Mass, culminating in the 1533 Brandenburg-Nürnberg Church Ordinance, which became one of the most influential guides for worship and belief in Lutheran lands. Nürnberg was also home to the Lutheran Reformation's most famous lay artisan pamphleteer, the shoemaker-poet Hans Sachs (1494–1576), whose *Wittenberg Nightingale* (1523) captured Luther's teaching in simple verse for the masses. As we have seen, in 1526, the Smaller Council welcomed Melanchthon to help establish a new school in the imperial city that adopted the humanistic curriculum favored in Wittenberg. Additionally, Nürnberg's leadership signed the Augsburg Confession (1530). Sixtus Oelhafen lived through all of these monumental changes in Nürnberg's religious life, and Hans Oelhafen grew up with them as an established fact of his life. Wittenberg was thus the natural place for him to study.

From Wittenberg, Hans went to Tübingen to study law, and after traveling for a while,[39] he eventually became a judge in Nürnberg (1548).[40] Like his father, Hans married twice: his first wife was Sybilla Paumgartner (d. 1566),[41] with whom he had six children; his second wife, whom he wed one year after Sybilla's death, was Susanna Harsdörffer, the mother of our Johann Christoph. The couple had seven children altogether.[42] Hans died when Johann Christoph was just five years old; Susanna never remarried.

Johann Christoph began his education at a Latin school in Nürnberg, and then, because of an outbreak of plague, in 1586 he transferred to the Altdorf Academy.[43] He did extremely well at the academy, winning first prize in Latin and Greek and being selected to hold a formal speech on behalf of his class at the annual school festival in 1587.[44] After spending five years in Altdorf, Johann Christoph, following in his father's footsteps, went on to study law in Strasbourg and Marburg and also traveled extensively for some seven years. His legal pursuits and wanderlust took him to the Netherlands, Belgium, England, Italy, Switzerland, Spain, Portugal, and France. The final country held both blessing and woe for Johann Christoph. In Anjou, he received a juristical licentiate degree,[45] but then in Montpellier, he had a close brush with death. In May of 1599, a barber surgeon accidentally cut a major blood vessel and nerve in Johann Christoph's arm while bleeding him. Johann Christoph, who was twenty-four at the time, at first feared he would lose his arm and then worried that his life was coming to an end. He even prepared his own epitaph, instructing his traveling companion, the Danish nobleman Otto Steensen Brahe (1578–1651), to arrange for his burial.[46] These provisions proved unnecessary, for after six weeks of extreme pain and great expense, the appointed cures worked, and he recovered sufficiently to return to Nürnberg. The experience made a lasting impression on him; he records in the *Pious Meditations* that he was still wary of bloodletting some twenty years later.[47]

In August of 1599, Johann Christoph was nominated to be legal counsel (*Ratskonsulent*) to the Nürnberg Smaller Council, even though he had yet to become a doctor of law, something that was unprecedented in Nürnberg's history.[48] After further study at the imperial chamber court in Speyer and the successful defense of his dissertation in Basel, he earned a doctoral degree in law and then returned to Nürnberg to take up his post as assessor for the municipal and marriage courts as well as legal counsel to the Smaller Council. Not long thereafter, he married Anna Maria, who, like his mother, was a Harsdörffer. (Johannes Christoph and Anna Maria were second cousins.)[49] Anna Maria's father, Lazarus Harsdörffer, was a member of the Smaller Council.[50] In addition to his legal duties in Nürnberg, Johann Christoph also served as legal counsel to numerous noble families and imperial cities throughout Germany.[51] Not later than 1602, Emperor Matthias (1557–1619,

r. 1612–1619) bestowed on him the lofty honor of imperial count palatine (*kaiserliche Hofpfalzgraf / Comitatus Palatinus*), which gave him the authority to dispense certain "graces" that belonged by right to the emperor (e.g., the conferral of honorary degrees or titles, the creation of notaries and poet laureates, and the ability to declare illegitimate children legitimate).[52] He and Anna Maria, along with their children, servants, and other family members, lived in the prestigious imperial mayors' residence (*Reichsschultheißenshof*) located a stone's throw from the imperial fortress.[53] By all accounts, during his marriage to Anna Maria, Johann Christoph was an enormously successful and highly esteemed individual.

A talented humanist, Johann Christoph was a bibliophile, and he was wealthy enough to indulge this love.[54] By the end of his life, his personal library contained some 1,900 works, an astounding collection for his day.[55] (After his death, the majority of these works made their way to the library of the University of Altdorf—the academy was raised to the level of university in 1622—and in 1818, after the University of Altdorf was closed, his collection was given to the library of the Friedrich-Alexander-University in Erlangen, where it is still housed.)[56] These volumes deal with numerous topics: jurisprudence, theology, history, politics, philosophy, and natural science, among others. Johann Christoph owned works by Cicero, Plutarch, Petrarch, Marsilius of Padua, Boccaccio, Bruni, Machiavelli, Lipsius, and Galileo, to name but a few. His impressive personal library also contains a diverse array of theological works by authors such as John Cassian, Thomas Aquinas, Johann Tauler, Desiderius Erasmus, Johann Eck, Martin Luther, Philip Melanchthon, Ulrich Zwingli, Urbanus Rhegius, Johannes Oecolampadius, John Calvin, Sebastian Castellio, Aegidius Hunnius, Robert Bellarmine, and Martin Becanus. He also owned a copy of the Formula of Concord and various works on the Council of Trent.[57] There is little in the way of consolation or devotional literature in his library, although it is quite clear from the *Pious Meditations* that Johann Christoph was familiar with this literature and its long history.[58] He must have owned such literature, but in keeping with the practice of the times, Johann Christoph likely bequeathed it to his children, wanting them to retain it for personal use.[59]

Despite the ecumenical character of Johann Christoph's personal library, he reveals no obvious sympathies for Catholicism in the *Pious Meditations*. As we have seen, his family had become enamored of Luther early on in the Reformation, and it even had ties with the leading reformers in Wittenberg.[60] As we have also seen, his home city had embraced the evangelical movement early on and had then sought to spread it elsewhere. Additionally, we know that in his official capacity as legal counsel, Johann Christoph urged the Smaller Council to assist the Protestant cause in Bohemia in the early stages of the Thirty Years' War, albeit without much success.[61]

While Nürnberg was firmly in the Protestant camp, its relationship with the emperor was still important to it, and thus the imperial city's political leaders frequently temporized in the face of confessional conflict. In the past, the Smaller Council had embraced the Augsburg Confession but had declined to join the Schmalkald League, a Protestant military alliance formed in 1531 to defend the evangelical faith. The Smaller Council had also chosen to remain neutral in the Schmalkald War (1546–1547), which saw Catholic forces defeat Protestant forces. After the conclusion of the war, Nürnberg was subject to the Augsburg Interim, an imperial effort to reimpose Catholicism on Protestants in the empire. It was not until the Peace of Augsburg (1555), which granted legal standing to Lutheranism in the empire, that Lutheranism could be officially reestablished in the imperial city. Nürnberg's patrician leaders continued to temporize during the early years of the Thirty Years' War.

This conflict was a central concern for Johann Christoph. He desperately wanted God to subdue the Catholic forces that threatened to become "destroyers of the Fatherland."[62] Johann Christoph feared the spread of war from Bohemia to the German lands. (His fears were later realized; Nürnberg itself was a site of a major battle in 1632, although Johann Christoph was no longer alive to experience it.)[63] The Nürnberg lawyer played a leading role in representing the imperial city and its interests in meetings of the Protestant Union,[64] a coalition of both Lutherans and Calvinists formed in 1608 by Frederick IV, Elector Palatine (1574–1610). The union sought to protect existing Protestant rights, possessions, and liberties against Catholic opposition and also to seek redress of long-standing grievances. In 1619, the meetings of the union dealt largely with the Protestant response to the outbreak of war in Bohemia, especially how best to support Bohemian Protestants, who sought admission to the union. Johann Christoph composed a number of the entries in the *Pious Meditations* while engaged in work for the Protestant Union;[65] even as he sought to avoid war with the "kings of the earth," he was fighting his own war with grief.[66]

As we have seen, he initially wanted the Smaller Council to support the Bohemian Protestants, and he did manage to persuade the patricians to offer some financial assistance. But once Frederick's son, Frederick V (1596–1632), accepted the Bohemian crown in early November 1619, Johann Christoph began to counsel restraint. (Frederick V had taken over leadership of the union after his father's death.) In his mind, the union's purpose was defensive, whereas Frederick's actions were offensive, intended to acquire new possessions for the Protestant cause. Still, Johann Christoph's restraint was motivated by political prudence, not by any misgivings about the truth of Protestantism.

Johann Christoph saw the Bohemian Protestants as his "brothers and sisters in faith,"[67] but there is no indication that he shared the Calvinist leanings of some of them. There were those in Nürnberg, however, who certainly did. In the late sixteenth century, the civic and religious leaders of the imperial city promoted a moderate form of Lutheranism that looked to Melanchthon as its guide and that accommodated other forms of Protestantism.[68] Altdorf, where Johann Christoph studied, was similarly "Philippist" in theological orientation,[69] and we know that he had heard lectures on Melanchthon's theology during his early years of study in Nürnberg.[70] The theological climate of Nürnberg and Altdorf began to change in the early seventeenth century when a more conservative version of Lutheranism emerged, owing in large part to the efforts of Johannes Saubert (1592–1646). He was clearly an important person in Johann Christoph's life.[71]

Saubert was born in Altdorf and, like Johann Christoph, had studied at its academy (1609, baccalaureate; 1611, master's). (Johann Christoph completed his studies there in 1591.) Saubert was especially influenced by the Orthodox Lutheran theologian Jakob Schopper (1545–1616), who had taught at Altdorf since 1598.[72] He was also exposed to Socinianism or anti-Trinitarianism, a position that a number of Altdorf professors advocated, including Ernst Soner (1572–1612), professor of medicine and philosophy (and sometime rector).[73] For a time, the Altdorf Academy emerged as an important outpost of Socinianism in the empire, although Saubert did not become a convert.[74] After leaving Altdorf, he soon came into contact with other Orthodox theologians at the University of Tübingen: Lucas Osiander (1534–1604), Matthias Hafenreffer (1561–1619), and Johann Valentin Andreae (1586–1654). From the University of Tübingen, he eventually made his way to Jena, where he studied with Johann Gerhard (1582–1637). The two developed a close relationship in which Gerhard shared with Saubert his deep admiration for the devotional writings of Johann Arndt (1555–1621).[75] Arndt was a Protestant mystic of sorts who stressed the importance of repentance in the Christian life along with the reality of the believer's union with Christ through faith and baptism.[76] One sees these distinctive emphases in his enormously popular *Four Books of True Christianity* (1610).[77] Saubert was a devotee of both Orthodox Lutheranism and Arndtian-style spiritual renewal, and he sought to spread them in Nürnberg and its surrounding environs.[78] Beginning in 1617, he ministered first as a chaplain and theologian in Altdorf and then moved to Nürnberg in 1622, eventually becoming one of the most influential clergymen (and librarians) in the imperial city.

Johann Christoph knew Saubert, and although the Altdorf preacher was eighteen years his junior, he must have had a close relationship with him. In 1616, Johann Christoph revealed in an opinion he wrote for the Smaller Council that he was in contact with Saubert, in this case regarding the Socinianism at the Altdorf Academy that troubled both men so much.[79] Once Johann Christoph completed his *Pious Meditations*, he shared the work with the Altdorf preacher, who was deeply impressed by its contents. Affixed to the first page of the *Pious Meditations* is a slip of paper with a handwritten Latin inscription that praises the deep faith that Johann Christoph displays in its pages; the slip of paper is signed by Saubert.[80]

We thus have good reason to believe that Johann Christoph was sympathetic to Saubert's version of Lutheran Christianity when he composed the *Pious Meditations*, although we cannot know if he agreed with Saubert on every point of doctrine.[81] One notable feature of Johann Christoph's prayers in the *Pious Meditations* is that they are thoroughly Trinitarian, in some cases including petitions to each member of the Godhead. Perhaps this feature may be attributed especially to the influence—or at least the support—of Saubert, a staunch champion of orthodox Trinitarianism over against Socinianism.

We know that Johann Christoph was familiar with the kind of mystically inflected Lutheran devotional literature of the late Reformation that Saubert affirmed.[82] In the *Pious Meditations*, he directly quotes Martin Moller's (1547–1606) *Manual on Preparation for Death* (1593).[83] He also records in his *Diarium* that he once made a gift of the Lutheran pastor's postils to a friend, no doubt the popular *Practice of the Gospels* (1601).[84] Moller was a pastor in Sprottau and then Görlitz, and although he lacked Saubert's extensive educational training—he never attended university—he shared Saubert's preference for what one might call "Protestant piety theology," which included sympathy for certain strands of medieval mysticism.[85]

The term "piety theology" (*Frömmigkeitstheologie*) was first coined by Berndt Hamm with reference to late medieval works of devotion. As one scholar explains, *Frömmigkeitstheologie* is Hamm's "designation for a genre of late-medieval writing and praxis, much of it derived from and directed toward pastoral care, which was especially concerned with the pursuit of an authentic Christian life as defined by the values and institutions of the day."[86] Late medieval *Frömmigkeitstheologie* was a form of practical theology or pragmatic mysticism whose primary concern was spiritual edification and comfort, not speculation.[87] Its most important contributors were Jean Gerson (1363–1429), Johann von Paltz (ca. 1445–1511), and Johann von Staupitz. Authors like Moller, along with Andreas Musculus (1514–1581), Philipp Nicolai (1556–1608), Philipp Kegel (?–1614), Arndt, Gerhard, and Saubert, may be seen as advocates of an evangelical version of *Frömmigkeitstheologie*; so, too, may Martin Luther. Johann Christoph's *Pious Meditations* is a rare and striking example of lay Protestant piety theology.

Image 1: Front cover of the *Pious Meditations* (*Gebetbuch des Hans Christoph Oelhafen*, GNM-HA, Familienarchiv von Oelhafen, Rep. II/80, Nr. 32)

Image 2: Back cover of the *Pious Meditations* (*Gebetbuch des Hans Christoph Oelhafen*, GNM-HA, Familienarchiv von Oelhafen, Rep. II/80, Nr. 32)

The *Pious Meditations*

The *Pious Meditations* contains seventy-five vernacular entries followed by two Latin ones; most entries are a couple of folio pages long, and all are in Johann Christoph's hand—the work was never printed. The Nürnberg widower dated each entry and also numbered the German ones (there are no folio or page numbers). The vernacular entries run from February 13, 1619, the day of Anna Maria's death, to December 31, 1619. The first Latin entry is dated January 1, 1620 (with a quotation from Boethius added on January 6); the second one, a later addition, is dated June 8, 1628. The entries take three basic forms: prayers, hymns/songs, and poems. Many of the prayers, which are really extended collects, appear to be original to Johann Christoph, although he does borrow now and again from various devotional works, usually supplementing or editing as he does so. The prayers that are original to him are replete with Scripture. Many incorporate themes from the lectionary readings for a given Sunday or feast day, while in others, Johann Christoph draws more freely on his impressive knowledge of Scripture. The hymns and songs in the *Pious Meditations* are clearly intended to be sung; Johann Christoph introduces these entries by listing the tune of the hymn/song and then provides the text. In some cases, he has simply copied down a well-known hymn and adjusted the incipits or initial letters of each stanza to form the acrostics that occur in many entries.[88] But other hymns and songs are original to him or are mostly original to him—at times, he incorporates a stanza or two from a well-known hymn into his own composition. As we have seen, Johann Christoph was in the habit of writing his own prayers and hymns before Anna Maria's death; this habit served him well as he composed the *Pious Meditations*. There are just a few poems in the work: some are borrowed, while others appear to be original to Johann Christoph.

It is not clear when Johann Christoph produced the *Pious Meditations* in its final form, although it is obvious that he took great care in its creation and hoped that it would survive for generations to come. Its pages are gilded vellum, and it is bound in red tooled leather (see images 1 and 2 and front and back covers of this book). In addition to the inscription by Saubert, which appears on the first page (see the following discussion), early on there is a color portrait of Johann Christoph by the well-known Nürnberg artist Lorenz Strauch (1554–1630; see image 5 and inside flap of book cover).[89] (Unfortunately, there is no portrait of Anna Maria.) This is followed by an ink drawing of Johann Christoph's epitaph (see image 6). Later on, the book includes an image of "Lady Patience" (see image 7). Both this image and the epitaph bear the date 1619, but it is unlikely that Johann Christoph completed his *Pious Meditations* in the year of Anna Maria's death. The dates of the first Latin entry militate against this possibility, as does the fact that Johann Christoph gave Saubert time to read the *Pious Meditations* in full. It is more likely that Johann Christoph completed his work on the book (minus the final Latin entry) shortly after the first Latin entry—that is, sometime in mid- to late January or early February 1620, probably before the one-year anniversary of Anna Maria's death on February 13.[90]

The entries in this extended lament are for the most part highly polished, although now and again there are signs of small revisions and mistakes. Black ink predominates, but Johann Christoph also employs red to signal acrostics or to emphasize important words, phrases, or numbers. He may have first composed and reworked the entries elsewhere before copying them down on vellum pages, or he may have simply written them directly on the costly material. The entries appear to be authentic—that is, there is every reason to believe that Johann Christoph composed them throughout the course of the year following Anna Maria's death rather than creating them sometime afterward and belatedly assigning dates and events to them. He refers throughout to feast and fast days in the Christian calendar and also to events in his own life and that of Nürnberg and the German lands. The fact that most entries fall on a Sunday suggests that Johann Christoph might have composed them on Sabbath afternoons or evenings, after having attended church in the morning. The *Pious Meditations* was Johann Christoph's attempt to find solace in his Christian faith in the period of considerable darkness that followed Anna Maria's death; his entries suggest that he needed such consolation every day.

The *Pious Meditations* and Modern Scholarship

The *Pious Meditations* is an important source for a number of contemporary scholarly conversations. As we have seen, the work provides unique insight into the evangelical *Hauskirche*, which Patrice Veit has examined. Veit has argued that the emergence of the house church may be seen as part of the domestication (*Verhäuslichung*) of the religious life in the late sixteenth and seventeenth centuries; he has also maintained that the house church and its piety provide evidence for a "sacralization of everyday life . . ." (*eine Sakralisierung des Alltags*)—Johann Christoph's extended lament illustrates both developments nicely.[91] As we have also seen, the *Pious Meditations* serves as a valuable example of lay Protestant piety theology.

The work additionally displays many of the assumptions and deploys many of the rhetorical devices that scholars have uncovered in their research on the consolation literature of early modern Lutheran Germany,[92] including the literature written by the bereaved for themselves and others—Johann Christoph was by no means alone in this endeavor.[93] He understands the consoling effects of writing, an insight that goes back to Seneca.[94] He especially understands the solace one can gain from the writing (and singing) of poetry and hymns.[95] Johann Christoph makes use of *apostrophe* (a speech directed to an absent being), *prosopopoeia* (the introduction of speech from a deceased or divine being), and also *dialogismus* (dialogue between two or more beings that constitutes a miniature drama).[96] In fact, Johann Christoph combines these rhetorical devices when he constructs a fictitious dialogue between himself and his deceased wife on what would have been their nineteenth wedding anniversary—one of the most moving entries in the work.[97] He also employs acrostics.[98]

As recent scholarship has demonstrated, all of this was typical in the consolation literature produced by the educated classes in early modern Lutheran Germany; in fact, it was typical of burgher family life, although we should not assume that every burgher was as devout or as talented as Johann Christoph—the Oelhafen *Hauskirche* had an exceptionally gifted *Hausvatter*. Still, early modern families were quite adept at consolation; parents like Johann Christoph were in the regular habit of teaching their children how to face death and how to grieve.[99] Johann Christoph had himself likely received such instruction as a youth. As Anna Carrdus explains, "The traditional consolatory forms and remedies were an integral part of an Early Modern family's day-to-day emotional and spiritual life. . . . They helped both parents and children to contain their fear and grief at times of almost unbearable crisis."[100] Carrdus emphasizes the role of the arts in helping families exercise this vital ministry of mutual consolation.[101]

Johann Christoph shares another important characteristic that scholars have identified in early modern Lutheran consolation literature, especially the literature dealing with grief: he gives rather full rein to his feelings of loss and despair in the *Pious Meditations*, even conceding that he was suicidal for a time.[102] Candor about spiritual and emotional suffering was a hallmark of Lutheran consolation literature in the early modern period,[103] something that, according to Johann Anselm Steiger, can be traced back to Luther himself, who was certainly forthright about his own inner turmoil.[104]

Johann Christoph does not seek to suppress or control his emotions through natural reason as the "constructive Stoic healer" Petrarch (1304–1374) urged in his famous *Remedies for Fortune Fair and Foul* (1366).[105] In this work, Petrarch has "Reason" respond to a grieving widower, "About what, then, do you complain? Yes, you have lost a wife. But you have gained liberty, bachelorhood, peace, sleep, rest, and are able to spend your nights without wheedling and jawing. . . . Only a fool loves the chains that fetter him, even though they be made of pure gold." According to Reason, the widower should, therefore, embrace his newfound freedom and dedicate himself to the undistracted pursuit of wisdom, setting grief aside.[106]

Such advice was present in Johann Christoph's day, owing to the rise of neo-Stoicism, a major intellectual current of the time that made its way into Lutheran devotional literature. The works of Justus Lipsius (1547–1606), a prominent neo-Stoic, were an important part of this current.[107] A baptized Stoicism had in fact influenced Christian consolation literature for centuries and had also shaped burgher piety in Germany, including during the Reformation, which in some ways reinforced it.[108]

This Stoicism existed in uneasy tension with the aforementioned emphasis on emotional candor in Lutheran devotional literature—both were present in early modern Lutheranism. Additionally, in the early modern period, members of the ruling class—the kind of people for whom Johann Christoph worked—looked increasingly to neo-Stoicism to help provide the stability and moral discipline that they believed their times required, especially in the midst of the social and political chaos unleashed by the Reformation. Stoicism was central to the formation of the early modern state.[109]

Johann Christoph was certainly familiar with the Christian Stoicism of his day. He was educated as a humanist, and as we have seen, he cites Boethius in the *Pious Meditations*. Johann Christoph may have even owned *Remedies for Fortune Fair and Foul*; we know he owned other works by Petrarch.[110] While there is nothing as crass and unfeeling as Petrarch's advice in the *Pious Meditations*, there is evidence of Christian Stoicism in some of his entries.[111] Johann Christoph existed in the aforementioned uneasy tension between Stoic self-management and a more expressive affectivity.

Still, the *Pious Meditations* has much more candor than Stoicism. To be sure, Johann Christoph heeds the Apostle Paul's warning that Christians must not mourn as those who have no hope (1 Thess 4:13), but this concern does not prevent him from expressing his deep grief, even as he seeks to hold on to his faith in the resurrection. Job and the Psalms are his models for coping with loss, not ancient or early modern (neo-)Stoics, certainly not in the first place.[112] Johann Christoph would have fully agreed with the judgment made by the Lutheran pastor Georg Walther regarding those who disallowed grief for Christians. In his *Consolation Booklet Drawn from Holy Scripture and the Books of Dr. Martin Luther* (Nürnberg, 1559, 1560, 1573, and 1600), Walther concludes that such people are "bestial" (*viehisch*).[113] Luther would have concurred.[114]

The *Pious Meditations* also provides a poignant example of an additional important theme that scholars have identified in early modern Lutheran devotion: the duty of self-consolation. Steiger has maintained that one of the hallmarks of the evangelical care of souls in this period was an emphasis on the obligation of laypeople to prepare themselves for difficult times through sustained meditation on Scripture. The clergy sought to teach the laity to become their own pastors by providing them with the "spiritual weapons" (*geistliche Waffen*) they would need for their inevitable duels with adversity.[115] Thus a number of the period's most popular works of devotion invoke the image of the spiritual knight in their titles and texts. To mention but two, there is Caspar Huberinus's (1500–1553) *On the Christian Knight* (1545; Nürnberg, 1558 and 1570) and Johann Spangenberg's (1484–1550) work by the same title (1541; Nürnberg, 1565, 1577, 1580, and 1598).[116] The latter work was frequently published with another treatise by Spangenberg, *A Booklet of Comfort for the Sick* (1542; Nürnberg, 1565, 1577, and 1598).[117] In this *Booklet*, the Lutheran pastor and superintendent discusses the importance of arming oneself spiritually for death and suffering before they arrive: "You should impress [*einbilden*] some comforting passages from Scripture and the gospel on your memory, passages to use against all temptations. Collect them as provisions [for the journey] and always carry them with you in your heart, just as a soldier carries his arrows in the quiver and has them ready to use whenever he needs them."[118] Johann Christoph refers to himself as a Christian knight three times in the *Pious Meditations* and throughout fights mightily to overcome his despair.[119]

This emphasis on spiritual self-preparation may also be seen in Lutheran funeral sermons, including those that appeared in and around Nürnberg during Johann Christoph's lifetime.[120] The sermons are full of references to how the deceased memorized or copied down consoling sayings from the Bible or devotional works to provide themselves with solace as they suffered and faced their end; the sermons urge survivors to do the same. Consider the example of Johann Will (1575–1641), a Lutheran pastor in Vorra, which lies fifty kilometers northeast of Nürnberg. He relays in a 1611 funeral sermon for Carl Tetzel (1557–1611), who served on the imperial city's Smaller Council and War Council, how the deceased consoled himself with verses from Jeremiah 23:6 and 33:16. Based on these verses, the deceased would say to himself, "Christ is my righteousness" (*Christus ist meine Gerechtigkeit*). Will praises Tetzel for this exercise of self-consolation and assures his hearers that Christ was indeed the deceased's righteousness and that he is now with his Lord in heaven.[121] Johann Christoph may well have known Tetzel and could have attended his funeral.

Steiger links this emphasis on spiritual self-care with the stress on physical self-care in the medical literature of the period; doctors of souls and doctors of bodies urged their patients to become their own (and each other's) physicians.[122] Of course, both the image of the spiritual knight and the emphasis on lay spiritual self-care were not unique to Protestant pastoral care and piety; one has only to think of Erasmus's famous *Handbook of the Christian Knight* (1503) and the late medieval *ars moriendi* (art of dying) tradition, which similarly assumed an important role for laity in ministering to the sick and the suffering and also emphasized the importance of spiritual self-care.[123] But the obligation to provide spiritual care for oneself and one's friends and loved ones clearly received new impetus from the Protestant movement through doctrines like the priesthood of all believers, which held that all the baptized were authorized to minister the Word to each other. The rejection of the cult of the saints placed a similar emphasis on this traditional obligation: this-worldly saints had to take over some of the functions attributed to heavenly saints in Catholicism, which included the consolation of the suffering. One also sees this new stress on spiritual self-care in the Lutheran treatment of private confession: evangelical laypeople were regularly instructed to become their own (and each other's) confessors, even as they were exhorted to seek clerical absolution whenever they required it.[124]

Johann Christoph's *Pious Meditations* provides important evidence for how creative and resourceful Lutheran burghers could be as they sought to console themselves and their loved ones in times of great suffering. This work also shows how the Lutheran emphasis on consolation could shape the emotional lives of Lutheran burghers in profound ways.[125] In *The Reformation of Feeling*, cultural historian Susan Karant-Nunn argues that *Trost* (consolation) was the telltale characteristic of Lutheran pastoral care and piety in the early modern period.[126] Karant-Nunn focuses primarily on the place of consolation in Lutheran Passion sermons and prescriptions for deathbed ministry, seeking to show how these sources provided an "emotional script" that the laity was expected to learn. Her study examines the creation and dissemination of early modern emotional scripts and thus naturally deals with clerical sources for the most part. She does not examine in detail the lay reception of these scripts—that is, she does not deal with so-called *Selbstzeugnisse* (self-narratives), or lay autobiographical sources.[127] Johann Christoph's *Pious Meditations* shows how the Lutheran reformation of feeling could extend to laypeople. His work may be seen as a self-conscious attempt on the part of an elite burgher to allow Lutheran-style consolation to shape, heal, and inform his own emotional life along with that of anyone else who read his work.[128] The *Pious Meditations* is an ideal example of how the confessionalizing impulse of late sixteenth- and early seventeenth-century Lutheranism, which has received so much scholarly attention, could achieve its goal of forming lay identities around the defining convictions and concerns of the gospel (as Lutherans understood it), especially in the face of suffering and death.[129]

Johann Christoph's extended lament is thus an important new source for the history of early modern emotions, a burgeoning field of scholarship,[130] and specifically for the history of loss and grief, a subfield within this larger field.[131] In the *Pious Meditations*, one sees Johann Christoph simultaneously inhabiting different "emotional communities," to borrow Barbara Rosenwein's important term. He seeks to navigate the boundaries and tensions between the private and domestic community, on the one hand, and the public and professional one, on the other, each of which had its own distinct "system of feeling," including with respect to grief and its remedies. In the former, one was allowed greater freedom of expression, while in the latter, one was expected to exercise stoical restraint.[132] Johann Christoph also encounters other emotional communities among his acquaintances that similarly urge emotional restraint. He complains now and again that people expect him to contain his grief when he finds it impossible to do so.[133]

The *Pious Meditations* also has obvious importance for the growing scholarly literature on attitudes toward death and dying in the Reformation period.[134] The unique contribution of Johann Christoph's extended lament is to provide sustained and intimate lay commentary on what it was actually like to deal with death and loss in this period. This perspective is largely lacking in the current literature, which focuses primarily on how, according to theologians and pastors, laypeople were supposed to confront death and loss, not on how they in fact did. In the *Pious Meditations*, we have a lay Protestant *ars moriendi* in action. To be sure, owing to his standing, Johann Christoph should not be viewed as a "spiritual everyman," as if he represented the lay masses in the late Reformation. Still, many shared his fervent devotion, if not his resources and skill in expressing it. The distance between the faith of Johann Christoph and, say, a Hans Sachs, while real, is not immeasurably far. The distance between the Lutheranism of Johann Christoph and that of a common peasant living in one of the villages outside of Nürnberg is likely considerably further.[135]

The *Pious Meditations* is additionally an important source for research into the history of the family. It adds to the sources that scholars such as Steven Ozment have examined in order to understand and underscore the emotional ties among early modern husbands, wives, and children. Ozment argued in a number of volumes that despite high infant mortality rates and the ever-present threat of disease and death, early modern families formed warm and affectionate ties; they did not remain emotionally aloof from one another to protect against the pain of loss and grief. The *Pious Meditations* provides even greater access to these ties than do the valuable letter collections that Ozment discovered in German archives.[136] Johann Christoph's work also furnishes insight into the experience of early modern widowers, an understudied group in the early modern family.[137]

Historians tend to see early modern Europe as an age of growing order and social discipline that contributed to the eventual emergence of the modern state; this is the primary focus of the aforementioned confessionalization thesis. Much recent scholarship has thus viewed the early modern period through the lens of a "Discipline Paradigm."[138] While the *Pious Meditations* can be fitted into this paradigm, for it is an exercise in a certain kind of discipline, and its author was also a member of a profession that played a key role in the aforementioned growth of *Ordnung*,[139] the work also provides important testimony to the presence of another side of early modern existence. This other side was characterized by rich affectivity, inspiring creativity, and deep faith. This other side of early modern existence has not received the attention it deserves because of scholars' preoccupation with what they see as the larger drive toward social and moral conformity in the period.[140] The human experience attested in the *Pious Meditations* requires us to complicate and challenge the rather monolithic narrative assumed in the Discipline Paradigm and also to supplement it with additional narratives that show the more human and intimate side of early modern existence. Without these additional narratives, our knowledge of the past is incomplete, and we fail to engage the human experience of previous generations as fully as we can and should.[141]

As indicated earlier, the *Pious Meditations* is what cultural historians call a *Selbstzeugnis* (a self-narrative)—that is, it is an autobiographical source that focuses on the life and experience of the writer and therefore provides unique access to people who lived in the past. The scholarly literature on self-narratives is enormous.[142] In addition to containing close analysis of the relevant sources, this literature also includes sophisticated methodological discussions about what kind of access these sources provide to lives of early modern people and also about what understanding of the self is present in them.[143] These discussions emphasize that self-narratives are a culturally mediated source that provide only limited and indirect access to the human beings who produced them, including to their emotional or subjective lives. Scholars of self-narratives emphasize that, first and foremost, one encounters early modern culture in these sources and, only secondarily, human beings who lived in the past. These scholars also warn against the temptation to see in early modern self-narratives evidence for the birth or evolution of the autonomous self that Jacob Burckhardt posited in his older but still influential works on the Renaissance.[144] There is a great deal of skepticism in this literature not only about the traditional story of the growth of the autonomous self in the West but also about whether human beings even have an essential self. These scholars argue that the human self—or sense of self—is extraordinarily malleable and capable of being formed and expressed in myriad ways.[145] It is shaped by numerous cultural factors, especially notions of gender and the perceived need to conform to various societal norms.[146]

Such cautions are important to heed, for, as finite and fallen creatures, we only ever see human beings in the past "in a mirror dimly" (1 Cor 13:12). In every age, time-bound human beings are also deeply shaped by culture, as are the historians who study them. The historian must furthermore be ever vigilant in avoiding teleological interpretations of the past, including where the history of the self is concerned—we have no God's-eye view of any aspect of history or its trajectory.[147] Still, if we are mindful of our limitations, careful in our research, and modest in our claims—that is, if we practice a "chastened realism"—I believe we can see something of Johann Christoph Oelhafen the human being in the *Pious Meditations* and not only his culture.[148]

What about the "self" that one encounters in the *Pious Meditations*? It is possible to fit Johann Christoph's sense of self into a narrative about the growth of what Charles Taylor has called "radical reflexivity," a form of heightened inwardness that he traces back to Augustine and that he argues has played a key role in formation of modern notions of the self.[149] Johann Christoph clearly had a highly interiorized sense of self. But his sense of self was "porous" or radically open to the divine and others, not "buffered," or closed to the transcendent and folded in upon itself, as Taylor argues is typical of much modern Western self-understanding.[150] Put differently, Johann Christoph had what the cultural historian Eva Kormann has called a "heterologous" sense of self that was defined through his relationship with God, others, and the external world and not simply with himself.[151] Or put differently again, Johann Christoph's sense of self was *perichoretic*, having much in common with the accounts of human personhood proposed by modern Christian theologians such as John Zizioulas, Stanley Grenz, and David Kelsey.[152]

Thus for a variety of reasons, the *Pious Meditations* is an important source for scholars of early modern self-narratives to consider. It is extremely rare and previously unknown. Beyond this, it reveals an early modern Christian whose self-understanding was shaped in profound ways by the Lutheran tradition of consolation and all that it assumed about

God, the world, and human beings. The experience and practice of this consolation helped form Johann Christoph's porous sense of self.[153] In the *Pious Meditations*, we find at least *one* important kind of early modern self-understanding that has contributed significantly, if in complicated, unintended, and utterly contingent ways, to at least *one* important kind of modern self-understanding.[154]

The *Pious Meditations* as an Evangelical Lament

Above all else, the *Pious Meditations* is a lament. It is an exercise in the honest and passionate expression of profound grief over painful loss. Early in the work, Johann Christoph cites the following lines from a well-known hymn: "Alone before you, Lord Jesus Christ, I now lament my distress. You are rich in consolation and help, let me not despair."[155] In hymns that he composes, he cries out, "Jesus Christ, graciously hear my lamenting voice, listen to my plea, I ask. My strength is completely spent in this dangerous time, have regard for my sighing."[156] Or again: "I can lament my misery to no one but you, my faithful God."[157] And finally: "Daily I make my lament, the water is almost up to my mouth, and I certainly cannot hold out if you do not help me bear my affliction."[158] While his laments do not typically have the sharp edges of some portions of the biblical lament tradition—especially Psalms 44, 80, and 88—they share in this tradition's searching honesty and, at least on occasion, something of its assertive and anguished protest. In one entry, Johann Christoph, quoting Psalm 13:1–2, probes, "Why, then, O God, my God, do you so utterly forget me? How long will you hide your face? Lord, how long must I seek counsel from my own sorrowful soul? How long will suffering afflict my heart?"[159] In another, responding to Catholic victories over Protestant forces, he asks God, quoting Jeremiah 14:9, "Why do you act as a hero who has lost heart and a giant who cannot help?"[160]

In recent years, there has been growing interest in lament among theologians of various stripes—systematic, historical, spiritual, pastoral—and also among philosophers and biblical scholars.[161] What much of the recent literature on lament claims, and largely with good warrant, is that the church quickly forgot or even suppressed the biblical tradition of lament, which has only recently been rediscovered.[162] I am sympathetic to this claim and have elsewhere reflected on the potential impact of the loss of lament on the growing implausibility of Christianity for many in the West.[163] I share the concern of this literature about the importance of the recovery of lament for the contemporary church. As noted previously, however, Johann Christoph's *Pious Meditations* demonstrates that lament was not completely lost in the past. It shows that at least some early Protestants developed their own version of lament that was directly informed by the central teachings and practices of the Reformation. In the *Pious Meditations*, one sees a distinctively Protestant—and specifically Lutheran—expression of lament from the early modern period. Many of the defining beliefs and practices of Wittenberg Christianity are on full display in this extended outpouring of grief and sorrow.

Johann Christoph believed he was a sinner through and through.[164] Indeed, in some entries, he interprets Anna Maria's death as a divine punishment for his sin, although this is neither his only nor his final word on the matter.[165] The fact that Anna Maria died at the beginning of Lent is significant. Johann Christoph was already in a penitential frame of mind, and her passing only deepened it. He constantly pleads Christ's work—and only Christ's work—on the cross for his forgiveness and salvation. He covers himself again and again with Christ's righteousness, always rejecting any human contribution to salvation.[166] Johann Christoph can also emphasize the reality of Christ's indwelling presence in his heart—for him, salvation involves both being covered by Christ's alien righteousness and being indwelled by Christ himself.[167] Johann Christoph refers a number of times to the "wonderful exchange" between Christ and the Christian that Luther discussed in *The Freedom of a Christian*,[168] a great source of comfort for him.[169] Yet he also believes that it is possible to forfeit salvation through the temptations of the world, the flesh, and the devil, a possibility he takes very seriously.[170] As was common among Lutherans of his time, there is an apocalyptic element in the *Pious Meditations* that includes a fascination with prodigies and signs in the heavens, along with prophecies of the same—Johann Christoph believes the end of the sinful world is coming soon, and he welcomes it.[171] He also welcomes his own end and the deliverance from grief and sorrow he believes it will bring.[172]

Johann Christoph believed that God was utterly sovereign over all things, including Anna Maria's death and other forms of suffering in his life and in the wider world. Early on, he uses lines from a contemporary devotional work to express his lament: "I have lost my most beloved treasure on earth, for you [i.e., God] have torn away a piece of my heart."[173] As we have seen, he can interpret suffering—his own and that of others—as a divine punishment for sin. But he can also employ a lay theology of the cross to arrive at a different conclusion, and this is where he is most distinctively Lutheran.[174] In one entry, he prays, "Help me in all of this so that my immature faith may be able to perceive the affection of your fatherly heart, which is frequently hidden under the cross."[175] Throughout the *Pious Meditations*, Johann Christoph asks the Holy Spirit to strengthen his flagging faith so that he may find the good and merciful God hidden in suffering;[176] he desperately seeks this God in his affliction.[177]

As a devout Lutheran, Johann Christoph rejected a number of traditional Catholic ways of making sense of suffering, including recourse to saints and their relics along with the belief that suffering, if patiently borne, could serve as a penance for sin and thus reduce time in purgatory. There is ample evidence in the *Pious Meditations* for what I have elsewhere called the "reformation of suffering," the effort of Lutheran theologians to purge Christianity of what they considered to be unbiblical means of coping with adversity and to replace them with ones they thought were grounded in Scripture.[178] Central to this reformation of suffering was the belief that adversity is in the first place a divine test of faith: by grace, one was to trust what the Word and its promises say about God (that he is good), not what fallen human reason concluded from suffering (that he is not). The theology of the cross is essential to the consolation that Johannes Christoph seeks for his troubled heart; it alone provides the assurance of divine goodness and mercy that he desires.

The term *heart* is important in the *Pious Meditations*, recurring throughout; Johann Christoph's piety is a piety of the heart, a fact that provides further evidence for his preference for the mystically inflected Protestant piety theology discussed earlier.[179] He even substitutes a heart-shaped symbol for the word *heart* in a couple of entries.[180] Above all, he wants to experience consolation in his heart: the seat of his deepest thoughts, affections, and desires; the center of his being; and the place where he believes he can know and encounter God.[181] In one entry, he prays to Christ, "Let me always feel your friendly sweetness in my heart."[182]

Johann Christoph does not always experience this sweetness—in fact, it frequently eludes him. In the *Pious Meditations*, he wrestles, Jacob-like, with God, now gaining the upper hand, now hanging on for dear life. Still, he resolves not to let go until he receives a blessing. In one entry, he prays to Christ, adapting lines from a contemporary work of devotion, "Open to me the door of your holy wounds, for I do not turn away from you. I will not stop pounding and knocking until you have mercy on me. I will not let up until you console my soul, bless me, and give me peace again."[183] Such persistence was also a fruit of suffering in Lutheran teaching, as was the patience that was necessary to endure the long intervals that seemed to hold no blessing at all.[184]

The sacraments were vital to Johann Christoph's piety. He dutifully records in his diary when his children were baptized and when he and his family went to private confession and the Lord's Supper, including when Anna Maria took Communion at home because of illness.[185] In the *Pious Meditations*, he even records the contents of his private confession.[186] While somewhat formulaic, this entry is extraordinarily rare; in fact, I know of no other source from the Reformation period in which a Lutheran layperson reveals what they have actually said—or claim to have said—to their pastor in private confession. Johann Christoph also records the prayer he prayed to prepare for confession along with the one he prayed after he received absolution.[187] Additionally, he includes prayers he prayed before, during, and after reception of Holy Communion.[188] The Lutheran means of grace were a primary source of consolation for him.

Johann Christoph was very conscious of his various vocations in the *Pious Meditations*, especially as legal counsel to the Smaller Council and as a father. In a number of entries, he prays for divine help in carrying out both vocations as he seeks to serve and love his various neighbors.[189] In an early entry, he reveals that one of Anna Maria's dying wishes was for him to be a good and faithful father to their children, now his "orphans," as he refers to them throughout the *Pious Meditations*.[190] His children figure prominently in a number of entries. Johann Christoph also comments on his new vocation as a widower, which he clearly does not like—he refers to himself numerous times as a "sad and miserable widower," or words to this effect.[191] In the final vernacular entry, he confesses that he has "found no joy in being a widower."[192] In part, as the *Pious Meditations* clearly attests, this is because he had found such great joy in being a husband, the vocation he has lost. Johann Christoph was a traditional Lutheran patriarch. At one point, he praises Anna Maria for her enduring beauty—no gray hairs even after thirteen births!—submissiveness, and fertility.[193] But it would be a mistake to reduce the reasons for his love for his AMICO to factors such as these. At least from Johann Christoph's point of view, their marriage was full of warm affection, friendship, and mutual support, especially in difficult times. She was his "most beloved treasure on earth," whom he admired and loved greatly.[194] We do not know if Anna Maria held the same lofty opinion of their marriage, as we have no sources from her own hand, a fact that is important to underscore. We only encounter Johann Christoph's AMICO in the *Pious Meditations*, not Anna Maria in her own voice.[195]

Johann Christoph also comments on the importance of friends who console him, the "visible angels" whom he believes God has sent him.[196] Luther urged the despondent and downhearted to avoid isolation at all costs, something Johann Christoph takes to heart.[197] Later in the *Pious Meditations*, however, he reproduces hymns that speak of abandonment by friends who grow impatient with those who do not overcome their grief in a pious and timely fashion. One stanza complains, "I am not permitted to lament my suffering, people ridicule me for doing so."[198] It is not difficult to imagine Johann Christoph making these words his own as time wore on and his grief did not subside in the way that others expected.[199] He might have felt unspoken—and perhaps spoken—criticism of his status or strength as a true Christian knight, even though he does finally appear to win his battle.

He had certainly heeded Johann Spangenberg's advice (see earlier) and armed himself well with Scripture. The Bible is by far and away the most important source for his reflections in the *Pious Meditations*.[200] In many entries, he indicates passages from Scripture in the margin and then composes prayers based on them. As noted earlier, in some cases, these passages correspond to the Lutheran lectionary, while in other cases, they do not.[201] The abundant biblical quotations in the *Pious Meditations*, which include citations from the Apocrypha,[202] come from the Luther Bible, which Johann Christoph must have owned, even though it does not appear in the inventory of his extant book collection. (Along with devotional works, he likely passed his personal Bible on to his children.) He knew the Luther Bible very well; its words flow effortlessly from his quill. In many ways, Johann Christoph was a lay Protestant version of a medieval monk: owing to a rule of life saturated with Scripture, the sacred text became part of him, with its words becoming his words, its story, his story.[203] In the *Pious Meditations*, Johann Christoph does not simply know Scripture, but he inhabits it, reading himself into its narrative: he becomes the royal official in John 4:46–54, waiting for divine visitation and healing; he is the debtor in Matthew 18:24 who owes God ten thousand talents.[204] As might be expected in a lament, Johann Christoph draws especially on the Psalms and Job. Echoing the Old Testament saint, he prays, "O dear God, I also asked you for a God-fearing, virtuous, chaste, and pious spouse, which you gave to me and also took away. Now, may your name be blessed [Job 1:21]."[205]

As we have already seen, Johann Christoph also knew Lutheran hymnody very well.[206] Similarly to the words of Scripture, the verses of many hymns had simply become part of the fabric of his being. He scatters hymns—both his own and those written by others—throughout the *Pious Meditations*, but he can also resort to hymns exclusively for significant stretches of time. From July 25 to September 12, nine successive entries are hymns, two by Johann Christoph, seven by well-known writers. During his year of lament, there were seasons in which he found that verse rather than prose could give best voice to his suffering.[207] *Fraw Musica* (Lady Music), as Luther once advised, played an especially important role in helping soothe Johann Christoph's *hertzeleid* (sorrowing heart).[208] Many of the hymns in the *Pious Meditations* fall under the rubric of "cross- and consolation-songs" (*Kreuz- und Trostlieder*), an important and ever-expanding category of hymns in late sixteenth and early seventeenth Lutheran hymnals.[209] The only other sources for Johann Christoph's lament, aside from the aforementioned concluding quotation from Boethius, are a few uncited works of Lutheran devotion.[210]

Genre and Audience

There is no record of the *Pious Meditations* in any of the summaries of Johann Christoph's life, whether early modern or modern.[211] His few writings on jurisprudence appear in these summaries but not his *Pious Meditations*.[212] The work was also not included in Johann Christoph's personal library. It wound up in the Oelhafen family archive, which is currently housed in the Historical Archive of the German National Museum in Nürnberg. This is where I discovered it. The Historical Archive's catalog lists the work as the *Gebetbuch des Hans Christoph Oelhafen*. This title is misleading, not only because the most important sources refer to the widower as Johann, not Hans, but also because the *Pious Meditations* is not really a *Gebetbuch* (prayer book).[213] In the early modern period, pastors and theologians would publish collections of prayers for lay use. Luther's prayers were especially popular in such *Gebetbücher*.[214] Devout laypeople would then create their own private prayer books by copying down inspiring sayings from Scripture, sermons, songs, clerical *Gebetbücher*, and other works of devotion to aid them in the life of faith, adding their own commentary here and there. A lay *Gebetbuch* was basically a compilation of the prayers and consoling or inspiring sayings of others.[215] Jill Bepler has discussed a number of such prayer books among early modern German noblewomen, and Patrice Veit has studied them among the upper classes through funeral sermons.[216]

As we have seen, while the *Pious Meditations* contains material borrowed or culled from other sources, much of it is original to Johann Christoph, or, perhaps more accurately, much of it is the result of his unique and original synthesis of the sermons, songs, prayers, biblical readings, and works of devotion that were so much a part of his life. It is in fact quite difficult to separate out what is original to Johann Christoph in the *Pious Meditations* from what he has borrowed, either wittingly or unwittingly, from elsewhere. There are numerous passages that refer to his own immediate and personal experience, and these certainly come directly from him. But in many other passages, the line between what is original and what is borrowed is indecipherable. I have tried to indicate obvious reliance on outside sources where I can, but I have not attempted to locate each and every source that might have informed Johann Christoph's *Pious Meditations*, an effort that would miss the true purpose of the work and misunderstand the author's attitude toward his sources. Johann Christoph's goal was not originality, and like his contemporaries, it was also not the strict avoidance of plagiarism that is so much a part of modern scholarship. His goal was consolation, and he drew instinctively and even feverishly on every source and resource he could, many of which he likely had memorized by this point in his life, the fruit of years of intensive reading and meditating on various works of devotion.[217] As we have seen, the sources of devotion in his life had simply become part of him.

Johann Christoph titled his work "Meditationes," not "Gebetbuch."[218] This choice of title is important; it indicates a greater authorial presence and creativity than was characteristic of prayer books. In terms of genre, it is perhaps closest to the "meditational diaries"—as opposed to the prayer books—of the ruling nobility that Jill Bepler has examined.[219] Like the *Pious Meditations*, these unpublished works contain dated entries of either prose or verse that consist of private meditations on the spiritual life. These meditations also contain the same hybrid mix of original and borrowed material that we find in Johann Christoph's work. Additionally, meditational diaries refer to places of travel.[220] Still, the *Pious Meditations* is unique in terms of its affectivity, interiority, and focus on a single life crisis over the course of one year; its verse entries also tend to be longer than those of the meditational diaries of the nobility.[221] Finally, Johann Christoph was not a member of the landed and ruling nobility; he was a well-to-do burgher, part of the urban nobility, but not a member of the patrician class. Thus, at least at present, there is simply nothing quite like the *Pious Meditations* in the extant lay consolation literature from early modern Germany.[222]

As we have also seen, it was never printed. Unlike much of the consolation literature of the period, the majority of it written by leading theologians, Johann Christoph did not intend the *Pious Meditations* for publication.[223] His audience was more limited, something that is also indicated by his decision to write in German, the language of his heart and family life and also the preferred language of devotion in his day.[224] At one level, his audience was simply himself. The work may be seen as an extended soliloquy in which Johann Christoph addresses his own soul—or, perhaps better, his own heart—seeking to console it with his Lutheran faith. The *Pious Meditations* is an exercise in the self-consolation that Steiger has studied, and it reveals the "radical reflexivity" that Taylor has examined. Johann Christoph speaks to himself in its pages, acting as a pastor to himself—this is perhaps the most striking feature of the whole work, for it is replete with self-consolation. His faith-self attempts to bring solace to his despairing-self. This self-consolation involves Johann Christoph stepping outside of himself, as it were, and reflecting on himself from an external vantage point, even as he remains firmly grounded in his current painful situation.

But the *Pious Meditations* is not simply an exercise in introspection; it is not merely an interesting example of early modern interiority, a category that Johann Christoph would have rejected in any case because of the porosity of his self-understanding. The work is too polished to have been intended solely for personal use, and yet it is also too unvarnished in its expression of personal pain to have been appropriate for the general reading public. We know that Johann Christoph had his children in mind as he produced the work, for, as we have seen, he mentions them several times. In at least one entry, he says that he has sung an original composition from the work in their presence.[225] As we have also seen, according to Anna Carrdus, early modern Lutheran parents were in the regular habit of teaching their children how to face death and how to grieve properly.[226] In keeping with the instructions of Luther's Small

Catechism, Johann Christoph was undoubtedly seeking to fulfill this duty as a faithful house father,[227] likely sharing portions of the *Pious Meditations* with his children, perhaps especially its hymns, during the gatherings of the Oelhafen *Hauskirche*. The age of his remaining children ranged from two-and-a-half to fifteen years old, so not all of the work's material would have been appropriate and accessible for all of them. But his children were certainly another audience for the *Pious Meditations*, and he likely bequeathed the work to them upon his death.

His posterity was another audience. Among other things, Johann Christoph was seeking to give a good account of himself as a faithful Christian who knew how to grieve well.[228] But the work also strikes one as a deeply honest account of his experience and not simply as an exercise in either witting or unwitting "self-fashioning," something that his decision to write in the vernacular and for a limited audience underscores.[229] As we have seen, the *Pious Meditations* is a work of art in its own right, and Johann Christoph clearly hoped that it would survive him. Given all of the effort and expense that he put into creating it, and given that he did not want it to be published, he must have had not only himself and his children in mind but also future Oelhafens as he did so. In one respect, he was simply providing an account of an extremely significant event in his life for his own sake and for his children and posterity. As was common in the early modern period, especially among the upper classes, he likely intended this work of devotion to be passed down from one generation of Oelhafens to the next. Members of the nobility would add personal reflections, devotional images, and even family portraits to Bibles, hymnals, prayer books, and works of devotion, effectively creating a *Familienreliquie* (a family relic) that would bear witness to their piety to future generations within their families.[230] Johann Christoph was doing something similar in the *Pious Meditations*.

There is another intriguing possibility as to the work's intended audience: Johann Christoph might have also written it with a proto-Rosicrucian gathering in mind. We know that he shared the *Pious Meditations* with Johann Saubert. Prior to taking up his posts in Altdorf (and later Nürnberg), Saubert had studied in Tübingen (1612–1614), where he had come under the influence of Johann Valentin Andreae (1586–1654),[231] the founder of a utopian brotherhood there called the *Societas Christiana*. This brotherhood was committed to a revival of evangelical Christianity in the vein of Johann Arndt's *True Christianity*, with a strong emphasis on practical piety (*pietatis praxis*).[232] (This group does not seem to have been committed to full-blown esoteric Rosicrucianism, with its interest in alchemy, astrology, and the kabbala, although Andreae's name is frequently associated with such a movement.)[233] Saubert was a member of this group and would plant a similar one, the *Unio Christiana*, in Nürnberg in 1628.[234] According to Donald Dickson, "This [Nürnberg] society was a support through which the brothers could encourage and comfort one another during their struggles with the world."[235] The symbol for this group was a cross covered with the rose-colored blood of Christ. The pastor who attended to Anna Maria on her deathbed and who granted Johann Christoph absolution during Lent,[236] Christoph Leibnitz (1579–1632), deacon at the St. Sebald Church since 1610,[237] knew Saubert and would later become a founding member of the *Unio Christiana* in Nürnberg.[238] So Johann Christoph was in contact with people who were interested in Andreae's efforts to revive evangelical piety through learned sodalities. (We do not know if Johann Christoph was a member of the *Unio Christiana* once it formed.)

Additionally, in the *Pious Meditations*, Johann Christoph quotes from a work associated with the nascent Rosicrucian movement in Germany, the anonymous *Simple Answer and Request of a Layperson Who Is Yet a Lover of Wisdom, to the Highly Illumined Brotherhood of the Rose-Cross* (1615).[239] Johann Christoph owned this work along with three others associated with the Rosicrucian movement: Andreae's *The Fame of the Fraternity or the Discovery of the Brotherhood of the Laudatory Order of the Rose-Cross* (1615),[240] Julius Sperber's *Letter or Report to All Who Have Read about the New Brotherhood of the Rose-Cross* [. . .] (1615),[241] and the anonymous *Letter to the Illustrious and Revered Brotherhood of the Rose-Cross* (1615).[242] Johann Christoph also refers to the "the precious rose-colored blood" of Christ in one entry of the *Pious Meditations*.[243]

It is thus possible that Saubert, perhaps along with Leibnitz, had already organized a proto–*Unio Christiana* group in either Altdorf or

Nürnberg and that Johann Christoph was part of it. He was definitely interested in the Rosicrucian movement, and he must have discussed this interest with Saubert. I am aware of no concrete evidence for the existence of such a group in Altdorf or Nürnberg at this time, but if one did exist, even as an informal gathering, it certainly would have been a fitting audience for the *Pious Meditations* and would help account for its highly polished yet still private nature. Johann Christoph was clearly in need of the comfort such a group could have provided in the midst of his struggles.[244]

If we were able to ask Johann Christoph who the intended audience for his *Pious Meditations* was, he would undoubtedly reply, "God." In the final analysis, his yearlong lament, with all of its heartfelt and heart-wrenching expressions of sorrow, confusion, and despair, along with all of its remarkable expressions of perseverance and faith—all of this was addressed to the Triune God, whom Johann Christoph saw as the ultimate cause of his grief and also as the true source of the consolation he so desperately sought in the midst of it. The work's considerable artistry could simply be an offering of a broken yet devout heart to its sovereign and merciful God.

Of course, Johann Christoph would be shocked to learn that his *Pious Meditations* now has a twenty-first-century audience and that, against his wishes, the work has finally been published, and in a language he never would have anticipated.[245] I can only ask forgiveness for this intrusion into his privacy, even as I am most grateful that he composed this remarkable work and that I was fortunate enough to discover it a number of years ago. We are separated from Johann Christoph by four hundred years, and it is important that we attend to this historical distance. Still, the *Pious Meditations* is his attempt to deal with some of the basic realities of human existence in every age: mortality, loss, grief, despair, the obligations of parenthood, and the frequently mysterious workings of fate or divine providence. There is wisdom in Johann Christoph's lament, although each reader will have to decide how much and of what kind.

A Note on the Translation, Dates, and Terms

I have striven in my translation of Johann Christoph's *Pious Meditations* to capture his meaning, and unfortunately, this has meant that I have been unable to express his full artistry. I have not sought to preserve the rhyme structures of the hymns, songs, and poems in the work, for doing so would have both exceeded my skill as a translator and also conflicted with my goal of rendering his meaning as faithfully as possible in English. Instead, I have simply indicated the rhyme structure for the relevant entries in the notes. I have, however, sought to preserve the appearance of the *Pious Meditations*, reproducing the spacing of words on the page and placing important words in red font where Johann Christoph used red ink. I have also sought to convey his emphases, arranging words in places of importance that reflect his concerns. I consulted with a couple of contemporary poets to learn how to hear, as best I can, his voice in his text.* Following their advice, I have read (and in some cases sung, albeit badly) each entry aloud in the original language and have then sought to translate with Johann Christoph's meaning and emphases—with his voice—in mind. I have also preserved, where possible, his acrostics, explaining their meaning in the notes. He uses "AMICO," or variants of it, as the pattern for many of his acrostics, a decision no doubt informed by the sentiment he expresses in entry 32 (stanza 10): "She remains constantly close to me, in my heart, and on my lips." Unless otherwise indicated, all biblical quotations are my own translations of Johann Christoph's use of Scripture, which closely follows the Luther Bible.

There were two calendars in Johann Christoph's lifetime, the traditional or old-style Julian one and the new-style Gregorian one. The

* I am grateful to my colleagues Mark Wagenaar and Chelsea Wagenaar, both talented poets, for this wise counsel as I have worked on this project.

latter was introduced into Catholic lands on December 21, 1582, while the former remained in force in Protestant lands for over a century or more, not being replaced until March 1, 1700, or even later. Initially there was a ten-day discrepancy between the two calendars and later an eleven-day one—the new-style calendar was ten (and later, eleven) days ahead of the old-style one. Early modern Nürnberg observed the old-style calendar, with the year beginning on January 1, as did Johann Christoph in his *Pious Meditations* and *Diarium*. I have, therefore, followed the old-style calendar in my translation. When Johann Christoph traveled to Catholic territories, which he frequently did, he operated on both calendars. To convert dates to the modern Gregorian calendar, simply add ten days: February 13, 1619, the day of Anna Maria's death, would be February 23, 1619.

Throughout, I use the term *evangelical* in the sense intended by early Protestants: those committed to the gospel. *Evangelical* is the term they, including Johann Christoph, used for themselves, and so I have employed it as frequently as possible, although I have opted now and again for *Lutheran*, which for the purposes of this volume can be treated as its synonym.

I also use the term *Late Reformation* throughout. It refers to the period between ca. 1580 and ca. 1620 in those portions of the German lands of the Holy Roman Empire that had adopted the Lutheran faith, even if, as in the case of Nürnberg, this confessional identity was contested. A synonym would be the *Confessional Age* (*Konfessionelles Zeitalter*), the term of choice in Germany.

Finally, in order to conform to the usage of the DB, NDB, SN, and UEN, in most instances, I have opted for "Johann Christoph Oelhafen" instead of one of the other versions of his name that appear in early modern and modern sources. The spelling of names was not uniform in the seventeenth century, in any case. "Johann Christoph Oelhafen" is attested in sources from the GNM-HA and the NStadtA, although these sources contain other spellings too. Based on how he refers to himself in the *Pious Meditations*, we know that Johann Christoph spelled his name "Iohannes Christophorus Ölhafius/Ölhafen" in Latin and "Johann

Christof Ölhafen" in German. I have retained these spellings a few times when it has made sense to do so. In the final vernacular entry of the *Pious Meditations*, Johann Christoph refers to his deceased wife as "Anna Maria Johann Christof Ölhafin," using the feminine form of their surname in German. He likely had this spelling in mind in each occurrence of "AMICO" and its variants, something that is not possible to capture in English translation.

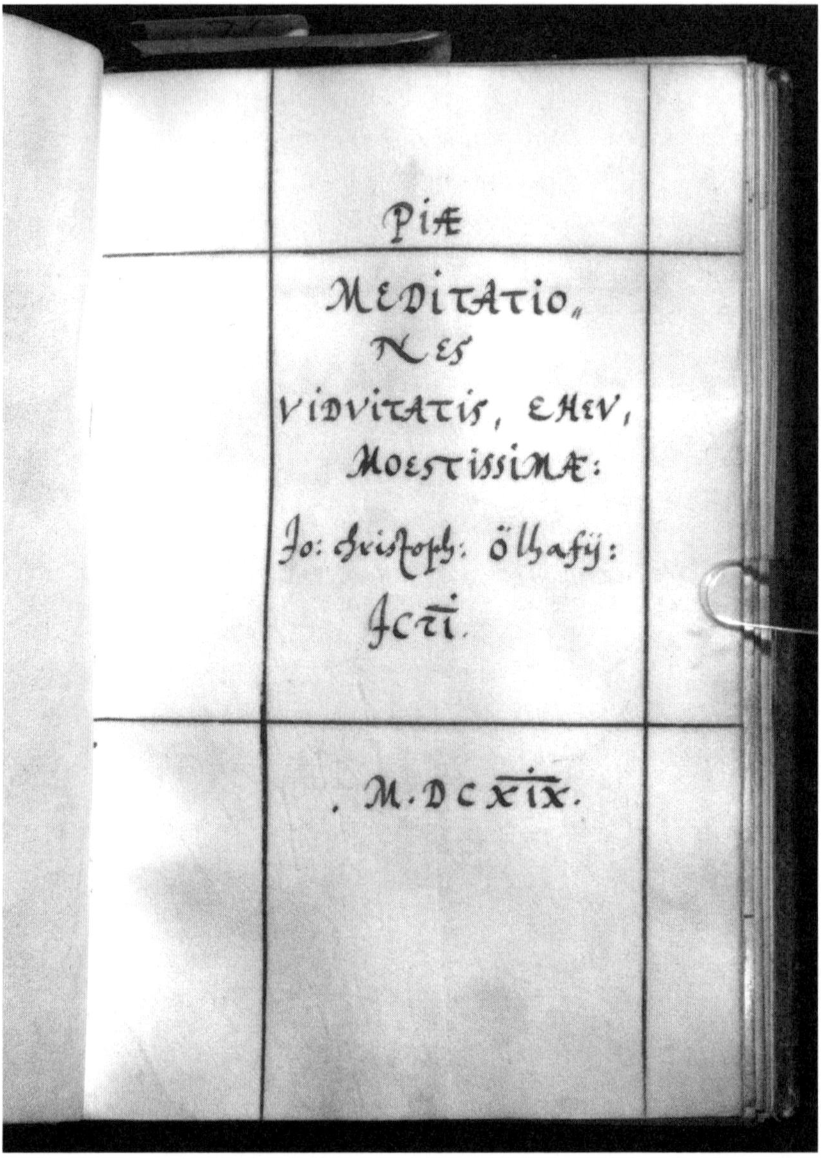

Image 3: Title page of the *Pious Meditations* (*Gebetbuch des Hans Christoph Oelhafen*, GNM-HA, Familienarchiv von Oelhafen, Rep. II/80, Nr. 32)

Pious Meditations
on the, Alas, Most Sorrowful Bereavement
of Johann Christoph Ölhafen, Lawyer

1619

Image 4: The Oelhafen coat of arms (*Gebetbuch des Hans Christoph Oelhafen*, GNM-HA, Familienarchiv von Oelhafen, Rep. II/80, Nr. 32)

Elsewhere, the way is safe for deceiving under the name of
FRIEND;[1]
but here, the way is safe even for trusting in the
FRIEND.
O remarkable testaments of remarkable faith! In
THIS FRIEND,
we learn who ÖLHAFEN is,
and what he loves.[2]
f. Johann Saubert[3]

---

1 The first line of this note—"Tuta via est alibi, per AMICI fallere nomen"—is similar to the first line in one of Ovid's maxims: "Tuta frequensque via est per amicum fallere nomen." See H. T. Riley, ed., *A Dictionary of Latin and Greek Quotations, Proverbs, Maxims, and Mottos, Classical and Mediaeval, Including Law Terms and Phrases* (London: George Bell & Sons, 1891), 470.

2 There are various ways of interpreting *FRIEND* in this note from Saubert. In the first occurrence (*AMICI*), Saubert, following Ovid (see preceding note), obviously has a generic false friend in mind. In the second and third ones—*AMICO* and *In AMICO HOC*, respectively—he appears to have the *Pious Meditations* in view, which he sees as a kind of true friend. Saubert commends the work as trustworthy and as an expression of exceptional faith. He also sees the *Pious Meditations* as being revelatory of Johann Christoph's true identity and his love for his deceased wife (and likely also for God). Alternately, given that Johann Christoph referred to Anna Maria as his AMICO in this work and elsewhere, something Saubert certainly knew, it is also possible to see the second and third occurrences of *FRIEND* as references to her. On this reading, Saubert was seeking to extol Anna Maria, who figures prominently in the work, as a true friend to her husband, by whom the reader learns who he actually is and what, or whom, he truly loves—namely, his deceased wife. Or Saubert may simply be playing with *AMICO* without intending to refer to Anna Maria exclusively. Finally, it is possible to see the

second and third occurrences of *FRIEND* as references to God, but this reading is less likely, as Johann Christoph never refers to God the Father as friend in the *Pious Meditations*, although he does refer to Christ in this way (see entries 62 and 67).

3 The *f.* is an abbreviation for *fidelis servus* (faithful servant). See the discussion of Saubert in the introduction.

To have had you with me, AMICO, has been happiness enough.[1]

I.C. Ölhafen, mourning
and grieving, [signed] by my own hand.

---

1 "Sat, AMICO te mihi, foelix." This phrase may be found in George Buchanan's *Psalmorum Davidis Paraphrasis Poetica* (Geneva, 1566), 4, as part of his paraphrase of Ps 4:7 (accessible via Post-Reformation Digital Library, http://www.prdl.org). "AMICO" could also be translated as "FRIEND." I have assumed that Johann Christoph is referring to his deceased wife.

Image 5: Portrait of Johann Christoph by Lorenz Strauch (see discussion in the introduction; *Gebetbuch des Hans Christoph Oelhafen*, GNM-HA, Familienarchiv von Oelhafen, Rep. II/80, Nr. 32)

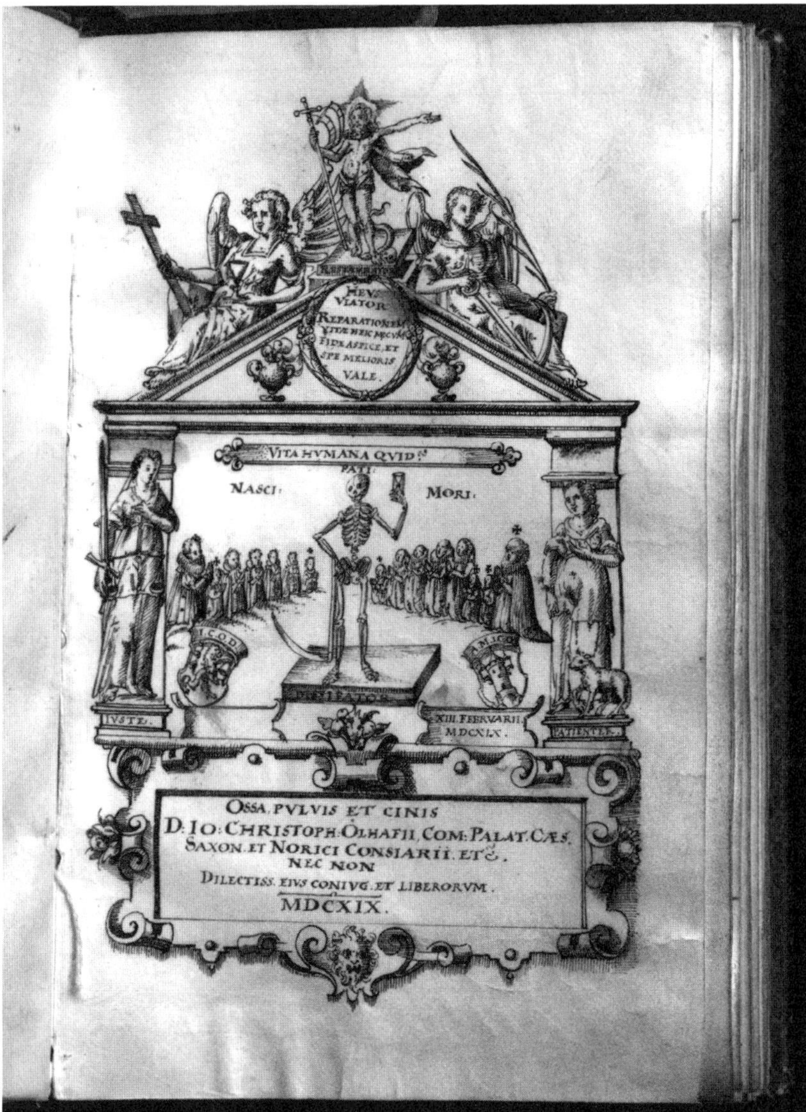

Image 6: Johann Christoph's epitaph in 1619 (*Gebetbuch des Hans Christoph Oelhafen*, GNM-HA, Familienarchiv von Oelhafen, Rep. II/80, Nr. 32)

This epitaph, to which Johann Christoph refers in entry 26, is based on the one that he had prepared already in 1599, when he thought he was going to die (see the introduction). A modified version of it also marks his grave in the St. Johannisfriedhof in Nürnberg, where Anna Maria and a number of their children are also buried (see the epilogue and image 9). The epitaph is composed of classical architectural framing elements—in this case, unadorned engaged columns supporting a simple pediment, crowned by reclining allegorical figures and the resurrected Christ. Beginning at the top, the resurrected Christ, still bearing the wounds of his crucifixion, stands triumphantly on the cover of an empty tomb. He has a cross-scepter and banner in his right hand, signifying his victory over the grave. His left arm is outstretched, with his thumb and first two fingers extended in a blessing gesture, a long-established attribute of the Salvator Mundi *in medieval art. The gesture was also typical of Lutheran images of the resurrected Christ and may be found in works by Lucas Cranach. Christ's left foot tramples the head of a serpent, an obvious reference to Genesis 3:15. The skull next to the serpent indicates that, like the serpent (or Satan), Christ has also vanquished death by his resurrection. Christ wears a cape that, along with the banner, is blown by the wind. Additionally, Christ has a halo or nimbus indicating his divinity, and aside from the cape, he wears only a loincloth to preserve modesty. The title on the facing edge of the tomb cover, likely added by Johann Christoph himself, reads "RESTAVRATOR" (Restorer). Interestingly, the Christ figure is smaller than the winged or angelic personifications, who recline atop the pediment on either side of him. The figure on Christ's right represents Faith; she holds a eucharistic chalice in her left hand, a cross in her right. The figure on Christ's left side signifies Hope; she has an anchor in her right hand (see Heb 6:19) and a palm branch in her left. The palm signifies peace but also, and perhaps more importantly here, victory over death.*

Below "RESTAVRATOR," on the pediment and at the intersection of the raking cornices, there is a wreathed cartouche flanked by two urns. In Roman times, people put the smoking ashes of the deceased in such urns for safekeeping. The inscription on the cartouche contains an invitation to the viewer:

HEVS
VIATOR

REPARATIONEM
VITAE HEIC MECVM
FIDE ASPICE ET
SPE MELIORIS

VALE

Hark,
Wayfarer!

In this place, with me,
look toward
the renewal of life in faith
and in hope of something better.

Farewell!

A grim reaper figure, representing Death, appears in the middle of the epitaph. The skeleton rests its right wrist on a sickle and holds an hourglass in its left hand. The sand in the hourglass appears to have run out. The inscription on Death's pedestal reads "DISSIPATOR" (Destroyer), the antithesis of "RESTAVRATOR" (Restorer). Above the skeleton's head, there is a question on a long, ornamental plate just below the cornice: "VITA HVMANA QVID?" (What is human life?). The skeleton's answer appears to its right ("NASCI" [to be born]), above its head ("PATI" [to suffer]), and to its left ("MORI" [to die]).[1] *To the skeleton's right, in the foreground, Johann Christoph's coat of arms appears with his initials, "I.C.O.D." (Johann Christoph Oelhafen Doctor). In the background, there are images of Johann Christoph himself and his six sons in order of birth, all kneeling with their hands folded in prayer, a pose traditionally identifying the donor and his family on devotional images and epitaphs. The crosses above the heads of two figures indicate that they were already deceased at the time the epitaph was made. To the skeleton's lower left, in the foreground, Anna Maria's coat of arms appears with "AMICO" at the top: Anna Maria Iohann Christoph Oelhafen. Below this coat of arms, Johann Christoph has inserted the date of her death: "XIII FEBRVARII. MDCXIX" (February 13, 1619). (Note that the corresponding frame on the other side is blank; Johann Christoph has left it open for someone to record his death.) In the background, Anna Maria and her seven daughters in order of birth kneel with hands folded in prayer; along with her, three have died, indicated by the crosses above their heads.*

Justice (or acting justly) stands in front of the column to the skeleton's right, holding an upturned sword in her right hand and scales in her left. Patience (or acting patiently) stands in front of the column to the skeleton's left, a lamb at her feet, which is reminiscent of Christ the Lamb of God, who exhibited long-suffering.[2] *These two figures without wings continue or establish the program of personified virtues that includes the winged figures atop the pediment. (The wings may have been added because the figures appear in the heavenly realm with Christ.)*

Beneath the central frame, the following words appear on a simulated engraved panel, framed by classical volutes, garlands, and grotesques:

OSSA, PVLVIS ET CINIS
D: IO: CHRISTOPH: ÖLHAFII, COM: PALAT. CAES.
SAXON. ET NORICI CONSIARII. ETC.
NEC NON
DILECTISS. EIVS CONIVG. ET LIBERORVM.
MDCXIX

The bones, dust, and ashes of
Dr. Johann Christoph Ölhafen, Imperial Count Palatine,
Legal Counsel to Saxony and Nürnberg, etc.,
and also
of his most beloved wife and children.
1619

Johann Christoph included this epitaph at the beginning of his Pious Meditations *in order to indicate his keen awareness of his mortality and also to testify to his faith and hope in Christ along with his resolve to live justly and patiently. For him, Christ is the great restorer of life and destroyer of death, the only one who can provide a more consoling response to the probing question and proffered answers of the skeleton. Christ is also the source of the virtues that the epitaph extols. The fact that Christ stands atop the whole structure may also indicate Johann Christoph's desire to extol Christianity over pagan religion and philosophy, which in his mind provided no solution to death, even though, as a humanist, he clearly admired classical literature. In sum, the epitaph seeks to convey the Christian piety of Johann Christoph and his family.*[3]

1 Johann Christoph likely has in mind here "Nasci, pati, mori/ Fortuna," Ludwig Senfl's (1486–1542/43) arrangement of the famous song "Fortuna desperata," which first appeared in fifteenth-century Italy. See Honey Meconi, *Fortuna desperata: Thirty-Six Settings of an Italian Song* (Middleton, WI: A-R Editions, 2001), 94–97, 180; and Arnold Geering and Wilhelm Altwegg, eds., *Ludwig Senfl, Sämtliche Werke*, vol. 6 (Wolfenbüttel: Möseler Verlag, 1961), 60–62. See also entry 48. On the popularity of Italian music, both sacred and secular, in late sixteenth-century Nürnberg, especially among the patrician class, see Butler, "Liturgical Music," 514–17. It is possible that the adverbs "IUSTE" and "PATIENTER" at the base of the two columns modify *NASCI* (to be born in the right manner / patiently), *PATI* (to suffer in the right manner / patiently), and *MORI* (to die in the right manner / patiently), but it is more likely that they simply indicate the actions or recommendations of the allegorical figures above them. See the following note.

2 These framing figures, along with those atop the pediment, are clearly meant as a riposte to Death's assertion that human life consists solely of birth, suffering, and death. Perhaps the adverbs *IUSTE* and *PATIENTER* could therefore be read as alternative responses to Death's query—human life consists of faith and hope and of living justly and patiently, all enabled by Christ's resurrection. Or, given the positioning of the two figures—Justice close to Johann Christoph and his sons, Patience near Anna Maria and her daughters—the inscriptions may be gendered, indicating that Justice (or acting justly) is an especially male virtue, while Patience (or acting patiently) is an especially female one. Still, patience is a dominant theme in the *Pious Meditations*, and there is no indication that Johann Christoph thought it was a virtue especially befitting the female sex. See entry 46.

3 I am grateful to Mitchell Merback for his assistance in interpreting this image.

I seek from you in great
distress
what is based on your teaching and own
commandment.
Grant this, you most exalted
triune God,
for the sake of your honor and my
salvation.[1]

1619

---

1 Original text:

Was, uf dein lehr, unndt selbst
Gebott,
Ich, bei dir such, in höchster
Nott:
das verleih du höchste
dreifaltigkeit,
dir zur Ehr; Mir zur
Seligkeit.

Rhyme structure is *aabb*. This prayer closely resembles a prayer to the Holy Trinity in *Precationes piae ab Friderico Wilhelmo Duce Saxoniae coll. et usurpatae / Christliche Gebet, so Fridrich Wilhelm Hertzog zu Sachsen selbst colligirt und gebrauchet* (Leipzig, 1605; there are no page numbers—this prayer is the final one before the concluding index; VD17 39:157054U—includes link to online version). Johann Christoph must have owned or had access to this book, as several of the entries in the *Pious Meditations* appear to come from it. Johann Wanckel (1544–1616), a talented intellectual who since 1595 had been employed at the court of Duke Friedrich Wilhelm, published the work in honor of his deceased benefactor. Unfortunately, he does not identify the authors of the prayers that Duke Friedrich Wilhelm assembled in his prayer book. On Wanckel, see the entry for "Wanckel, Johannes" in DB. In 1602, he became a professor at the University of Wittenberg, where he served in various capacities until his death. It is likely that Johann Christoph knew both Wanckel and the duke, as the Nürnberg jurist provided legal counsel for electoral Saxony. Wanckel may have even presented Johann Christoph with the *Precationes* as a gift, although this is only a speculation; the work does not appear among Johann Christoph's extant books.

Take me, LORD, from myself,
and give me to yourself;[1]
turn away from me what turns me
away from you.[2]

---

1 Original text:

> Nimb mich HERR mir,
> unndt gib mich dir,
> wende von mir, was mich
> wendet von dir.

This prayer bears close resemblance to a prayer in *Morgen vnnd Abendts Gebete / sampt einem Vatter vnser / Gebetßweiß* (Nürnberg, 1573; VD16 M 6331—includes links to online versions). The prayer, intended for daily use, appears on the penultimate printed page of the work—there is no page number. The first two lines of the prayer are also nearly identical to a prayer in the works of an English poetess. See Adah Blanche Roe, "Anna Owena Hoyers: A Poetess of the Seventeenth Century" (PhD diss., Bryn Mawr College, 1915), 76.

2 Rhyme structure is *aaba*.

1[1]

O living God and consoler of all the sad-hearted, I have lost my most beloved treasure on earth, for you have torn away a piece of my heart. You gave her to me and let me have her for eighteen years. Now you have taken her out of this miserable existence to yourself as your beloved child, because she gratefully acknowledged your Son and called to him from her heart as her Bridegroom in the middle of death's despair. Console me, a sad and miserable widower, and help me to bear my suffering and to rear up my small children. According to your divine will, send that blessed hour when I and those who belong to me will come together with her before your face in true joy and eternal love. May you, who can bring eternal joy and delight out of suffering, be highly praised in all eternity. Amen.

February 13, 1619, the evening of the
same day that my beloved wife,
AMICO, fell asleep in the Lord at a
quarter to one in the morning.

May God give her a joyful resurrection and me a blessed following after her.[2]

---

1 This prayer closely follows "Ein Gebet für ein Hausvatter/dem sein Weib stirbet" ("A Prayer for a Housefather Whose Wife Has Died") in Peter Streuber, *Ehespiegel* (Leipzig, 1589), Mv v-Mvi r (VD16 S 9554—includes link to online version). (This prayer appears in Johann Mathesius, *Oeconomia oder Bericht vom Christlichen Haußwesen. Sampt kurtzen Haußgebetlein*, which Streuber reproduces at the end of his work. The

Oeconomia was first published in 1564 [VD16 M 1421—includes link to online version].) Johann Christoph has personalized this prayer, adding that he had Anna Maria for eighteen years, but he otherwise reproduces the prayer largely verbatim.

2 "Eine Seelige nachfarth."

2

Almighty and eternal God, you true and faithful Father of all widowers and orphans, you have now taken away from my dear children, their mother, and from me, my earthly helpmate. Nevertheless, have mercy on them and me in a fatherly way according to your promise.[1] Give us grace and grant that I may bring them up in all fear of God, discipline, and virtue. And if it is your divine will, for the sake of what is best for them, preserve me in good health for a time longer so that I can lead them honorably and, as a faithful father, fulfill the desires and wishes of their dear mother of blessed memory. If you find it good and useful for these poor orphans, bestow on my life, O righteous God, what you, according to your alone wise counsel, took away from their dear mother in recent years so that I, with your grace, may help them along a little better. And turn away your great rod of wrath, which you have wielded against us. Regard us with the eyes of your mercy and compensate her and us with eternal goods in exchange for the temporal goods that you have taken away from us.[2] Do this for the sake of Jesus Christ, your beloved Son. Amen.

February 14, 1619, as my beloved wife of
blessed memory was laid in her coffin.[3]

---

1 Johann Christoph may have 2 Cor 6:2 in mind, part of the Epistle reading for Lent 1.

2 Luther could also speak of such divine compensation or exchange for the loss of temporal goods, including loved ones. See Tappert, *Luther*, 39, 54, and 56.

3 Johann Christoph records in his *Diarium* that Anna Maria was laid in her coffin on the evening of this day. He also records that he composed this prayer "for comfort and help" (*umb Trost vnndt beistandt*). See the entry for February 14, 1619. February 14 was the first Sunday of Lent in 1619. On February 15, Johann Christoph additionally records that he began to write an account of Anna Maria's life story, although it does not appear to be extant.

3[1]

When I consider my misery
    and cast my eyes here and there,
all help and consolation from people and the wide world
    fail me.
But I say to you, faithful and merciful God,
    help me, because urgent aid is necessary.
If you do not provide counsel and rescue,
    I will very soon have death as my portion.
If you do not take away this burden,
    my heart will have neither peace nor rest.
Ah, Father, regard with grace
    my sighs and tears so that I can
endure this heavy hardship
    into which my wife's death has plunged me.
If your helpful hand would only extend
    a small finger, there would be nothing to fear.
I would be wholly strong, calm, and healthy,
    and would have peace and rest at the same hour.
It is the merit and great work of your Son
    by which he redeemed us
that I seek and desire from the heart
    and humbly grasp in faith.
If you would also come to my aid
    against Satan's murderous and shameful designs,[2]
I would then live as pleases you
    as long as I am a pilgrim on earth.
I would keep my conscience pure
    until my soul (O, let it be soon)

journeys to my AMICO's throng,
where continual joy is unending,
where the devout in the heavenly hall
loudly praise and laud
the highly exalted Trinity
from now into eternity.
Amen. Amen.

February 17, 1619, as the coffin of my
beloved wife of blessed memory
rests on the wagon.[3]

---

1 This poem closely follows a prayer for true penitence that appeared in *Precationes piae* [. . .] *Christliche Gebet*, 187–91. In the original, the poem comprises a series of rhyming couplets. Johann Christoph has personalized it here and there.

2 As later entries suggest (see especially 73), for Johann Christoph, these diabolical designs may have included the temptation to take his own life.

3 Johann Christoph records in his *Diarium* that Anna Maria was buried on this day. He writes, "Gott verleihe Ihr vnnd vnß allen, Eine fröliche auferstehung. Amen. Ach herr Jhesu. Amen" (May God give to her and all of us a joyful resurrection. Amen. Ah, Lord Jesus. Amen). In the entries for February 18 and 26, 1619, Johann Christoph records that he has designed and ordered an epitaph for Anna Maria. This epitaph does not appear to be extant, unless it was incorporated into Johann Christoph's epitaph, something he does not indicate. Their common grave in the St. Johannisfriedhof in Nürnberg has only Johann Christoph's epitaph (see the epilogue and image 9).

4[1]

Ah, LORD, you great and frightening God, I have sinned and done what is not right. I have been godless and by my deeds have turned from your commandments and laws. Therefore, your wrath and curse have begun to strike me. But hear my prayer and pleading and look upon me graciously with the eyes of your mercy. Forgive me my sins and misdeeds, and hear me for the sake of the Lord Messiah, your most beloved Son Jesus Christ. Give to me a penitent heart and grant that I may refrain from sin and live according to your divine will and pleasure. Renew in me your goodness and mercy. Then I will render thanks to you and praise you eternally. Amen.

February 21, 1619,
on Reminiscere Sunday.[2]

Ah, Lord, listen. Ah, Lord, be gracious. Ah, Lord, attend to me and act on my behalf. And do not delay for your own sake, my God, because I am called by your Name.[3]

---

1 As Johann Christoph indicates in the left margin, this entry is based on Dan 9 (:4–5, 17–18). Dan 9:15–19 was the traditional lesson for the Monday Mass after the Second Sunday in Lent. See MRM, 72. (The SM does not contain readings for most days of the week.) Perhaps Johann Christoph anticipates the Monday reading in this entry.

2 The Second Sunday in Lent.

3 As Johann Christoph indicates in the left margin, these lines are based on Dan 9 (:19).

5

Ah, that I had enough waters in my head and that my eyes were springs of water, so that I could bewail day and night the loneliness of my life. For death has broken in and strangled my most beloved.[1] Now my household has been destroyed and my honor turned to shame.[2]

But, LORD, you are the one who has created everything in heaven, on earth, and in the sea. You alone are the one who kills and brings to life, for you are righteous, gracious, merciful, patient, of great goodness, and you abandon no one but give your good Spirit to instruct us. And when one who is anxious cries to you, you listen from heaven and give your Savior to those who hope in him. Now, you great God, powerful and frightening, do not consider as insignificant the fear and need that have struck me. To be sure, you are justified in all that you have brought upon me, for you have acted righteously while I have been godless and not lived according to your law. I have also ignored your commandments and testimonies. But, Lord, make with me a firm covenant, for I pledge to live according to your commandments and to uphold your ordinances and regulations, Lord our ruler.[3] Amen.

February 28, 1619, on Oculi Sunday.[4]

---

1 "Dann der Todt ist herein gedrungen, unndt hatt mein Allerliebste gewurget."

2 As Johann Christoph indicates in the left margin, the first part of his entry is based on Jer 9 (:1).

3 As Johann Christoph indicates in the left margin, the second part of his entry is based on Neh 9 (:6, 13, 17, 20, 28, 32, 33, 38).

4 The Third Sunday in Lent.

6

Ah, LORD, do not punish me in your wrath nor discipline me in your anger.[1] Ah, LORD, do not deal with me according to my just deserts and misdeeds, but according to your great grace and mercy.[2] In your wrath, Father, consider and regard the weakness of your child. Why allow me to be asked, where is your God now?[3] Righteous God, because as an unworthy servant I certainly cannot request to be set free from the well-deserved punishment of my sins against your divine majesty, ah, LORD, let me fall into your hands. For you, faithful God, will finally have mercy on me as your poor creature. You will not discard the broken reed,[4] rather, you will soften your heart toward me, a miserable person of flesh and blood, and allow your grace to shine forth. I ask this of you in the name of your Son Jesus Christ. Amen. Amen.

March 7, 1619,
on Laetare Sunday.[5]

---

1 See Ps 6:1 and 38:1.

2 See Ps 103:10. There are also parallels between this line and the collect for Lent 4 in the SM: "Concede quesumus omnipotens deus ut qui ex merito nostre actionis affligimur, tue gratie consolatione respiremus" (Grant, we beseech thee, almighty God, that we who are deservedly punished for our deeds, may be relieved by the consolation of your grace), fols. XXIIII v–XXV r/Bildnr. 70–71.

3 See Ps 42:3.

4 See Isa 42:3.

5 The Fourth Sunday in Lent. Johann Christoph records in his *Diarium* that on March 1, 1619, he was ill with stomach pains and an unusual

or irregular heartbeat. He sought a remedy through purgative sweating. He may have these physical struggles in mind, along with his grief, in this entry.

7[1]

Yes, LORD, I have sinned and unfortunately have been godless and acted against your commandments. Ah Lord, relent from your anger toward me. Hear my prayer and pleading, and help me for the sake of the honor of your Name. Let me find grace so that the whole world may know that you are my God. Incline your ears and listen; open your eyes and see. For the dead in hell, whose spirit has left their bodies, do not praise the glory and righteousness of the Lord. Rather, a soul that is downcast and bent over, going about in a miserable state, and whose eyes have cried out their last tear—Lord, this soul praises your glory and righteousness.

Now LORD, my God, I lie here before you with my prayer, not on account of my righteousness but because of your mercy. Be my God and do not leave me. In this great distress and need, I cry to you. Lord, listen and be gracious to me, the one who is in the jaws of death. For you are my Savior and Helper. Then I will praise you and say, "O blessed am I, for God has revealed his will to me."[2] Amen.

March 14, 1619,
on Judica Sunday.[3]

---

1 As Johann Christoph indicates in the left margin, this entry is based on Bar 2 (:11–19) and 3 (:1–2).

2 See Bar 4:4.

3 The Fifth Sunday in Lent. Johann Christoph records in his *Diarium* that on March 13, 1619, "Mein Epitaphium" (my epitaph) was finally ready. It may be that he feared for his life because of the illness mentioned in the March 1 entry and thus had his own epitaph updated.

But it is more likely that he has Anna Maria's epitaph in mind (see notes to entry 3). In the entry for March 14, he records that he has traveled to Neustadt an der Aisch on business. Johann Christoph remained there until March 18. He was clearly healthy enough to travel.

8

Ah, why do I cry out? Why do I lament, worry, and torment myself day and night without end? Why does my heart eat away and gnaw at itself regarding my loss and almost unbearable pain?

This is the reason: I must freely confess and say that God has sent all of this to me himself, and as faithful father, because of my sin, he let me see and recognize this fact a good time ago, for it is his work to punish on account of sin.[1]

For you, O merciful God and Father, have chastised me in a fatherly manner by taking away my beloved spouse. Yet, at the same time, she was relieved of her many anxieties of heart and her burdensome temporal condition, and instead was raised up to eternal joy and blessedness. But I, on the other hand, have become a miserable, forsaken, and sad widower, and my innocent children have become motherless orphans. Ah, nevertheless, I know that your work is also to have mercy on poor sinners through grace.[2]

So, have mercy on me now. O Jesus, you Son of David, be gracious and merciful to me, a poor sinner. [Father,] for the sake of Jesus Christ your Son, forgive me all of my sins and misdeeds by which I have provoked this your gracious chastisement and fatherly discipline.[3] Amen.

March 21, 1619,
on Palm Sunday.

---

1 As Johann Christoph indicates in the left margin, the first portion of this entry is based on Jer 30 (:15).

2 As Johann Christoph indicates in the left margin, the next portion of this entry is based on Jer 51 (:6, 52, 56), Hos 6 (:5), and

Jonah 3 (:8–9). Taken together, these verses are meant to support Johann Christoph's concluding assertion that God punishes on account of sin.

3 As Johann Christoph indicates in the left margin, the final portion of this entry is based on Luke 18 (:13, 38–40). Johann Christoph references Luke 18 to support his preceding assertion about God having mercy on sinners and also his petition for the same that follows.

9[1]

O LORD, I must confess, I cannot ignore it, I have sinned against your commandments and am not worthy to enter under your roof.[2] But you, LORD, are full of goodness and grace; your mercy far exceeds my sin. Therefore, O Lord, be gracious and merciful to me.

You do not will the death of the sinner and you have no pleasure in the destruction of anyone.[3] If a mother cannot forget her child, LORD, you will also look after my children in grace.[4] Therefore, extend your gracious hand to me as well, tear me away from all my sins,[5] so that my enemies do not rejoice and the devil does not gloat over me, as if he has overpowered me in my sins.

This is, to be sure, a great and frightening day; there has never been one like it. This is a true time of fear. But I will be helped out of it.[6] Therefore, Lord, I flee under your wings and place myself under your protection and *salva guardia*.[7] Open to me the door of your holy wounds,[8] for I do not turn away from you. I will not stop pounding and knocking until you have mercy on me. I will not let up until you console my soul, bless me, and give me peace again. Amen.

March 23, [1619], as I
prepare for confession.[9]

---

1 This prayer closely follows a prayer for the forgiveness of sin in the *Precationes piae* [. . .] *Christliche Gebet*, 341–45. See the following notes for additions that Johann Christoph makes to this prayer.

2 See Matt 8:8. Johann Christoph says he is not worthy to enter under "dein Tach" (your roof), whereas the centurion in Matt 8:8 says that he is not worthy to have Christ enter under "mein Dach"

(my roof). Johann Christoph adds this reference to Matt 8:8 to the prayer in the *Precationes piae* [. . .] *Christliche Gebet*. He may have taken it from the pre-Communion prayer that he adapts in entry 12 (see following notes), which contains language from Matt 8:8 about the communicant not being worthy of having Christ come under his roof.

3 See Ezek 18:23, 32; 33:11.

4 See Isa 49:15–16. Johann Christoph adds this reference to Isa 49 to the prayer in the *Precationes piae* [. . .] *Christliche Gebet*.

5 "reiß mich auß allen meinen sunden."

6 As Johann Christoph indicates in the left margin, this portion of the entry is based on Jer 30 (:7). See entry 8, where he references the same chapter. Johann Christoph adds this reference to Jer 30 to the prayer in the *Precationes piae* [. . .] *Christliche Gebet*.

7 See Ps 57:1 and Ps 91:4. *Salva guardia* (Spanish and Italian) is usually a military term and refers to a civilian safeguard from attack; it can also mean *custody* or *care*. Johann Christoph adds this reference to *salva guardia* to the prayer in the *Precationes piae* [. . .] *Christliche Gebet*.

8 On the place of Christ's wounds in late medieval Catholic devotion, see Rittgers, *Reformation of Suffering*, 66, 68, 82. On Christ's wounds in Lutheran devotion, see Rittgers, 97, 114, and 207. Johann Christoph adds the reference to Christ's wounds to the prayer in the *Precationes piae* [. . .] *Christliche Gebet*.

9 On the Lutheran practice of private confession, which Johann Christoph has in mind here, see Rittgers, *Reformation of the Keys*.

10

Confession[1]

Reverend sir,[2]
In my great sadness, I appear before you with this confession and acknowledge before God and your reverence,[3] as a poor and miserable person, that I was conceived and born in sin.[4] In particular, I confess that I have often moved my beloved God to wrath and punishment with the manifold sins that I have committed against his divine majesty and my neighbor in thought, word, and deed. All of this, I am sorry to say, is abundantly clear to him, for he knows the heart.[5]

I feel all of this keenly, and it causes me great sorrow from the depths of my heart, apart from all hypocrisy. Yet I console myself and firmly believe that my Lord Jesus Christ also came into the world on account of My sins,[6] and that he offered his true body on the tree of the holy cross for Me, a poor sinner, and poured out his precious blood and thereby delivered Me from my sins and from eternal death, enabling me instead to inherit righteousness and eternal life.[7] Therefore, I flee to the unfathomable grace and mercy of Almighty God and seek there help and consolation. I also forgive all who have ever trespassed against me. I now ask Your Reverence, as a called servant of God,[8] in light of my acknowledgment and confession, and admission and recognition [of my sins],[9] that you would absolve me from my sins and count me free and loose from them. In order to provide steadfast consolation, assurance, and strengthening for my weak faith, I also ask that you would give and administer to me the most worthy Lord's Supper, the true body and true blood of Jesus Christ, who established this sacrament himself.[10] For I intend, with God's help, to strive earnestly from this point on to improve my life, to refrain from sin, and to have a pious Christian conduct through the help of the Holy Spirit.

I composed this and read it out
[to my confessor] on March 24, 1619.[11]

---

1 Johann Christoph records in his *Diarium* that on March 24, 1619, he and his family received absolution from Christoph Leibnitz (1579–1632), the deacon at the St. Sebald Church who had ministered to Anna Maria on her deathbed (see the introduction).

2 "Ehrwhürdiger Herr." Johann Christoph uses formal address for his confessor, as was customary at the time. The 1531 edition of Luther's Small Catechism also uses formal address for the confessor. See WA 30/I: 385.4–5; and BC, 360.21.

3 "Euer Ehrwürden."

4 See Ps 51:5.

5 See 1 Sam 16:7; Acts 1:24.

6 See 1 Tim 1:15. The uppercase "My" reflects Johann Christoph's emphasis.

7 See 1 Pet 2:24. The uppercase *M*s in first-person singular pronouns in this sentence reflect Johann Christoph's emphasis. He does not capitalize all such pronouns, though, which is also reflected in my translation.

8 One of the two proffered forms for absolution in the 1533 Brandenburg-Nürnberg Church Ordinance instructed the confessor to refer himself as "ein berufener diener der christlichen kirchen" (a called servant of the Christian church). See EKO, XI, 187. This church order governed church life in the imperial city, at least in theory.

9 "vf solch Erkandt- vnndt bekandtnuß, an- vnndt vfnemen."

10 Johann Christoph did not receive the Lord's Supper on this day. See entries 12–14.

11 "Conscripsi Et Raecitavi." Johann Christoph indicates here that he has composed this prayer himself. Rather than having read it out to his confessor, it is possible that he instead recited it to himself in order to memorize it in preparation for confession.

11

After Receiving Absolution

Almighty God, you who have invited me via the gospel to the inheritance of your Kingdom[1] and who now, through the announcement of the forgiveness of my sins by your servant and the wonderful consolation it has provided to my saddened heart, have not allowed my small part of this inheritance to be taken away—ah, complete the good work you have begun in me and be near to me with your grace.[2] Uphold me with your powerful hand and strengthen me through your might[3] so that I, in knightly fashion, am able to fend off the assaults of Satan with the weapons of righteousness,[4] and so that I never again allow myself to be led into my previous sins, but instead through the power of God am preserved unto eternal life. Amen.

On the same day,
March 24, 1619.

1 See Matt 25:34.

2 See Phil 1:6.

3 See Isa 41:10; Ps 139:10.

4 See 2 Cor 6:7. See the discussion of the theme of spiritual knighthood in late medieval and early modern Christian devotion in the introduction.

12[1]

Before the Reception of Holy Communion

O LORD Jesus Christ, you Son of the living God, I acknowledge and confess at all times that I am certainly not worthy of this high kingly and heavenly meal of your body and blood in Holy Communion. For I am a poor, sad sinner and you are the Lord of heaven and earth.

But because you yourself will have it this way and prepare this heavenly meal for everyone, and have so joyfully invited penitent sinners, especially, to it, if they only believe in you—ah, I also now come, dear Lord Christ, at your behest, command, and invitation, and I ask you most earnestly to accept me as a guest. Consider my neediness, revive and now feed my sad soul with your body and blood, and give me your grace so that I may bring to this holy meal a truly penitent and broken heart,[2] and thus in true and firm faith may share in all of your heavenly goods and benefits that you set before and offer me in it.

O dear LORD, may this holy Sacrament always be in my heart a sure pledge, seal, and assurance of the promised forgiveness of my sins for the strengthening of my faith and for the nurturing in me of ardent love of my neighbor.[3] Allow this so that in and through the use of this most worthy holy Sacrament, faith may be daily increased in me, hope strengthened, and my fearful conscience always consoled. And may my soul also enjoy your divine favor and everlasting atonement in a way that I can truly sense,[4] and thus, may my soul finally be blessed in you eternally. Amen.

March 25, 1619,
on Green Thursday,[5]

as I receive holy Communion
at the St. Sebald Church.[6]

---

1 This prayer closely follows a pre-Communion prayer in the *Precationes piae* [. . .] *Christliche Gebet*, 465–71. Johann Christoph's version is somewhat shorter than the one that appears in this work.

2 See Ps 51:17.

3 In the Large Catechism, Luther refers to the Lord's Supper as "ein gewis pfand und zeichen" (a sure pledge and sign of forgiveness); Johann Christoph's prayer refers to it as "ein gewißes vnderpfandt." See WA 30/I: 225.4; and BC, 469.22. One finds similar language in the 1533 Brandenburg-Nürnberg Church Ordinance. During the liturgy of the Lord's Supper, pastors are to say in reference to the bread and cup, respectively, in the voice of Christ, "Dez zu einem gewisen anzaigen und zeugnus gib ich euch mein leib zur spies" (For a sure sign and testimony [of the forgiveness of sins], I give you my body as food) and "Des zu einem gewisen anzaigen und zeugnus gib ich euch mein blut zu trinken" (For a sure sign and testimony [of the forgiveness of sins], I give you my blood as drink). During the prayer of thanksgiving after Communion, the pastor is to say that divine grace, forgiveness, union with Christ, and eternal life have been "angezaigt and zugesagt" (signified and promised) in the sacred elements. EKO, XI, 196, 197.

4 Johann Christoph asks God that he might "empfindlich genieße" God's divine favor and everlasting atonement.

5 That is, Maundy Thursday. As the following entries make clear, Johann Christoph was quite busy on this day crafting prayers and a hymn for his *Pious Meditations*.

6 Johann Christoph records in his *Diarium* that on March 25, 1619, he, his son Christoph (1603–1634), and the other members of his household (*haußgenossen*) received Communion at the St. Sebald Church. In the January 10, 1619, entry, he also records that he took Christoph to the Lord's Supper. Christoph would have been fifteen years old on both occasions. It is not clear if Johann Christoph's other children took Communion on March 25 or not, for he only mentions

Christoph by name. *Haußgenossen* can refer to family members or more generically to members of a household, including servants. At least one more of Johann Christoph's eight children may have been old enough to take Communion—Johann Jacob (1606–1634), who was twelve, the typical age for first Communion in many Lutheran lands, although this age could vary from city to city and region to region. See Arthur Repp, *Confirmation in the Lutheran Church* (St. Louis, MO: Concordia, 1964), 56–57.

13[1]

At the Reception of Holy Communion

O you Son of the one true God, you who as the true bread of life satisfy,[2] feed, and slake all sad souls, fearful consciences, and hungry and thirsty hearts with your true body and blood, graciously grant that I may now worthily receive your most holy body and most costly blood in your most worthy Communion so that my faith may be strengthened by the forgiveness of my sins and my love for my neighbor may be inflamed and increased more and more. I ask this of you, who with the Father and the Holy Spirit, true and eternal God, live and reign forever. Amen.

On the same day, March 25, 1619.

---

1 This prayer closely follows two prayers in the *Precationes piae* [. . .] *Christliche Gebet*. "O you Son" to "true body and blood" follows a Communion prayer (507), while "graciously grant" to "Amen" follows a pre-Communion prayer that Johann Christoph modifies into a Communion prayer by adding "now" (*itzunndt*) (493).

2 See John 6:35.

14[1]

After Reception of Holy Communion

LORD almighty, triune, and eternal God, with what heart, tongue, and words shall I declare your great goodness, which you have now allowed me to experience, in that you yourself have given to me as a gift everything that is yours and belongs to you?[2] But may you be pleased by the thank-offering of my heart and mouth, which in this poor flesh and blood I now am able to give until I finally come to you.[3]

I thank, laud, honor, and praise you, almighty God, Father of our Lord Jesus Christ, that you have sent into this world your beloved Son, our Lord and eternal Savior. He took our flesh and blood on himself and thus became an offering for our sin, through which he revealed your divine will, saving us from your righteous wrath, the power of the devil, and eternal death.

I ask you, further, faithful God, that you would give me your Holy Spirit so that I may know you from my heart and also the One you have sent, Jesus Christ,[4] and that I may call upon you in true faith and heartfelt confidence. May I console myself with Christ's merit and may I benefit from it and make it my own in all times of need, cross, trial, and adversity. Yes, may I entrust myself to Christ and hold fast to him in life and in death so that, for his sake, I may have and receive from you, righteous Father, forgiveness of my sins, righteousness, and after this life, an eternal one.

LORD Jesus Christ, to you may praise and thanks be expressed now and always for your holy and most worthy sacraments, which you commanded and established in the church and, as signs and seals of grace,[5] have made to depend on your divine promises. Give to me your Holy Spirit so that, according to your institution, I may often make use of these holy signs of the covenant in true and steadfast faith for the salvation of my soul. You are especially to be praised and thanked, Lord Jesus Christ, for the most worthy sacrament of your true body and blood. You have left it behind for me as a reminder so that as often and as soon as I acknowledge my sins and experience true remorse and sorrow for them and have a good intention through your divine help to improve my life, I can obtain absolution and truly receive and use the sacrament of your true body and blood as it was instituted by you for the forgiveness of my sin and the strengthening of my weak faith.

O, give me your Holy Spirit so that I may at all times live a penitent life, appear often in church with true remorse and penitence for my sins, worthily receive the holy and most worthy sacrament of your body and blood according to your divine institution, and use it for the strengthening of my weak yet true faith, for the forgiveness of my sins, and for remembrance of you. Grant also that I may proclaim to my small children your death and satisfaction for sin, and especially that I may finally die, believing with firm faith your promise that all of my sins have been forgiven and pardoned and that eternal life is mine.[6]

For you yourself say, "The one who eats my body and drinks my blood will have eternal life, etc."[7] O LORD, you yourself should be a witness to this my faith, as should your holy angels, the priest who has given me the sacrament on the basis of such faith,[8] and the people who have seen me receive it. It should also be my last will and testament to die in such faith in your promise based on your pure mercy.[9]

And even if I, because of pain, foolishness, and trials come to hold, or wish to hold, a different opinion, now as then and then as now, this opinion will certainly not be valid; rather, my above stated faith and last will remain unretracted,[10] and I will be judged accordingly before you on the basis of your mercy. In this way, death, hell, sin, and the devil will not harm me. Your word is stronger than these and everything else, etc.[11]

Further, I praise and thank you, O God the Holy Spirit, you third person of the Godhead, true God with the Father and Son, for you rule and preserve all of Christendom through the revealed word via preaching and through the holy sacraments. And I ask you, awake in my heart true fear of God, right knowledge of him, and faith. Be my consoler and help in all of my times of need, especially in my present trials. Enlighten and rule me so that I, in proper obedience and all humility, may call upon, laud, honor, and praise God the Father, God the Son, and you, God the Holy Spirit, forever and forever. Amen. Amen. Amen.

On the same day, March, 25, 1619.

---

1 The opening paragraph of this prayer closely follows a post-Communion prayer in the *Precationes piae* [. . .] *Christliche Gebet*, 579–81.

2 See Luther's language of the "joyful exchange" (*der froelich wechßel*) in the German version of *Freedom of the Christian*. See WA 7: 25.34. See the discussion in the introduction of the importance of this phrase in Johann Christoph's piety.

3 The remainder of this entry comprises Johann Christoph's "danck-hopfer" (thank-offering) to the Triune God. See Ps 50:14; Heb 13:15. Much of it appears to be original to him.

4 See John 17:3.

5 For similar language regarding the sacraments, see entry 12.

6 The following two paragraphs closely follow a post-Communion prayer in the *Precationes piae* [. . .] *Christliche Gebet*, 595–99.

7 See John 6:54.

8 Lutherans could still refer to their pastors as *priester*. See EKO, XI, 195.

9 In the preceding two sentences, *should* (*solt/soll*) could also be translated as *are* in the first two occurrences and as *is* in the third one. I have translated the modal verbs literally.

10 "mein obgesatzer glaub vnndt will, vnwiderrufen bleiben."

11 See Heb 4:12; 1 Pet 1:23.

15

AMICO

Spiritual Song. To the tune of "All Mankind Fell in Adam's Fall"[1]

1.

Alone before you, Lord Jesus Christ,
I now lament my Distress.
You are rich in Consolation and Help,
Let me not despair.
In you alone my Hope stands;
Give me your Grace, Lord,
So that I may obey you
And not be [further] harmed by this Cross.

2.

My Eternal Refuge, O Faithful God,
To you my Suffering is well known.
Extend to me your hand in this Distress,
For, in my heart, the loveliest one upon the Earth
Has been separated from me;
My Consolation, my Joy, my Delight,
Who loved and honored me in Christian fashion,
Is now in the heavenly throne room.

3.

I certainly do not begrudge her the highest Joy
That she has now received
In Heaven at this time;

All Suffering has been taken away from her.
But, unfortunately, I still lament and bewail
With my tender Children
The unexpected Day of Separation[2]
That met us so harshly.

4.

Christian patience, give to me,
Now and at all times,
Then I will thank you eternally
And spread abroad your Divine Praise.
Preserve me also by your Word,
Which I bear in my heart,
And turn away Satan's murderous exploits
So that nothing brings me [more] pain.

5.

O God, you who are a Father
To orphans and those in misery,
To you I cry out at this time,
Turn yourself toward me.
Send me your help and give me grace
So that I may order and lead
My whole life according to your Counsel
And not oppose it, following the example of AMICO.

On the same day, March 25, 1619.

---

1 The Nürnberg City Council secretary, Lazarus Spengler (1479–1534), authored the nine-stanza "Durch Adams Fall ist Ganz Verderbt" in 1524 (see the discussion of Spengler in the introduction). It was included in one of the earliest evangelical hymnals, Johann Walter's *Geistliches Gesangbüchlein*, which appeared late in 1524 with a preface by

Martin Luther. It was also included in a hymnal that Johann Christoph owned, Ammon's *Neuw Gesangbuch*. The hymn quickly became one of the most popular in the Lutheran Reformation, and its opening lines served as a standard statement of the evangelical belief in original sin. See BC, 531n20; 535.23. For a critical edition of this hymn, see Berndt Hamm and Wolfgang Huber, eds., *Lazraus Spengler Schriften*, Band 1, *Schriften der Jahre 1509 bis June 1525* (Gütersloh: Gütersloher, 1995), 398–405. The hymn appears in abbreviated form in the LSB (562) but not in ELW. See also Wackernagel, III, 48–49 (no. 71). The text of this entry appears to be original to Johann Christoph. Both in the original German and in my translation, the initial letters of the first word of each of the five stanzas of this poem form the acrostic *AMICO*—Anna Maria Iohann Christoph Oelhafen. Johann Christoph's use of capitalization with the initial letters of several nouns in this song appears to be intentional, whereas in other entries, it is not. I have preserved this intentionality in my translation. Johann Christoph also capitalized the initial letters of the words that begin each line. The rhyme structure is *ababcdcd*.

2 "den unverhofften Trennungs Tag."

16

I thank you, you eternal Son of God, you who loved me so ardently that you gave yourself over to death for me and poured out your blood for the forgiveness of my sins.[1] I ask you with my whole heart, do not allow your supremely important payment [for sin] to be lost on me; rather, enlighten me through your Holy Spirit so that I may console myself in death and life with your suffering and death. May I also by the power of your Cross patiently overcome all of my crosses and suffering, and through crosses and death press on to you in eternal life.[2]

In the meantime, Lord God, Heavenly Father, you who allowed your Son to die for me on the Cross, be gracious to me, a poor sinner.

Lord Jesus Christ, you eternal Son of God, you who became a human being for me and who gave yourself over to death and poured out your blood for me, do not let your precious payment [for sin] be ineffectual nor in vain for me, a poor sinner.

O God, Holy Spirit, you who have revealed such things to me and also graciously called me to the knowledge of Jesus Christ, complete the work of grace you have begun in me.[3] Strengthen, increase, and preserve me in true faith; rule, lead, and guide me, that I may live Christianly, die blessedly, and rise again joyfully.[4] Amen.

March 26, 1619,
on Holy Good Friday.

---

1 See Eph 5:2.

2 See Phil 3:14.

3 See Phil 1:6.

4 "das ich christlich lebe, seelig sterbe, vnndt frölich widerauferstehe."

17

O you righteous, eternal, merciful, almighty, gracious, and wise God, the Father of my Savior, Jesus Christ;

O you faithful Savior, Jesus Christ;

O you good Consoler, Holy Spirit,

You know well in what sadness and distress both the departure of my beloved treasure and her leaving behind of our many small children have placed me. Since then,[1] I have daily lamented such things [to the Father] and confided them to his fatherly heart.[2]

You faithful shepherd and bishop of my soul,[3] you will also allow me to confide these things to you once again and to commend them to you in all grace. For as your Son, Jesus Christ, my only Savior, still walked upon the earth, his gentle heart never despised nor disparaged any sad person. You will not begin to do so with me; rather, in the power of the promise he made that you will listen as often as we call upon you in his name, etc.,[4] you will help me out of my great sadness. In this help you will allow me to experience your wonderful goodness and sweetness, and as a faithful father, you will know how to make all of this work for the salvation of my soul, [the benefit of] my neighbor, and your honor.

Consequently, from a heartfelt, unwavering, fervent love and confidence, I will commend my sad condition and life to you, Almighty God, in your divine omnipotence. I will commend them to you alone, the only wise and understanding God, in your understanding and divine wisdom; to you, merciful and good God, in your great goodness and immeasurable mercy.

You will not allow this situation to destroy me, for no one who waits upon you will be put to shame.[5] Ah, so I also will not be put to shame. Rather, you will stand by me in all situations—in life and death, in crosses, fear, distress, suffering, and adversity—and with powerful might and for the sake of the honor of your name, you will help me out of all of them. Therefore, I commend myself to you, with body and soul, with all that I am, have, and can do—all of it is in your hands. Protect my going out and my coming in, from now into eternity.[6] Amen, Lord Jesus, Amen.

March 28, 1619,
on Holy Easter Day.[7]

---

1 "Als deme [*sic*]."

2 The prayer in this paragraph appears to be addressed to either Christ or the Holy Spirit. Johann Christoph says that he has "gebeichtet" (confessed) his sadness and distress to the fatherly heart of God (*in sein vätterliches hertz hinein*), but he does not appear to see this sadness and distress as sinful, even though here and immediately following, he uses the verb associated with private confession. I have thus opted for "confided" as an alternative translation of "gebeichtet" that better captures its meaning.

3 See 1 Pet 2:25. Johann Christoph now appears to be addressing God the Father, even though the verse in 1 Pet to which he alludes refers to Christ.

4 See John 16:23.

5 See Ps 25:3.

6 See Ps 121:8.

7 In this Easter entry, Johann Christoph does not celebrate Christ's resurrection with much gusto, perhaps because his heart remained heavy following his wife's death.

18

O Jesus Christ, Son of God and Child of the Virgin Mary, you who alone give and produce devout children, I ask you from the bottom of my heart and for the sake of your obedience [to the Father] that you would also make my children devout. I ask that you would keep them in the fear of God and in proper obedience so that they may be seedlings[1] that grow to worship and praise your kingdom, and that extol you both here in this life and there in eternal life with me, their faithful father. Ah, Lord, protect them from sin and shame. Bless them, body and soul, and allow me to see and experience joy and consolation in them, both here, temporally, and there, eternally. Amen.

March 29, 1619,
on the day after Easter.

Hope constantly in Christ,
Commend your concerns to him;
His door of grace stands open,
Despite the one who has led you astray.[2]

---

1 "pflántzlein." For the use of this term to refer to young children, see "pflántzlein" in Grimm.

2 Original text:

In Christum Stetiges Hofe,
Dein Obligen Ihm Commendir,
Sein Gnadenthür steht ofen,
Trotz dem, der dich verfuhr.

The final line could also be rendered, "Despite (or, to spite) the one who leads you astray." I have not been able to locate the origin of this poem. The rhyme structure is *abab*.

19

O God, a Father of all grace and mercy, I ask you with great earnestness that you would generously give me grace, because you first created me according to your image, and when I was lost, created me anew through your beloved Son—that is, you saved me from the devil, sin, shame, and eternal damnation, and you made me a partaker of eternal blessedness. Please also grant that, in the future, as your purchased and redeemed child, I may never ever let your holy word depart from my eyes or my heart; rather, may you preserve me in the same in a fatherly way so that I may triumph over my weak flesh and blood, the sinful world, and, yes, the devil himself.[1] May you also be gracious and merciful to me through the holy and bitter suffering and death of your dear Son, and may you console my heart through the same in crosses and temptations so that, through faith, I may have certain hope in the forgiveness of sins.[2] And if I should stumble, still sanctify me through your word so that I do not give room to sin in my life, but instead completely suppress it and put it to death, and conduct myself in complete accord with your will. Amen.

April 4, 1619,
On Quasimodo Sunday.[3]

---

1 Johann Christoph may have 1 John 4:4 in mind here, part of the Epistle reading for Easter 1.

2 Johann Christoph may have John 20:23 in mind here, part of the Gospel reading for Easter 1.

3 The First Sunday after Easter. In his *Diarium*, Johann Christoph records that he declined an invitation to a wedding on April 5, 1619, because of his "Laid" (sorrow or suffering). The loss of Anna Maria was clearly shaping his social life as well as his inner life.

20

Almighty, eternal, merciful, and good God, I thank you from the bottom of my heart for all of the favors that you have graciously shown me from my youth up to this hour. I especially thank you for allowing me to be born of honorable Christian parents who, later on, allowed me to be educated in the praiseworthy studies[1] so that I might enter the service of the Fatherland. In addition to this, you have given me your blessing and benediction so that I, with the help of your Holy Spirit, am able to be of some use to this city and its citizenry, along with other estates of the Empire. I ask you that you would continue to increase such great gifts in me out of sheer grace and mercy, for I recognize that, apart from you, I neither know anything nor can do anything—everything is in your hands.

O dear God, I also asked you for a God-fearing, virtuous, chaste, and pious spouse, which you gave to me and also took away. Now, may your name be blessed;[2] you can and do make all things well.[3]

Third, along with my beloved wife, I asked you for young seedlings,[4] and these you gave to me, from both sexes, and you have allowed the same number of each to live up to now.[5] Help them, LORD, and allow me to instruct them properly in your divine word so that they may truly know you from the heart and the one you have sent, your dear Son, our Lord Jesus Christ.[6] May they also call upon you and your Son from the heart in true trust and steadfast faith, and thus, along with me, be eternally blessed.

Finally, O faithful Father, I asked you for a bit of daily bread, which you have generously and faithfully given to me. I thank you for this. I laud, praise, and honor you, and also ask that, in addition to my daily bread, you would [continue to] give me your generous blessing and benediction. Lead, govern, and guide me so that, according to your divine counsel, I may properly enjoy these your favors and, as always, carry out my vocation and complete my life so that everything redounds to the adoration and praise of your most holy Name, to the benefit of my neighbor, and to the salvation and blessedness of my soul and the souls of those who belong to me.[7] Amen.

April 11, 1619,
on Misericordia Sunday.[8]

---

1 "in den löblichen studiis, erziehen laßen."

2 See Job 1:21.

3 See Mark 7:37.

4 "Iunge Pfläntzlein" (i.e., children). See entry 18.

5 As indicated in the introduction, Johann Christoph had eight surviving children: four sons and four daughters.

6 See John 17:3.

7 "auch mein vnndt der meinigen, seelen hail vnndt seeligkeit." Johann Christoph uses the phrase "die meinen" frequently, which I have translated throughout as "those who belong to me." The phrase certainly includes his children, but it also encompasses his domestic servants. In short, it refers to his whole household, to all of those under his care as a *Hausvatter*. His servants must have played a significant role in caring for his children after the death of his wife.

8 The Second Sunday after Easter.

21

"In You Have I Hoped"[1]

1.

Attend to my misery in grace, LORD;
my soul has its refuge in you,
because in a time of great distress
you have protected me
through your goodness
so that no misfortune has put me to death.

2.

Mortality had almost enveloped me,
but you, gracious LORD, my God,
held me in your hands.
    The death of my beloved
    brought to me such distress;
I still have not fully overcome it.

3.

I confess my sins and misdeeds,
    which make me so utterly weary
    that all power escapes me;
    all my bones
    are wasting away;[2]
sorrow has enveloped me.

4.

Christ, without your consolation, I would now stand
naked,
and my suffering would be even greater
if you did not preserve me
with strong deeds
so that no [further] harm
nor suffering may befall me.

5.

O God, therefore, I do not despair
and have wagered it all on you,[3]
holding fast and constant [in faith] without wavering.
At the right time
you will help me to have joy
so that I may thank you for it.

6.

Delivery from worry comes, Lord,
from depending fully
on your goodness,
which is truly great,
although not always apparent,
and frequently hidden in affliction.
Amen.

Let us be patient in our crosses
and console ourselves with your great suffering,
deriving from the same the confidence
that you will not forsake us,
but will most faithfully stand by us
until we go from death
into life.[4]

April 13, 1619.
I took medicine and tomorrow
will distribute [Anna Maria's] personal effects.[5]

---

1 Johann Christoph usually prefaces the name of the hymns he records or refashions with "To the tune of" (*Im Thon*), but here he neglects to do so. Adam Reusner (1496–ca. 1575) wrote "In dich hab ich gehofet," which is based on Ps 31 (there are allusions to this psalm in Johann Christoph's rendering). On its publication history, see Wackernagel, III, 133 (no. 170); and V:1, 373–74 (no. 587). There are clear parallels between Johann Christoph's third and sixth verses and the tenth and eighteenth verses, respectively, of the version in Wackernagel V:1. The text of this entry appears to be otherwise original to Johann Christoph. LSB 734. Both in the original German and in my translation, the initial letter of the first word of each of the six stanzas of this poem form the acrostic *AMICOD* (Anna Maria Iohann Christoph Oelhafen Doctor). The spacing of the lines in each verse reflects Johann Christoph's original text. The rhyme structure is *aabccb*.

2 See Ps 32:3.

3 "vnndt hab es gantz auf dich gewagt." Alternative translation: "and have entrusted the whole matter to you."

4 Original text:

> Laß vns im creutz gedultig sein,
> vnndt trösten deiner schweren pein,
> auch schöpfen drauß die zuversicht,
> das du vnß wirst verlaßen nicht,
> sonder gantzt Trewlich bei vnß stehn,
> biß wir von Todt ins leben
> gehen.

I have not been able to locate the source of this poem. The rhyme structure is *aabbcc*.

5 "cum medicina uterer, et seq[uenti] die, legg[ata] distrib[uam]." Johann Christoph records in his *Diarium* that he took a purgative of some kind on both April 11 and April 12, although he does not

disclose the nature of his malady. He must have continued this medical treatment on April 13. Johann Christoph also records on April 12 that he composed a spiritual song ("doch Ein geistlich lied gestellt"), no doubt referring to this entry in the *Pious Meditations*. He records that on April 13, he organized Anna Maria's clothes and that on April 14, he distributed her personal effects (*legata*). I assume that Johann Christoph wrote this entry in the *Pious Meditations* on April 13 and have therefore taken "distrib." in the concluding line as referring to Johann Christoph's intentions for the following day (*distribuam*—future tense). It is possible that he wrote this entry—or at least the final version of it—after April 13 and assigned this date to it later. In this case, one could render the verb in the imperfect tense (*distribubam*), indicating that Johann Christoph was looking back on the day on which he distributed Anna Maria's personal effects.

22

O God, heavenly Father, you who know the heart and who see the thoughts of all people,[1] you know well that I have not set out upon this trip in a frivolous way or because of vain curiosity or greed; rather, it is because of pressing need and the demands of my calling, even though I am a sad widower. I ask with my whole heart that you would guide me with your eyes and surround me with the protection of your holy angels.[2] I also ask that you would safeguard me on the roads from robbers, evil company, and menacing threats, and protect me from tempestuous weather, dangerous storms, and utterly dark nights. In addition, protect me in all inns and hostels from thieves, murderers, evil odors,[3] and all assailing pestilences so that I may arrive at my intended destination with favor and bodily health.

Meanwhile, LORD, watch over my bewildered household. Protect my poor people from fire, the orphans I have left behind and all those who belong to me from sickness and sudden death,[4] so that when I return home, I may receive them with joy and look upon them in all respects with no sadness. In addition to this, LORD, give me your grace so that during my necessary time away I am able to carry out my dealings successfully and perform them in a useful way to the honor of your Name, especially in light of my sad condition.[5]

And when I have completed my work, lead me safely on the way home and bring me in all happiness, fresh and healthy, to all who belong to me. Then we will all extol your Name together and praise you, our righteous Father, in Christ Jesus your dear Son, along with the Holy Spirit. Amen.

April 18, 1619,
on the trip to Leipzig

with the Overseers of the Gräfenthal Company.[6]
On Jubilate Sunday.[7]

---

1 See 1 Sam 16:7; Acts 1:24.

2 See Ps 32:8; 34:7; 91:11; Ex 23:20.

3 Early modern people frequently associated foul smells with demonic activity and presence. See Ronald K. Rittgers, introduction to "Preface to 'A True Account of What Took Place at Stassfurt on Christmas Eve, 1534 (1535),'" LW, vol. 60 (St. Louis, MO: Concordia, 2011), 74–81.

4 A sudden death prevented one from properly preparing for one's end, which for Johann Christoph likely would have included private confession and the Lord's Supper. See Rittgers, *Reformation of Suffering*, 169–70.

5 As Johann Christoph wrote these two lines, juxtaposing sadness and joy, he may have had in mind the Gospel reading for this Sunday, John 16:16–23, which contains a similar juxtaposition.

6 Johann Christoph records in his *Diarium* that on April 15, he left for a trip to Leipzig accompanied by Endres (Andreas) Imhoff (1572–1637), who served as an imperial sheriff (*Reichsschultheiß*). On Imhoff, see "Imhoff, Andreas" in DB. (Biedermann, CCLV, states that Andreas III Imhoff was born in 1562, not 1572.) Johann Christoph would not return home from this trip until mid-May (see entry 28). While he lists just one traveling companion in his *Diarium*, in this entry in his *Pious Meditations*, he clearly references multiple people—"mit den hrn. Gräventhalischen." Johann Christoph does not specify who these "herren" were, but in addition to Endres Imhoff, they likely included Wilhelm Imhoff along with Martin and Georg Pfinzing (or some combination thereof). We know from Johann Christoph's *Diarium* that on April 17 he and Endres Imhoff visited the "Saigerhütte" (the smelting and liquidation furnace) near Gräfenthal. From 1616 on, the two Imhoffs and the two Pfinzings composed the "Gräfenthalische Gesellschaft" (Gräfenthal Company) that oversaw this Saigerhütte, which derived silver from copper ore. See Mark Häberlein and Johannes Burkhardt, *Die Welser. Neue Forschungen zur Geschichte und Kultur des oberdeutschen Handelshauses* (Berlin:

Akademie, 2002), 252–57. The relevant documents in the NStaatsA record that the Smaller Council had approved Johann Christoph's trip to Leipzig to deal with matters relating to the Saigerhütte in Gräfenthal, likely its sale to the Leipzig city council, which took place in 1619. See Ratsverlässe der Herren Älterern, Rep. 60 d, Nr. 30, 8 April, 1619, fol. 6v, 9 April, 1619, fol. 7v. Leaders of the Saigerhütte industry gathered annually at the Leipzig trade fair to conduct business. See Philipp Robinson Rössner, ed., *Martin Luther: On Commerce and Usury (1524)* (London: Anthem, 2015), 64. By 1615, Johann Christoph had been involved in assisting the two Imhoffs and the two Pfinzings with business related to the Saigerhütte industry in Gräfenthal. See NStadtA A 1 Nr. 1615-01-28. The Smaller Council was directly involved with another Saigerhütte in Eisfeld, which lies about forty kilometers southwest of Gräfenthal. See Häberlein and Burkhardt, *Die Welser*, 253. It is possible that Johann Christoph began his journey to Leipzig with Endres Imhoff, as his *Diarium* attests, and met up with other representatives of the Gräfenthal Company in Gräfenthal, continuing on with them to Leipzig from there. This explanation would make sense of what he says about his traveling companions in the *Pious Meditations*. On Nürnberg's long involvement in the Saigerhütte industry, see Pfeiffer, *Nürnberg*, 98, 187–88, 297; and "Saigerhandel" in the SN.

7 The Third Sunday after Easter.

23

Almighty and eternal God, you who govern all things according to your unsearchable wisdom and who wisely rule over the whole world and all that lives within it according to your divine will,[1] you have provided me with a profession through which your praise and honor, along with the salvation and blessedness of my soul, and also the benefit and welfare of my neighbor, can all be promoted. Ah, especially now on this trip that I have undertaken in keeping with my office and calling, illumine my heart, mind, and soul so that I may carry out this profession as pleases you, as benefits my temporal and eternal welfare along with that of my neighbor, and not least, as is helpful to my kin and to everyone in general in both body and soul. For, O LORD, I am a fallible human being and my reason can easily err; I can do either too much or not enough in these situations. Therefore, I ask you from my heart that you would govern, lead, and direct me so that, first and foremost, I may accomplish your will; that I may show loyalty, love, justice, and righteousness to my neighbor; and then, in general, may fulfill my calling in such a way that you will be my gracious and merciful God at the Last Judgment. Amen.

April 25, 1619,
as I approach Dresden[2]
in the name of the
Gräfenthal Company.
On Cantate Sunday.[3]

1 See Rom 11:13.

2 Apparently, Johann Christoph made a detour to visit Dresden before continuing on to Leipzig.

3 The Fourth Sunday after Easter.

24

Contrasting Echo[1]

O beautiful and loveliest season of May,
what do you bring to me this year
for my pleasure and joy?
Misery.[2]

Misery? Ah, misery drives away all
playful jesting,
but must it also bring inner
pain?
Heart.[3]

Pains of the heart are difficult to bear,
my God;
but what is the cause of this
great distress?
Death.[4]

Ah, death itself drives away
all pain;[5]
how does it then bring such anguish
to my body?
Wife.[6]

My pious wife was instead the
preserver of my joy;

now what can reduce the sorrow
her death has created?
Time.[7]

Precious time cannot lessen this
growing suffering;
I ask, what may relieve this
painful torment of my heart?
Children.[8]

No, children cannot help one withstand
this sorrowful separation.
But why was the life of the one
who bore them shortened?
Given.[9]

Given, in all seriousness? Ah, tell me when,
where, and who the giver is?
I will seek him without any
delay.
Christ.[10]

Christ? The one who, out of concern,
has often delivered us;
can he also provide freedom from this
evil?
Consolation.[11]

Consolation is very necessary for the
weary soul;
do you perhaps mediate God's
oil of joy?[12]
Choose.[13]

Choose? I choose such healing oil
for all of our guilt,
but what good does such a choice do,
does it bring hope or patience?
Grace.[14]

Eternal grace? For me, my blessed
wife, and our seed?
Yes! I will thus give praise, honor, and thanksgiving
to your Name, LORD Christ.
Amen.

May 1, 1619, on the trip
to Leipzig with the
Overseers of the
Gräfenthal Company.

---

1 "Widersinnigen Eccho." "Widersinnig" may also be translated as absurd or paradoxical. In this poem, the final word in each stanza rhymes with the penultimate word, for which it usually provides an answer—in some cases a seemingly absurd or paradoxical one, in other cases not. It has not been possible to preserve these rhymes in my translation, although I have provided them in the notes. In the original German, the initial letters of the first word of each of the stanzas of this poem form the acrostic *ÖLHAFEN ICDWE*. The meaning of this acrostic is unclear: Iohann Christoph Doctor Widersinnigen Eccho or, perhaps, Iohann Christoph Doctor Witwer Einsam (lonely widower)? In this entry, Johann Christoph works his way to the grace and consolation in Christ that he believes he needs by entertaining objections and obstacles to this quest along with possible deviations from it.

2 "Frewdt?—Laid."

3 "Schmerz?—Herz." Johann Christoph here indicates that he experiences the pain that misery brings in his heart.

4 "Not?—Todt."

5 Johann Christoph likely means here that death puts an end to pain.

6 "Leib?—Weib." Johann Christoph likely has in mind here the Christian teaching that husband and wife are one flesh (see Gen 2:24; Matt 19:5; Mark 10:8; Eph 5:31); in Anna Maria's death, he has lost part of his flesh or body. Or he could be saying that he experiences the loss of his pious wife in his body—grief grips his very flesh and bones.

7 "Laid?—Zeit."

8 "Lindern?—Kinder."

9 "Leben?—Geben." It is not clear what Johann Christoph means by "Geben" (Given) here. As in entry 20, he may be saying that Anna Maria was given to him by God for a time and then taken away (see Job 1:21). He might also be referring to his children as a temporary gift from God.

10 "Frist—Christ."

11 "Bösem?—Trösten." Johann Christoph here suggests a positive answer to the preceding question—yes, Christ can bring consolation.

12 Here Johann Christoph seems to be asking Consolation itself if it mediates God's oil of gladness or joy. See Ps 45:7.

13 "Öel?—Wehl." It is not clear what Johann Christoph means by "Wehl" (Choose). He seems to be saying that the grieving person (i.e., himself) must choose the consolation that is to be found in Christ. Indeed, one can see the whole of the *Pious Meditations* as a conscious choice to seek such consolation in the midst of grief. Johann Christoph may also be alluding to the optional use of chrism oil in baptism. He could be indicating here that one should choose to reappropriate the divine healing and grace that this oil symbolizes, especially in times of distress.

14 "Gedult?—Huldt." Johann Christoph seems to indicate that choosing the healing oil brings grace.

25

Ah, most beloved LORD and God, how true it is that there is no constancy to be found in this world of inconstancy, nor any rest in this world of unrest! Yesterday, we began the loveliest season of May; today, we enter into the cross-week.[1] In fact, our entire life is nothing but crosses, angst, and sorrow.[2]

Therefore, the beloved elders placed the teaching about prayer right in front of the door of this cross-school[3] so that, before all else, we would seek refuge in prayer. You saving cross-bearer, teach me to know how I may order my prayers according to your command[4] so that my prayers may assist me in bearing more easily the cross that has been placed upon me. For my worthiness does not help me, nor my unworthiness hinder me, but mistrust damns me.

Placing my confidence in you,[5] however, makes me worthy and preserves me, for three things move you to this end: (1) your fatherly heart, (2) your great mercy, (3) your unfailing truth. Ah, turn toward me also, my Lord and God, and be gracious to me.

For I am alone and miserable, full of trouble, adversity, worry, and angst. Make known to me the way I should walk in, lead my soul out of distress for the sake of your mercy, destroy my enemies for the sake of your goodness, and drive away all that frightens my soul. For I am your servant, bless me. Make your face to shine upon me and be gracious to me.[6] As I bear my cross,[7] I commend to your fatherly protection my soul and body; what I do and cause to be done; my thoughts, words, and work; my living and dying; my children, friends, and household; what I have and possess; and all that I have received from your divine grace.

I know that without you I can do nothing[8] and that I cannot retain what you have given me without your help. I also know that all of my efforts are in vain if you do not lend your aid. Finally, I know that my grieving and lamenting do not make my cross any lighter but instead make it heavier.

Therefore, O Lord, may you, today and at all times, be my cross-bearer, my housefather, both for me and for those who belong to me. Govern all of us according to your will, give us the grace we need to live so that we may proclaim your glory, honor, and praise, along with your grace, love, and mercy, both here in this temporal life and there into all eternity. Amen.

May 2, 1619,
on Sunday Vocem Iucunditatis.[9]

---

1 "Creutzwochen." Johann Christoph likely has in mind here the Rogation Days leading up to the Feast of the Ascension.

2 Johann Christoph may have the Gospel reading for this Sunday (John 16:23–30) in mind here, or perhaps the verses that precede it (19–22), which speak of the Christian's sorrow in this world.

3 "Creutzschuel." It is not clear who Johann Christoph has in mind in this reference to "die lieben alten" (the beloved elders) and "die lehr vom Gebett" (the teaching about prayer) that they have provided. He may have been influenced here by Johannes Saubert's *Schola crucis oder christliche kreutzschule* (*School of the Cross or Christian Cross-School*; 1619). (Unfortunately, this treatise does not appear to be extant.) Or Johann Christoph may simply be referring to the framers of the lectionary, who placed the Gospel reading for this Sunday (John 16:23–30), which teaches about praying in Christ's name, at the beginning of the cross-week or cross-school—that is, at the start of the Rogation Days leading up to the Feast of the Ascension. The term *Creutzschule* occurs frequently in the devotional works and funeral sermons of the day.

4 See John 16:15, 24, part of the Gospel reading for this Sunday.

5 It is somewhat difficult to know which member of the Godhead Johann Christoph is addressing throughout this prayer. He appears to have God the Son in view in the opening two paragraphs and then switches to God the Father in the third paragraph, as the reference

to "dein vätterliches hertz" (your fatherly heart) suggests. But at the end of the prayer, he refers to "mein Creutzträger, mein haußvatter" (my cross-bearer, my house father), which appears to invoke Christ, or Christ and the Father. It may be that he has Christ in view throughout the whole prayer. It is interesting to note that Johann Christoph, who undoubtedly took his role as *Hausvatter* very seriously, looked to Christ as his own *Hausvatter*.

6 See Num 6:25.

7 "in dießem meinem creutzstandt." Here Johann Christoph appears to be thinking of his condition as a widower and not simply of the Rogation Days that he is entering into with other Christians.

8 See John 15:5.

9 The Fifth Sunday of Easter (also Rogate Sunday).

26

Merciful, eternal, and benevolent God, I have no other confidence, hope, and refuge, I can also boast of nothing else than that you were born, put to death, and especially, raised from the dead and ascended to heaven for me. In order to give public testimony to this fact, I have had you depicted on my gravestone as the one and only exultant and rejoicing Prince of victory, as the One who has powerfully broken through death, and as the One who has brought us life again.[1]

And when you now require merit from me, I bring before you the merit of your most holy suffering, the merit of your cross, and the merit of your death. According to your inexpressible mercy, you, most gracious God, have allotted to me all of this merit together, so much so that I can call it my very own.[2]

Through this your great and glorious triumph, I, my beloved AMICO, our children, and the whole wide world have all obtained reconciliation with God the heavenly Father and therefore also eternal blessedness. O LORD, be gracious to me, turn my heart from what is earthly and give me a desire for what is heavenly so that I may avoid sins that damage my soul.[3] Then I will say to my soul, "Raise yourself up, be joyful and consoled, for the Lord, the King of Israel, is with you."[4] It is my greatest joy, in any case, to give you honor, and my greatest pleasure, to praise you with fervent thanksgiving, because everything on earth is transitory, but your holy Name remains eternal. Accept my prayer and have mercy on me. Amen.

May 6, 1619,
on Ascension Day.

1 See both the image of Johann Christoph's epitaph that he placed at the beginning of the *Pious Meditations* (image 6) and the picture of the epitaph that adorns his grave in the St. Johannisfriedhof in Nürnberg (image 9). He had the former in mind in this entry, of course.

2 Johann Christoph again references the "wonderful exchange" between him and Christ that allows him to call Christ's merit his very own. See entry 14.

3 The collect for the Feast of the Ascension in the 1533 Brandenburg-Nürnberg Church Ordinance, which Johann Christoph likely knew, asks, "O almechtiger Gott. Wir bitten dich, verleihe, das wir auch mit dem gemüt im himel wonen, was himlisch ist, suchen und gesinnet sein, wie wir glauben, das dein eingeborner Sune, unser seligmacher, gen himel ist aufgefahren" (O almighty God, we ask you to grant that we may also live with our souls in heaven, and that we may seek and be inclined toward what is heavenly, for we believe that your only begotten Son, our Savior, has ascended to heaven). EKO, XI, 193.

4 See Zeph 3:15.

27

To the tune of "Lord God, you who search me, etc."[1]

1.

Arise, arise, my soul, and from the ground of your heart
praise God your righteous Lord,
sing unceasing praise to him with tongue and mouth,
and exalt his honor highly.
Thank and honor him your whole life long
for all of his benefits,
which are richly given to you
upon this earth,
including that he will also henceforth
keep your children under his protection.

2.

My God, the Lord, I constantly invoke
and entrust myself to him completely;
I go to him in times of distress and death
and build upon him in my heart,[2]
for he will not allow anything to harm me,
because he takes what is mine upon himself
and protects me completely.[3]
In his hands are inscribed[4]
those he has saved from all punishment,
therefore, I will not despair.

3.

In this world no one is able
to escape death's fierce arrows,
which in a moment take away our bodies, our gold, our
hearts, our senses, our good fortune, our courage, and
our happy days.[5]
Death powerfully destroys all authority
and all consolation; hope quickly comes to an end
and many plans fall to the ground.
When true distress presses in on us,
human actions all go awry
and earthly joy does not last long.

4.

Christ, however, will and can help,
his power has no end;
therefore, he is praised as the Man
who has everything in his hands.[6]
I call upon him at all times
and believe that his promises are certain.
He can turn aside all sorrow;
this consoles me and causes me to be joyful.
In the end, he will give abundantly
what I now grasp in faith.

5.

O God, take my orphans to yourself,
for you wish to keep them innocent of harm.
Nourish me, the widower, spiritually
and protect me according to your will.
Enable me to behave righteously in my distress,
and protect us from sudden death,
which threatens us more and more.

I seek to act uprightly and I trust in you;
I build on your goodness, grace, and truth;[7]
you will be pleased with this.[8]

May 9, 1619, with the Overseers of the Gräfenthal Company,[9] three months after beloved AMICO's death. From then until now, I have daily mourned her departure with sighs, tears, and sobbing.

But when I am the weakest, then through your divine grace, I am the strongest.[10]

On Exaudi Sunday.[11]

---

1 Heinrich Vogther (1490–1556), an artist, poet, printer, and medical author in Strasbourg, authored the text of "Herr Gott der du erforschest mich," which was based on Ps 139. On its publication history, see Wackernagel, III, 508–9 (no. 560). It was also included in a hymnal that Johann Christoph owned, Ammon's *Neuw Gesangbuch*. The text of this song appears to be original to Johann Christoph. Both in the original German and in my translation, the initial letters of the first word of each of the five stanzas of this poem form the acrostic *AMICO* (Anna Maria Iohann Christoph Oelhafen). The rhyme structure is *ababccdeed*.

2 "von hertzen auf ihn bawe." See Matt 7:24–27.

3 Johann Christoph again emphasizes the "wonderful exchange" between Christ and the Christian. See entries 14 and 26.

4 See Isa 49:16.

5 "Gstalt, gold, hertz, sinn, gluck, mutt, gutt Tag." Alternative translation: "outward appearance, gold, strength to live, meaning, happiness, courage, and good days." Each of the words that Johann Christoph uses to describe things that are threatened by death has a wide semantic range in the original German.

6 "Mann" might be an allusion to the second stanza of Luther's *Ein feste Burg*, where the Wittenberg theologian writes, speaking of Christ,

"es streit' für uns der rechte Mann" (Were not the right Man on our side). See Wackernagel, III, 20 (no. 33); LSB 656, 657; and ELW 503–5.

7 See Matt 7:24–27.

8 "Das wirst dir laßen belieben." Alternative translation: "You will be happy to comply."

9 In the original German, it is unclear whether Johann Christoph was in Gräfenthal, likely on his return journey from Leipzig, or if he was stating in abbreviated form that he was still traveling with the Overseers of the Gräfenthal Company, the translation for which I have opted. After the date in the postscript, he writes, "Gräventhal[ischen?]" with no preceding preposition or article and with no reference to "Herren."

10 See 2 Cor 12:10.

11 The Seventh Sunday after Easter.

28

Almighty God, without whose help, grace, and assistance we neither can nor are able to do anything, I give you great thanks from my heart for the strong support you have clearly shown to me on my recent trip, especially given how important this matter has been, having to do with five tons of gold.[1] Truly, I would not have been able to deal with this matter satisfactorily without you. You alone are the wisdom, you alone are the strength, in which I have done everything. Therefore, it is fitting for you alone to have the praise, along with my most submissive request: just as you have helped me bring my work to completion, may the work also please you, and may you allow me together with my neighbors to prosper in body and soul.

And if on account of the unexpected pungent odor that now fills the air, my children and relatives both here in Nürnberg and in Altdorf are found to be sick, or if my own bodily condition is changed, I will not allow my trust in you, my righteous God, to falter.[2] Rather, through such discipline,[3] I will be strengthened in my confidence that you love me dearly and will see it as nothing other than when a father teases and jests with his beloved child. Therefore, I call upon you just as the ten lepers called upon Jesus:[4] dear Father, have mercy on those who belong to me, give us your generous grace so that the remedies prescribed for us promote good health, and so that with healthy bodies and joyful consciences we may thus express to you eternal and unceasing thanks, glory, honor, and praise. Amen.

May 14, 1619, on St. Job day.
I took medicine and
returned home two days ago.[5]

1 "funf thonnen goldts betrefenden sachen." One should not take "ton" literally here, as the actual weight to which the word referred varied in the early modern period. Johann Christoph could also be using the word to refer to large earthen pots that held gold or money (see "Tonne" in the FWB). In any case, there was a great sum of money at stake in this business dealing. This fact bespeaks how important the copper smelting industry in Gräfenthal and elsewhere was to the Nürnberg Smaller Council and also how much the city fathers trusted Johann Christoph in such dealings.

2 It is not clear what kind of health threat Johann Christoph has in mind here, although given his reference to the "unexpected pungent odor that now fills the air" (*unverhofentlich, eingefallenen scharfen lufft*), it is likely plague or fear of the same. Contemporaries believed that plague could be caused by poisoned air.

3 See Prov 3:12 and Heb 12:6.

4 See Luke 17:11–19 (especially v. 13).

5 "Cum Medicina uterer, et biduo ante, domum reversus."

29

O righteous LORD and God, you who with your outstretched arm created heaven and earth out of nothing,[1] relying on your divine grace, I am intending to be bled for the maintenance of my health, following the recommendation of my good friend and doctor,[2] Herr Hieronymus Peßler.[3] And even if it is painless, I certainly know from my experience in Montpellier, France, on March 15, 1599,[4] that there is always the danger of death in such procedures. Therefore, please give me your divine blessing so that this bleeding may prosper my health. Amen.

May 16, 1619,
on the Holy Feast of Pentecost.

---

1 See Jer 32:17.

2 Johann Christoph refers to Peßler as his "leiblichen Artzts," presumably to distinguish him from a doctor of the soul. In his *Diarium*, Johann Christoph notes that Peßler attended to Anna Maria during her extended illness in 1617. See the entry for October 26, 1617. On Peßler, see the following note.

3 Hieronymus Peßler (Beßler; 1566–1632) was a prominent doctor and botanist in Nürnberg. See "Besler, Hieronymus" in DB. See also Will, *Nürnbergisches Gelehrten-Lexicon*, vol. 1, 104–5. For access to the letter correspondence between Johann Christoph and Beßler, search (Author) "Oelhafen von Schöllenbach, Johann Christoph" in the UEN online catalog.

4 See the discussion of this event in the introduction.

30

I thank you, O Eternal Son of God, for this your special grace and favor, that, for my good and that of all Christians, you have established the Holy Feast of Pentecost, on which you sent forth your Holy Spirit and richly poured him out upon your disciples. I ask that you would keep me, as one of the least of your disciples,[1] eternally in this grace. I also ask that you would allow the Holy Spirit to dwell constantly in my heart and to be powerful so that he might lead me into all truth and console me in all sadness.[2] Above all, may he be with me in the hour of my death and protect me at my end, when I travel to my home and leave this miserable life.

Lord God Holy Spirit,[3]
strengthen me in faith most of all
so that at my final end I may joyfully
depart out of this miserable life.
Be with me in my hour of final need;
accompany me into life out of death.
O Lord, prepare me through your power
and strengthen the weakness of my flesh
so that I may fight as a knight and
press through death into life.

Amen.

May 17, 1619,
on the Monday of Pentecost.

1 See 1 Cor 15:9.

2 See John 16:13.

3 The following paragraph is clearly a hymn—or a composite of a couple of hymns—but Johann Christoph does not format it as such. Rather, it appears on the page as a normal prose paragraph without the typical spacing and indentations that he employs elsewhere, aside from the first word, *Herr*, which is slightly indented. I have formatted the paragraph as a hymn. Lines 1 to 4 follow closely the third stanza of "Kyrie Gott Vatter in Ewigkeit" ("Lord God Father in Eternity"). See Wackernagel, III, 226 (no. 250). Lines 5 and 6 follow closely lines 3 and 4 of the third stanza of Martin Luther's hymn, "Erhalt uns, Herr" ("Lord, Keep Us Steadfast in Your Word"). See Philipp Wackernagel, *Das deutsche Kirchenlied von Martin Luther bis auf Nicolaus Herman und Ambrosius Blaurer* (Stuttgart: S. G. Liesching, 1841), 149 (no. 217); Wackernagel, III, 26–28 (nos. 44–48); LSB 655; and ELW 517. Among other places, the hymn appeared in the hymnal that Johann Christoph owned, Ammon's *Neuw Gesangbuch*. This hymn was also a staple of liturgical life in Nürnberg. See Butler, "Liturgical Music," 376, 378, 380, 381.

31

I thank you now once more with my whole heart, most beloved heavenly Father, that you have so loved me, my dear AMICO, our children, and all people that you have not spared your only Son, our Lord and Savior Jesus Christ, but have given him up to death for us so that we and all good-hearted Christians who believe in him may not be eternally damned but may rather receive forgiveness of all our sins and eternal life.[1] Grant, dearly beloved Father, that we never forget such benefits, but instead at all times console ourselves with them and rejoice over them, in joy and sorrow, whether things go well or badly for us. May we also at the same time thank you for your benefits from now and into eternity. Amen.

I thank you also from the deepest part of my heart, Lord Jesus Christ, the only-begotten Son of God, my dearly beloved brother,[2] that you were born as a human being and were put to death for me, my dear AMICO, and all other poor sinners, and that with your innocent and bitter suffering and death, holy resurrection, and ascension, you have won for us forgiveness of all our sins, the Holy Spirit, and eternal life. Through these same acts, you brought us—each and every one of us—before your heavenly Father in grace so that he is and will remain our dear and faithful father and protector. For all of this, I express eternal praise, honor, and thanksgiving to you, O most faithful brother, Lord Jesus Christ, now and without end. Amen.

I thank you also, Lord God Holy Spirit, from my heart, that you have illumined me,[3] my dear AMICO of blessed memory, and our young children with true faith, in that we hear God's holy word, speak about it frequently, and gladly occupy ourselves with it.[4] This faith allows us to be certain in our hearts that God the heavenly Father is gracious and merciful to us for the sake of his beloved Son. Therefore, O God the Holy Spirit, for such illumination and consolation, I express eternal praise and thanks to you, and I do not desire to die [any longer] but to live for the highly exalted Trinity in everlasting praise.[5] Amen.

May 23, 1619,
on Trinity Sunday.[6]

---

1 See Rom 8:32 and John 3:16.

2 See Heb 2:11.

3 See the explanation of the third article of the Creed in Luther's Small Catechism, BC, 355.6.

4 See the explanation of the Third Commandment in Luther's Small Catechism, BC, 352.6.

5 "begere nit zusterben." This phrase suggests that Johann Christoph had desired to die, so great was his grief.

6 It is fitting that Johann Christoph composed a prayer to the Father, Son, and Holy Spirit on Trinity Sunday, although this was not the first time he had done so in the *Pious Meditations*. See entries 14, 16, and 17.

32

[To the tune of] "The Shepherdess"[1]

1.

AMICO, beloved darling, where have
you gone?
Has the beloved God taken you
to himself?
Or have you been completely taken away from me
for some other reason?
On our anniversary,
speak or cry out,
and help me lessen
my heart's sorrow.

2.

In this world, ICO, you shall not
find me,
therefore, bravely leave your searching
behind now.
You also cannot discover the place
with your own skill,
for I am, praise God,
without pain, in the hall of joy;
so now let your worry
completely pass away.

3.

My darkness[2] I will certainly still
grieve in my heart;
I will build a wall, as it were, against all joy
there,
even if it means that death awaits me
all the sooner.[3]
I constantly bear my sorrow
on account of her at all times;
I endure it the whole night until
early morning.

4.

Christian heart, but a good thing has happened
to me:[4]
now, I truly stand
before God's face
and behold with pleasure
all of his glory.
I live at all times
in peace and joy;
why then do you live with such sadness
on my account?

5.

Beloved, I have good reason,
for our children
painfully shatter my heart
almost every hour.
Ah, that you could still be with them,
but healthy.
Still, I console them, telling them that
God cares for those

whose genuine love for him remains
unvanquished.

6.

O faithful heart, how does your love actually
help me now?
Do not let my departure
sadden you so much;
rather, from now on give yourself fully
over to peace.
May your heart be still,
for according to God's will,
I passed away in your arms,
as I had wished.

7.

Saddened as I am, should I no longer think about
our separation?
O' no,[5] for you only make your heart sick
by doing so.
Rather, give to my children the gift of your faithfulness,
protection, and love.
Surrender yourself to God,
do not give in to distress;
my soul's rest should not be an occasion for
walling yourself in.[6]

8.

How? Must I then commend our marital bond
to God?
And even if it should help your
dear soul rest,
should I not still torment myself about
your grim death?

No, no, instead of suffering,
I wish you great joy.
God himself will count us
among the elect.

9.[7]

AMen: My blessed heart,
you should not now accept
ten thousand worlds if they were
offered to you, nor should you come back to us
in sinful flesh, which shames us
before God.
But believe me,
I wish to come to you
along with our children,
free from grieving.

10.

This song I have sung
out of fidelity and love
on the day of our Anniversary, because AMICO
was swallowed up by death,
which I bewailed along with my
children, who have been left behind.
To be sure, as long as I live,
she remains constantly close to me,
in my heart, and
on my lips.

On the day of our anniversary, May 25, 1619,
eighteen years since I led
my beloved Anna Maria
Harsdörffer, now of blessed memory,
to the altar at the St. Lorenz Church.

I chose this tune because she often used to sing the secular Shepherdess with a joyful soul to my lute-playing.[8]

---

1 This may be a reference to "Filli die schöne Schäferin," which appeared in Johann Hermann Schein's popular *Venus Kräntzlein* (Wittenberg, 1609). I am grateful to Prof. Dr. Thomas Gerhard Wilhelmi of the University of Heidelberg for this reference. On Hermann, see Arthur Prüfer, *Johann Hermann Schein und das weltliche Lied des 17. Jahrhunderts* (Leipzig: Breitkopf & Härtel, 1908). Johann Christoph might have also had in mind "Gott grüß euch schöne Schäferin so reine," which appeared in *Drey Schöne Lieder* (Augsburg: Valentin Schönig, 1600; VD16 ZV 15924). The text in this entry has every sign of being original to Johann Christoph. The song is a dialogue that he has constructed between himself and his deceased wife, in which she consoles him from heaven. The dialogue alternates between Johann Christoph and Anna Maria, with Johann Christoph speaking in the first stanza and Anna Maria in the second, and so on, until the seventh stanza, in which both speak. Johann Christoph alone speaks in stanzas 8 to 10. The rhyme structure is *aaabba*.

2 "Mein Schwartze." Johann Christoph uses red ink here to emphasize how strong his experience of sorrow and grief is. He uses red ink for similar emphasis in other parts of this entry.

3 Johann Christoph's comment in the final line of the preceding entry that he no longer wishes to die seems to have been put to the test on his anniversary.

4 "mir ist gar wol geschehen." Alternative translation: "It has turned out well for me."

5 Here Anna Maria speaks.

6 "die Rhue meiner seelen thue Ja mitt nicht verschrenckhen." Alternative translation: "Do not erect a barrier against the rest of my soul."

7 As in the concluding lines of the preceding stanza, Johann Christoph is here speaking to Anna Maria.

8 It seems that Johann Christoph was in the habit of rewriting both spiritual and secular songs that his family would sing at home. See the discussion of his habit of writing hymns in the introduction. See also the discussion of how he learned to play the lute in France, during his tour of Europe as a young man.

33

O Almighty and good God, you who are a source of strength for the weak, of healing for the sick, of might for those who labor, of solace for the sad hearted, of joy for the sorrowful, of refuge for the abandoned, of help for the afflicted, you who are a God of patience and all consolation—you know, and I see and sense it myself in all my members and their powers, that I cannot bear my heavy cross without your divine help and assistance. (This cross does not stem from the loss of temporal goods, which really cannot be considered a loss; rather, it comes from the death of my pious wife and the resulting loss of fresh courage, which means "to lose much" and "to lose the half.")[1] Therefore, I call to you, now after my sorrowful anniversary day has passed (the day you chose for me eighteen years ago as a day of matrimonial honor and joy). I not only ask you with my whole heart that you would keep me firm in faith and constant in hope in this adversity that has come upon me and caused such pain; I also express fervent thanks to you for sending me visible angels, as it were, in the form of my faithful, upright, and honorable friends, who have exhorted me in such a heartfelt and faithful way to suffer your fatherly hand and discipline with a gentle spirit and quiet heart.[2]

Ah, LORD, give me patience, which is absolutely necessary for me, and teach me to keep still before you, my God,[3] to regard this affliction not as a sign of your disfavor but of your fatherly affection, and never to murmur against you in my heart nor to be otherwise impatient. Rather, let me recognize from day to day, ever more and more, that you have intended all of this only for my edification,[4] and that hitherto you have delivered me from six troubles, and that, for the sake of my beloved Fatherland and my young children, you will not leave me stranded in the seventh.[5]

So, help me now, you strong and faithful helper; help so that in the future I forget what cannot be brought back, that I possess my soul in patience, and that in the certain hope of the eternal life to follow, I remain constant, without turning from you or from my vocation. Help me in all of this so that my immature faith may be able to perceive the affection of your fatherly heart, which is frequently hidden under the cross.[6] Armed with your strength, power, and might as a Christian knight,[7] standing fast, may I finally, with a cheerful and thankful soul, walk before you and exalt and praise you. May I also in this way be certain that, because I am patient and suffer here, there, with you, I shall be raised up to eternal glory. Amen.

May 26, 1619, the day after the feast of St. Urban,
on which, eighteen years ago, my postnuptial
celebrations took place with my beloved
AMICO.[8]

---

1 "so, nicht von verlust zeitlichen guts, welches, aigentlich, kein verlust zuachten, sondern, von abgang meines Ehelichen frommen weibs, vnndt entweichung frischen muts, so viel vnndt halb verloren haist, herrhuret." Johann Christoph here appears to be citing a popular German proverb: "Gut verlohren, nichts verlorhen / Mut verlohren, halb verlohren / Ehr verlohren, alles verlohren." Other versions replace "halb" with "viel" and have either "Freiheit" or "Seele" instead of "Ehr." See Friedrich Heinrich Wilhelm Körte, *Die Sprichwörter und sprichwörlichen Redensarten der Deutschen* (Leipzig: F. A. Brockhaus, 1837), 183, nos. 2482, 2483; and Johann Georg Seybold, *Selectiora Adagia Latino-Germanica* (Nürnberg: [Sum]ptibus Wolfgangi Mauritii Endteri & Johannis Andreæ Endteri, hæredum, 1677), 255.

2 See Prov 3:12; Heb 12:6. See the discussion in the introduction of a possible proto-Rosicrucian group in Nürnberg to which Johann Christoph may have belonged.

3 See Ps 46:10.

4 "zu meiner beßerung." See Rom 8:28. Luther interpreted suffering in an identical fashion in his *Sermon on Indulgence and Grace*. See WA 1: 244.40–245, line 4; and Timothy J. Wengert, ed., *The Annotated Luther*, vol. 1, *The Roots of Reform* (Minneapolis: Fortress Press, 2015), 62. See

discussion in Rittgers, *Reformation of Suffering*, 106. Johann Christoph is here clearly displaying one of the central tenets of the Lutheran approach to suffering, which insisted that, for the faithful Christian, suffering was an expression not of divine punishment but of divine testing or proving, for Christ had borne all such punishment on the cross. See Rittgers, *Reformation of Suffering*, 108, 134, 147–48, 173, 217, 247–49.

5 See Job 5:19.

6 This is the clearest evidence in the *Pious Meditations* that Johann Christoph was familiar with Luther's theology of the cross.

7 See the discussion of the importance of the theme of the Christian knight in early modern Lutheran devotion in the introduction.

8 The feast day of Saint Urban is May 25.

34

O Merciful God, I ask you that you would give me your divine grace to trust you steadfastly in all things and to fear, praise, love, and honor you, whether things go well or badly for me.

To you be thanks, praise, and honor into eternity.[1]

Your will be done in heaven and upon earth.[2]

Your judgments are righteous; we, however, are poor, sinful creatures.[3]

May your name be blessed into eternity.[4]

O my God, you who have created and redeemed me and, in addition, eternally decreed what I am and shall be, you know what you will do with me. You know what is most useful and beneficial for the salvation of my soul. Do with me at all times what is in accordance with your divine pleasure and mercy. Amen.[5]

May the name of the LORD be praised, for when you are wrathful, you show grace and goodness, and in the midst of tribulation, you forgive the sins of those who call upon you. To you, my LORD, I turn my face, to you, I lift up my eyes, for I truly know that after affliction, the one who serves you will be consoled and rescued from tribulation, and after the discipline, he will find grace. For you have no pleasure in our destruction, rather, after the storm, you allow the sun to shine again, and after the weeping and wailing, you pour out joy upon us. To your name be honor and praise eternally, you God of Israel. Amen.

May 30, 1619, on the trip to Heilbronn,[6]
on the First Sunday after Trinity.[7]

---

1 See Rev 2:7.

2 An obvious reference to the Lord's Prayer.

3 See Ps 119:75, 137; Rev 16:7.

4 See Ps 72:17; 113:2; Dan 2:20.

5 As Johann Christoph indicates in the left margin, the following paragraph is based on Tob 3 (:14–15, 22–23), here reproducing the relevant verses verbatim.

6 Johann Christoph was traveling to Heilbronn to participate in a meeting of the Protestant Union. He would remain away from Nürnberg until late July. See the discussion of his involvement in the Protestant Union in the introduction.

7 While Johann Christoph does not cite the Epistle reading for the First Sunday after Trinity, 1 John 4:16–21, his overall attitude toward his tribulation in this entry may well have been influenced by v. 18, especially.

35[1]

Almighty, strong, and eternal God, a God of peace and a lover of Christendom,[2] you who are frightening, strong, and righteous; you who alone are the true King and Anointed One who gives all kinds of gifts[3]—how long will you remain so relentlessly wrathful toward this your evangelical people (who are your own inheritance and whom you have purchased at such a high price)[4] and not turn away from them the tumult of war? How long shall we drench our bread in tears and mix our drink with gall?[5] Is our sin so great that it can receive no forgiveness, or are our wounds so severe and dangerous that they cannot be healed,[6] and must we alone remain placed for conflict with all people? Look upon the deeply troubled hearts, the poor and innocent widows and orphans who are not guilty of this bloodshed.

Yes, as those in Nineveh (where more than 120,000 people lived), they do not know their right hand from their left,[7] but nevertheless must be liable to the same danger of destruction and death.

Have mercy on us and strike terror into all people who hide themselves from you[8] and undertake what is against you, which is in vain. Lift up your hands against the strangers, punish those who oppress us and who with great boasting seek to humiliate us so that they see and acknowledge your power.

Ah, LORD, the Spanish and the Italian[9] destroyers of the Fatherland—the kings of the earth—they gather themselves and already move over all of our roads. Your sword of wrath threatens the land from one end to the other. No flesh will have peace because of these destroyers.[10]

Just as you will be hallowed by us before their eyes, so show yourself glorious to them before our eyes so that they acknowledge, just as we confess, that there is no other God than you, LORD, alone. Perform new signs and wonders by your strong hand and outstretched right arm, through the name of your Holy Child Jesus.[11] Then we shall be saved, but our enemies will shrink back, become weak, and acknowledge that you are our protector. But if, on the contrary, they, out of hard-heartedness, do not want to acknowledge you, then arouse your fury toward them. Pour out your zealous wrath on them, tear into your adversaries, and smash their godless followers. Be quick to act in this way and think on your oath so that people may praise your wondrous deeds.[12]

For our help is in your Name alone,[13] you who created heaven and earth. Without you, all of our strength and power is in vain and of no use.[14]

But through you, the Lord of all lords, we shall accomplish deeds of great strength and you shall trample down our enemies and reduce them to nothing.[15]

Therefore, look down from your holy heaven, be gentle, dear LORD, and soften all of those hearts and souls that advise and authorize the spilling of blood, or let the fire of your wrath consume them.

Allow those who do harm to your people to be overcome and reduced to nothing. Crush the heads of the princes who are our enemies and who say, "We are the only ones." Protect and gather your people who are called by your Name, which they love, laud, and praise eternally.[16] Cause your word to go forth again, that your honor may be great among the people. Fulfill the prophecies that have been proclaimed in your Name. Reward those who wait upon you so that your prophets may be found to be truthful.[17] Hear the prayer of those who call on you according to the blessing of Aaron upon your people.[18] Do all of this so that all who live upon the earth may acknowledge and with humble hearts again say, "You, You alone are the LORD, the eternal God."[19] Amen.

June 6, 1619,
during the Union Meeting in Heilbronn,
on the Second Sunday after Trinity.[20]

1 In entries 35–40, Johann Christoph appears to have in view events leading up to and following the Battle of Sablat (June 10, 1619), in which Catholic forces defeated Protestant ones.

2 As Johann Christoph indicates in the left margin, this portion of the entry is based on Sir 36 (:1, 22).

3 As Johann Christoph indicates in the left margin, this portion of the entry is based on 2 Macc 1 (:24–25).

4 See 1 Cor 6:20. Here "Evangelisch" includes Protestants in Bohemia, some of whom were Lutherans.

5 See Ps 42:3; 80:5; 102:9; Matt 27:34.

6 As Johann Christoph indicates in the left margin, this portion of the entry is based on Jer 15 (:18).

7 As Johann Christoph indicates in the left margin, this portion of the entry is based on Jonah 4 (:11).

8 "Erbarme dich vnßer, vnndt erschreckhe alle völckher, die sich, wider dich entbehren." See "entbehren" in Grimm, option 5. Alternative translation: "Have mercy on us and strike terror into all people who reject/remove themselves from you."

9 "Welsche." Johann Christoph might also have the French in mind, as "Welsche" could refer to this people group as well. Charles Bonaventure de Longueval, leader of an Imperial Army that would soon clash with Protestant forces at Sablat, was French.

10 As Johann Christoph indicates in the left margin, this portion of the entry is based on Jer 12 (:12).

11 As Johann Christoph indicates in the left margin, this portion of the entry is based on Sir 36 (:4–7).

12 As Johann Christoph indicates in the left margin, this portion of the entry is based on Sir 36 (:8–10).

13 As Johann Christoph indicates in the left margin, this portion of the entry is based on Ps 124 (:8).

14 As Johann Christoph indicates in the left margin, this portion of the entry is based on Ps 124 (:1–2).

15 As Johann Christoph indicates in the left margin, this portion of the entry is based on Ps 108 (:13).

16 As Johann Christoph indicates in the left margin, this portion of the entry is based on Sir 36 (:11–17).

17 Johann Christoph may well have Martin Luther in mind here, as many Lutherans saw the Wittenberg reformer as a prophet, both in his own day and throughout the early modern period. See Ronald K. Rittgers, "The Word-Prophet Martin Luther," *Sixteenth-Century Journal: The Journal of Early Modern Studies* 48, no. 4 (Winter 2017 [2018]): 951–76. As noted in the introduction, Johann Christoph was also living in a period of increased fascination with prophecy among Lutherans. He might, though, simply have in mind the fulfillment of the biblical prophecies he cites in this entry.

18 Johann Christoph likely has the Aaronic blessing in mind here. See Num 6:24–26.

19 See Sir 36:20–22.

20 Although Johann Christoph does not cite the Epistle reading for the Second Sunday after Trinity, 1 John 3:13–18, he may have had v. 13 in mind in this entry.

36

To the tune of "Lord, how long will you forget me?"[1]

1.

Ah, LORD, incline your ear to me
and have mercy on me because of your grace.
All of my desires are directed to you alone,
strengthen me with your arm.
I am surrounded by the enemy
and have no idea where to turn
than to you alone, LORD.

2.

My poor soul is full of great fear and terror,
the spirit within me is perishing from longing [for mercy].
My heart gnaws and eats away at itself in my body;
it ponders and considers my situation
and finds neither rest nor peace anywhere.
O dear God, spring to my rescue
or I must sink without a trace.

3.

Jesus, my God, have mercy on me
and forgive me my sins, LORD.
Graciously set me free
from distress, worry, misery, affliction, and pain.
According to your wise counsel, give me help

and do not snatch me away in wrath,
much less, those close to me.

4.

Christ, turn to me, you faithful God,
and let my request soften your heart.
Protect me in this distress
and make of me a sign
so that everyone truly understands
that no righteous person perishes
who trusts in your word.

5.

O, may it never be that with an insolent spirit
I ask something against your will.
Whatever is good for my body and soul,
this you alone will bring to pass.
Do what is beneficial for me, as you alone know,
and allow your Spirit to teach me
that you wish to defend me.

6.

Devoting myself entirely to you,
I trust steadfastly in your might.[2]
Those who belong to me hope in you
day and night, as long as they live.
My soul is also joyful in you,
for I am certain that you yourself are with
all who put their hope in you.

June 13, 1619,
during the Assembly of the
Protestant Union in Heilbronn,
on the Third Sunday after Trinity.

1 The famous Nürnberg shoemaker-poet Hans Sachs authored this hymn, "Herr, wie lang wilt vergeßen mein," which is based on Ps 13 (see the brief discussion of Sachs in the introduction). See A. von Keller and E. Goetze, eds., *Hans Sachs Werke*, vol. 22 (Hildesheim: Olms, 1964), 117; and Wackernagel, III, 63–64 (no. 91). Among other places, the hymn appeared in the hymnal that Johann Christoph owned, Ammon's *Neuw Gesangbuch*. Aside from original incipits to form his acrostic, Johann Christoph's text closely follows Bartholomäus Ringwaldt's "O Herr dein ohren naig zu mir." Wackernagel, IV, 910–11 (no. 1343), vv. 1–2, 6–7, 8–9. In the original German and in my translation, the initial letters of the first word of each of the six stanzas form the acrostic *AMICOD* (Anna Maria Iohann Christoph Oelhafen Doctor). The rhyme structure is *ababccd*.

2 Original text:

> Dann Ich Traw, stetigs, deiner macht,
> Thue mich dir gantz ergeben.

Alternative translation:

> For I trust steadfastly in your might
> and submit myself entirely to you.

37

Almighty and eternal God, you who are at the same time a strict judge of the unrepentant and also a loving and merciful Father toward those who have sorrow for their sins, do not punish us in your wrath nor repay us according to our misdeeds.[1] Have mercy on us and our brothers and sisters in faith.[2] Look upon how miserably and mercilessly your sheep have been martyred, tortured, murdered, and hacked to pieces by the Spaniards and other enemies of your holy gospel. Allow yourself to be moved by the cries of the innocent infants who have been ripped from their mothers' breasts, by the laments of the wives and virgins who have been so indecently put to shame, and by the fact that much innocent blood has been spilled.[3] In particular, though, may you be moved by the arrogant blaspheming of your holy and divine Name.

O LORD, turn away all such severe punishments and grant that we, the neighboring people, since we acknowledge and confess our sins, may not be overtaken at any time by this bloodthirsty enemy.

O LORD, scatter all of the enemies who do not honor your Name and cause them to flee, as you have done in the past when you rescued your people from the Egyptians, who were plunged into the Red Sea.[4]

O LORD, you who have no regard for the size of a people's army,[5] drive back those who boast of their power and grant our praiseworthy governing officials, along with all of the Christian rulers who support them with their collectively smaller forces, victorious triumph against all of their enemies. And give to all of us together the true peace that we desire for our bodies and souls through Jesus Christ, the true Prince of Victory. Amen.

June 20, 1619,
at the Assembly of the Protestant Union in Heilbronn,[6]
on the Fourth Sunday after Trinity.

1 See Ps 6:1; 38:1; 103:10.

2 "vnßerer Mitbrüder vnndt Schwester." Johann Christoph has Protestants in view here who have suffered at the hands of Catholic forces in Bohemia.

3 It is not clear if Johann Christoph has the Battle of Sablat in mind here, or simply the general effects of the early conflicts of the Thirty Years' War on Protestants.

4 See Ex 14 and 15.

5 See Ps 33:16.

6 Johann Christoph can refer to the gathering of Protestant Union officials as either the "Unionstag" as in entry 36 or, as here, the "Unions Convent." In subsequent entries, he continues to use both terms.

38

Ah, LORD, please tell your slaying angel to desist so that he does not cause the land to be completely barren and does not put all living souls to death.[1] Accept our deep sighs and graciously turn away from us this wretched warfare. All anxious hearts, including my own, would hear of this with great joy and together we would therefore exalt, honor, and praise you. For we know that if you do not preserve us with your fatherly protection, we are finished.[2] Therefore, we commend our bodies and souls, possessions, honor, goods, and all that we have to your fatherly safekeeping. O LORD, preserve and guard us. Amen.

June 21, 1619, at Heilbronn,
during the Assembly of the Protestant Union, etc.

---

1 See Ex 12:29; 2 Kgs 19:35.

2 "das es vmb vnß geschehen sei." Alternative translations: "We are lost/condemned" or "The same may happen to us."

39[1]

I have Jesus in my heart,
Outside of Jesus, I am not able to be anything.[2]
Alone and only in Jesus do I believe;
Nothing but Jesus does my heart embrace.

Christ is mine and I am his;[3]
Hold as insignificant everything in comparison with Christ.
Rich enough, am I, with Christ,
In grain and wine,[4] as long as Christ is with me.
Send consolation, O Christ, when death, fear, and pain
Threaten soul and body (Christ).[5]
O Christ, may I remain unharmed by them,
For I will fear you, Christ, alone.

On the other hand, if misfortune comes my way,
Let it simply be commended to God.
Hold firmly onto Christ, for he alone helps
All those who hold firmly to him.
From all threats, insults, and torments of
Enemies, he powerfully preserves me.
Now, since I trust in Christ alone,
Devilish enemies gain no ground from me.[6]

My only hope is Jesus Christ.

June 24, 1619,
during the Assembly of the Protestant Union in Heilbronn,
on the Feast of St. John [the Baptist],
which is rich in mercy and grace.[7]

1 In this entry, Johann Christoph forms an acrostic of his name—*IOAN CHRISTOF OLHAFEND*. In the original German, each line rhymes with the next, concluding with words ending in *-ein*. I have preserved the acrostic but not the rhyme scheme.

2 "Ohn Jhesu, Ich nichts vermocht zu sein." Alternative translation: "Without Jesus, I am nothing."

3 See Song 6:3.

4 "korn und wein."

5 The somewhat awkward inclusion of *Christ* in this line is mirrored in the original German, where, as an expression of his devotion, Johann Christoph places *Christ* within parentheses. He does this so that either *Jesus* or *Christ* appears in every line of the first two stanzas of this poem, thus confirming what he has confessed in the opening stanza—that he is nothing without Christ.

6 "Den feinden Ich nichts raume Ein." I have supplied *devilish* to complete the acrostic. It is not clear whether Johann Christoph had physical or spiritual enemies in mind in this entry, but even if it is the former, he thought the latter were still present, as the following entry makes clear.

7 Original text:

> Vnder wehrenden
> VnionsTag zur hailbronn,
> Am Fest Johannes,
> Id est: (huld)
> Reich.
> (gnad)

In this wordplay with "Huldreich" (rich in mercy) and "Gnadenreich" (rich in grace), which could also be translated as "mercy- and grace-rich," Johann Christoph may have Zechariah's Song (Luke 1:67–80, especially v. 78) in mind, which was part of the Gospel reading for the Feast of Saint John the Baptist. Alternately, instead of referring to the saint's day, Johann Christoph may have the place name "Heilbronn" in mind as a source or spring (*Brunnen*) of salvation or healing (*Heil*).

40

Stay with us, dear LORD JESUS CHRIST, stay with us, for evening draws near, the day has passed,[1] and we have been moved nearer to the end of the world.[2] Turn aside to us and do not abandon your poor little band [of evangelical Christians] in this dangerous warfare, for the devil and his followers are seeking to extinguish the light of the gospel.

Ah LORD, you are the consolation of Israel and her Helper in times of distress, why do you act as if you were a guest in the land and as a foreigner who will only stay overnight in it? Why do you act as a hero who has lost heart and a giant who cannot help? Yet you are with us, LORD, and we are called by your name. Do not abandon us.[3]

Are you not the God in heaven and ruler of all kingdoms, in whose hands are power and might, whom no one can withstand? Our God, have you not driven the Spanish from our land in the past and powerfully preserved the inhabitants of the land by the light of the gospel?[4] Now, see, they are making us pay for the past, and they are coming to cast us out of your inheritance, which you have given to us and in which we have praised your Holy Name. Will you not judge them? We do not know what we should do; instead, our eyes look to you, the preserver and propagator of all earthly rule.[5]

O LORD, let your Spirit give counsel to our teachers and preachers, as happened in the past with the Levites so that they inspire in us true consolation and courage. We should neither fear nor despair in the face of this large army, because the struggle is not ours but yours, the most high God. We shall, accordingly, see your salvation, you who are with and among us. And we shall, as a result, give thanks to you as we ought, for your mercy endures forever. Amen. Amen. Amen.

At the conclusion of the Assembly
of the Protestant Union in Heilbronn,
on June 27, 1619,
the Fifth Sunday after Trinity.[6]

---

1 See Luke 24:29. Johann Christoph may be citing the opening lines of "Ach bleib' bei uns, Herr Jesu Christ" by Philip Melanchthon and Nikolaus Selnecker, which appeared in *Geistliche Psalmen, Hymnen, Lieder und Gebett* (Nürnberg, 1611). See Wackernagel, IV, 286–87 (no. 392); and LSB 585. These lines are also part of a traditional vespers collect.

2 "Bleib bei vnß, Lieber HERR JHESUS CHRISTE, bleib bei vnß, dann es will Abend werden, der Tag hat sich genaiget, vnndt sindt [*sic*] ans Endt der welt hinan geruckhet."

3 As Johann Christoph indicates in the left margin, this portion of the entry is based on Jer 14 (:8–9).

4 Johann Christoph likely has in mind here the series of military engagements between Catholic imperial forces—many of them Spanish—and Lutheran forces that took place from the late 1540s to the mid-1550s (the Schmalkald War and the Princes' Revolt) and culminated in the Peace of Augsburg (1555), which granted Lutherans official legal standing in the Holy Roman Empire.

5 As Johann Christoph indicates in the left margin, this portion of the entry is based on 2 Chr 20 (:6–7, 11–12).

6 In addition to the biblical passages that Johann Christoph cites in this entry, he may also have had in mind the Epistle reading for the Fifth Sunday after Trinity, 1 Pet 3:8–15, especially vv. 12 and 14.

41

O God and LORD of all goodness, you who have formed the human being in such a way that he should not only rule over the creatures that you have made but also judge the world with holiness and righteousness, give me the wisdom of your majesty that constantly surrounds your throne. Do not cast me out from the number of your servants, for I am your slave,[1] a weak person, short-lived, and with minimal understanding. Even if there were one among the children of humankind who had perfect knowledge of your rules and laws, it would count for nothing if he lacked the wisdom that comes from you alone.[2]

Ah, so send forth this wisdom from your high heaven and from the holy seat of your glory,[3] as you began with me years ago during my blossoming youth, and as you have also begun now with my dear sons, Christoph and Hans Jacob,[4] providing public testimony to the progress of my and their studies at the Altdorf Academy on the Feast Day of Ss. Peter and Paul.[5]

Send this wisdom once more, I ask again, that she may always be with us,[6] work with us, and, from year to year, increase among us.[7] May this also apply to my other sons, Hans Christoph and Wolf Hieronymus,[8] so that we all, each one of us, may discern according to his calling and office, and also the dictates of his stage of life, what would be pleasing to you.

Allow wisdom, as the one who knows and understands all things, to lead us in all that we do and to protect us securely through her perfect might. Then all of our work will be pleasing to you and will finally be worthy before your throne. For what person knows the counsel of God in any other way? Who can discern what God wills? Since all mortal thoughts are unreliable and human plans, deceitful, they rarely understand even what takes place on earth and can only discover with difficulty what is at hand. How, then, can they investigate what is in heaven above, unless you, LORD, give wisdom?[9]

O faithful God, therefore send your Holy Spirit out of the great heights so that what is done on earth may proceed in the right way and so that I, along with my dear sons, may finally be blessed through your very own wisdom and knowledge.[10] Amen.

June 29, 1619, in Göppingen,[11]
on the Feast Day of Ss. Peter and Paul.

---

1 "verwirfe mich nicht, auß der zahl deiner diener, dann, ich bin dein knecht."

2 As Johann Christoph indicates in the left margin, much of this entry is based on Wis 9 (:1–6).

3 See Wis 9:10.

4 Christoph Oelhafen (1603–1634), who was fifteen at this time, matriculated at the Altdorf Academy on February 2, 1617. He would eventually marry in 1627 but then die from a shot to the head sustained in a battle with imperial forces outside of Nürnberg. He had no children. Hans Jacob Oelhafen (1606–1634), who was thirteen at this time, matriculated at the Altdorf Academy on August 11, 1618. He married in 1633 but died of plague the next year, leaving no children. See Biedermann, CCCLVIII; and Elias von Steinmayer, ed., *Die Matrikel der Universität Altdorf (1576–1809)*, 2 vols. (Würzburg: Königl. Universitätsdruckerei H. Stürtz A.G., 1912), vol. 1, p. 144 (entry no. 4302 from February 13, 1617); p. 153 (entry no. 4566 from August 11, 1618); and vol. 2, pp. 407–8. It was these two sons whom Johann Christoph summoned home from Altdorf as their mother lay dying.

5 As noted in the introduction, Johann Christoph had studied at the Altdorf Academy and had given a prestigious address at the annual school festival on the feast day of Saints Peter and Paul, which marked the beginning of the summer vacation period. He here prays that his two sons at Altdorf may continue to be blessed

with the same heavenly wisdom that he had received, especially on the occasion of the festival. Neither held a public address at it.

6 Wisdom is referred to with the feminine pronoun throughout Wis 9, and thus I have translated *sie* as *she* instead of *it* in this entry.

7 See Wis 9:10.

8 Hans Christoph Oelhafen (1614–1660), who was four at the time, would eventually marry and continue his father's line, having nine children by two successive wives. Wolf Hieronymus Oelhafen (1616–1656), who was three, would eventually study at Altdorf and later marry, although he had no children. See Biedermann, CCC-LIX and CCCLVIII. Johann Christoph does not pray for wisdom for his four daughters here, likely because, in keeping with customs of the time, he did not envision providing for further study for them at Altdorf or elsewhere.

9 See Wis 9:11–14, 17.

10 See Wis 9:17–18.

11 As Johann Christoph makes clear in the next entry, he traveled about seventy kilometers from Heilbronn to Göppingen in order to receive treatment in the famed natural springs there. In his *Diarium*, he records on June 25 that he had head pains in Heilbronn.

42

O eternal and faithful God and Father, you created all of your creatures in their essence, good, and also the human body, perfect and healthy, but on account of the fall of our first parents, you imposed weakness on us as a fitting punishment. Nevertheless, from your inexpressible mercy, you also created and provided all manner of salutary means through which our life may be preserved. I thank you, first of all, from the bottom of my heart, that you have graciously kept me healthy and well in all of my members up to this point. I ask you, further, for the sake of the bitter suffering of your dear Son, Jesus Christ, that insofar as it would not be of harm to my soul or otherwise oppose your unfathomable plan, you would again generously grant full strength to my bodily members and also allow me hereafter to carry out my appointed office in good health.[1] Grant this for the improvement of my sinful life, for the honor of your divine Name, and for the promotion of the common good.

In particular, now that I have begun to partake of the means of the noble mineral springs, grant that I may do so in fear of you, with humble gratitude, and in full acknowledgment that they are ordained by you. Grant that I may also avoid all presumption and temerity, and with firm faith, trust, depend, and build upon you alone as the only true doctor,[2] through your most beloved Son, our Lord and Mediator,[3] Christ Jesus. Amen.

On July 2, 1619,
as I have begun to drink from the mineral springs
at Göppingen in an orderly fashion.[4]

1 It seems that Johann Christoph was healthy enough to carry out his duties in Heilbronn but that his health had flagged near the end and was now in need of restoration.

2 See Matt 7:24–27.

3 Earlier in this prayer, Johann Christoph refers to various creaturely means (*Mittel*) through which God preserves human life, including the mineral springs at Göppingen, which he also calls a *Mittel*. By referring here to Christ as the Mediator—*Mitler*—Johann Christoph is expressing his belief that Christ is finally the one true divine means of health and salvation.

4 Johann Christoph records in his *Diarium* the amount of water he drank on each day, working his way up from one and a half glasses twice a day to six glasses in the morning and five in the afternoon by the time he departed. See the entries for July 3, 4, and 12, 1619.

43

Although I am a poor sinner, as are my fellow brothers, and neither should nor can rely on my own righteousness, as the Pharisees and scribes did,[1] yet I know that you, O Righteous God, do not look on my unworthiness, but on the perfect worthiness of your most beloved Son, Jesus Christ, who made complete satisfaction for my sins to you and thus won for me true righteousness.

In the same holy merit, I now appear before your face, and in his Name I ask on the basis of his righteousness: do not abandon me, etc.[2] You will certainly allow me to enjoy the intercession, reconciliation, and advocacy offered by your dear Son. Amen.

July 4, 1619,
at the mineral springs in Göppingen,
on the Sixth Sunday after Trinity.

1 Johann Christoph likely has Matt 5:20 in mind here, part of the Gospel reading for the Sixth Sunday after Trinity.

2 See Ps 38:21.

44

Almighty and good God, you are my father and preserver and also the father and preserver of all those who belong to me. From you we possess all that we have received in terms of body and soul, honor and goods, intelligence and understanding, so that we have you alone to thank. And we can thank you for so much more, because you can take the little that your divine hand has given and graciously multiply it, just as your own blessed Son, with seven loaves and a few small fishes, richly fed four thousand people so that there were seven basketfuls of broken pieces left over.[1]

O LORD, since birth, and now especially in this my most grievous widowerhood, along with my dear children, I have placed my trust and confidence in you alone. I also know that you care for the poor widowers and orphans, yes, that you are the true helper of all of those who are in need.[2] Therefore, I again seek no other help in all of my distress than from you alone. In my concerns at home and work, in the conduct of my life, and in what I do and do not do—I cast all of these upon you, you who nourish and quicken all that has life in it. I also fervently ask that you would protect me from excessive concern about my bodily well-being and,[3] much more, that you would regard me with the eyes of your mercy and graciously bless my few loaves and fishes. I furthermore ask that you would bless me, my dear children, and all of those in my household, by turning away from us all sin, shame, fire, flood, and other kinds of distress, and by feeding, satisfying, and preserving us in body and spirit. Please do all of this so that I at all times set my heart on you as the eternal good, that I never strive after what is earthly, nor place my hope in transitory riches, but in you, the eternal God and Lord of my life. Do this also so that I seek the lasting treasure that is in heaven, where neither moth nor rust consumes it, nor thieves can break in and steal,[4] through Jesus Christ together with the Holy Spirit. Amen.

July 11, 1619,
at the mineral springs in Göppingen,
on the Seventh Sunday after Trinity.

---

1 See Mark 8:1–9, the Gospel reading for the Seventh Sunday after Trinity.

2 See Ex 22:21–24; Deut 10:18; Ps 68:5; 146:9.

3 "Bitte dich, inniglich, du wollest mich, vor der Schendlichen bauchsorg, behutten." Johann Christoph is not here referring to a literal concern for his stomach—rather, he is referring to his overall bodily well-being, asking that he not be overtaken by concern for it. See "Bauchsorg" in the FWB.

4 See Matt 6:20.

45

To the tune of "Salvation unto Us Has Come, etc."[1]

1.

Ah, how miserable is my time
here on this earth,
how quickly a person can be brought low.
I wish that I could die,
because this whole vale of tears
is everywhere full of trouble and toil,
even if one's life in it achieves much success.[2]

2.

My dear soul,[3] what torments you so much?
Hold fast and do not waver;
the source of my protection, defense, consolation, and
salvation still lives!
I shall constantly thank him for the same.
Humble yourself and suffer a little while;
after affliction great joy will certainly come to you,
for God will preserve you.

3.

"Yes," they ask, "where is your God?
See how he comes to you."[4]
This torments my heart, marrow, and blood,
so that I weep from such affliction,
especially when the lying mob

still despises and mocks me,
as if I were not in distress.

4.

A Christian soul grows tired
when, day and night, it wails,
and all that is good turns away from it,
as if God did not wish to come to it.
Let your strong wrath subside
and accept me again in grace,
O God, for the sake of your Son.

5.

O, be patient, grieving soul,
patience is here necessary,
until the beloved Immanuel, according to his will,
brings us to death himself.[5]
God is righteous, as is his judgment.
All such things happen because of our sin,
therefore, do not try to push him toward your own goal.[6]

6.

You should not despair in the midst of distress;
rather, you should remain still
and know that whatever happens,
it is God's wise will.
Through his hidden and secret counsel,
he wants to move you
from evil deeds toward moral improvement.

7.

He knows what is needful for each person,
death or life;
believe this always, firmly, and free from care.

Give over to him all crosses and concerns.
If someone takes away even a hair from your head in this life,
it is in accordance with his will.[7]
So, place your hope and trust in him.

8.

Laud and honor, with high praise,
be to God the Father, the Son, and the Holy Spirit
for such care.[8]
With grace he will complete
what he has begun in us,[9]
to the honor of his majesty,
so that his name may be hallowed.

9.

Your kingdom come, your will be done,
on earth as in heaven.
Give us today our daily bread;
forgive us our debts,
as we also forgive our debtors.
Do not let us remain in temptation,[10]
but deliver us from evil. Amen.

July 18, 1619,
soon before I depart from the mineral springs at Göppingen,
on the Eighth Sunday after Trinity.

---

1 Paul Speratus (1484–1551) provided the text for "Es ist das Heil uns kommen her," which appeared in *Etlich Cristlich lider* or the *Achtliederbuch* (Nürnberg, 1524). See Wackernagel, III, 31–33 (no. 55). It also appeared in the hymnal that Johann Christoph owned, Ammon's *Neuw Gesangbuch*. LSB 555; ELW 590. There are clear parallels between

portions of Johann Christoph's text and portions of Philipp Nicolai's (1556–1608) "So wünsch ich nun ein gute Nacht der Welt." Johann Christoph's stanza 2 draws on Nicolai's stanza 7, his stanza 3 on Nicolai's stanza 5, and his stanza 5 on Nicolai's stanza 12. See Philipp Nicolai, *Freudenspiegel des ewigen Lebens* (1599), (Soest: Westfälische Verlagsbuchhandlung Mocker & Jahn, 1963), 413; and Wackernagel, V:1, 259–60 (no. 396). Otherwise, the hymn appears to be original to Johann Christoph. In the original German, the initial letters of the first word of each of the nine stanzas form the acrostic AMICODESS. The meaning of the acrostic is not clear: Anna Maria Iohann Christoph Oelhafin Die Ewig Selig Sei (Anna Maria Johann Christoph Oelhafen, may she be eternally blessed)? I have not preserved the acrostic. The rhyme structure is *ababccd*.

2 "Wann es schon woll gelinget."

3 Here Johann Christoph speaks to his own soul.

4 See Ps 42:3.

5 "Biß vnß der lieb Emanuel, Nach seim willen, selbsten tödtet."

6 "Drumb thue ihm kein ziel strebhen."

7 See Matt 10:30; Luke 12:7.

8 The care promised in Matt 10:30 and Luke 12:7 appears to be in view here.

9 See Phil 1:6.

10 "Laß vns nicht in versuchung stahn." This is an interesting variation on the Lord's Prayer, which in Luther's translation as well as in the 1533 Brandenburg-Nürnberg Church Ordinance runs, "und führe uns nicht in Versuchung" (and do not lead us into temptation).

Image 7: Lady Patience[1] (*Gebetbuch des Hans Christoph Oelhafen*, GNM-HA, Familienarchiv von Oelhafen, Rep. II/80, Nr. 32)

46

PATIENCE[2]

The noble virtue of Patience
has favor with God and people;
with God, because she waits upon the Lord,
with people, when help is distant.
A crown adorns her head, because in distress
she remains true unto death.
The book, God's holy word,
guides her to her source of protection and refuge.
The candle that burns in her hand
shows the way to the heavenly fatherland.
When death, the world, the devil, and hell bestir themselves,
she places them under her feet
through the death and painful suffering of Christ,
and, especially, the joyous victory of his resurrection.
As a lamb lives quietly in hope,
so, Patience awaits her bridegroom's will.
Christ sends her the garland of honor
that was bound together in heaven by an angel,
in the middle of which the name "Eternal Life" appears.[3]
Help us to reach this end, faithful Jesus.
Amen.

July 21, 1619,
while preparing to depart from Göppingen
and its mineral springs.

1 This image of "PATIENTIA" may have been created by the master portrait painter Leonhard Riehl (1582–1620). See Andreas Tacke, ed., *"Der Mahler Ordnung und Gebräuch in Nürmberg." Die Nürnberger Maler(zunft) bücher ergänzt durch weitere Quellen, Genealogien und Viten des 16., 17. und 18. Jahrhunderts* (Munich, 2001), 551. I am grateful to Jeffrey Smith for this reference.

2 This poem is a series of rhyming couplets.

3 The Hebrew at the top of the image reads "YHWH."

47

To the tune of "The Lord is My True Shepherd, etc."[1]

1.

Jesus Christ, you highest good,
fountainhead of all grace,
see how I am burdened with pain
in my soul
and have many arrows in me[2]
that press upon my conscience
without end as a poor sinner.

2.

Christ, take this heavy burden
from my sick heart,
for you have atoned for it
on the wood of the cross with the pains of death.
Do this so that I do not
drown in my sins and despair eternally
from great pain.[3]

3.

O God, when the things I have done during my days on earth
come upon me,
a stone falls upon my heart,[4]
and I am surrounded by fear.
Yes, I have no idea where to turn

and would immediately be lost
if I did not have your word.

4.

It is your salutary word alone, with its
sweet singing, that makes
my heart free and able to laugh again,[5]
as if it were going to leap for joy,
because your word promises grace to all
who with a truly penitent spirit
come to you, O Jesus.[6]

5.

Since, in my mind, I am,
as I previously lamented,
a truly aggrieved sinner,
whose conscience gnaws at him,
I would gladly like to be
absolved from my sin by your blood,
as were David and Manasseh.[7]

6.

As I now come to you, Lord,
approaching you in my distress
and asking with my whole heart
on bended knee,
forgive me in your grace
what I have done against you
during my life on earth.

7.

My Lord and my God, for the sake of your Name,
forgive me my sins
and remove the heavy yoke

that knowledge of my transgressions has created
so that my heart may be given over to peace[8]
and may hover before you with the angels,
in constant praise and adoration.

8.

Strengthen me with your Spirit of Joy,
heal me with your wounds,[9]
wash away from me the sweat of death
that is felt in the last hours,[10]
for you have brought me by faith
out of the evil world under the tent
of your elect. Amen.

July 25, 1619,[11]
on the Feast of St. James,
the Ninth Sunday after Trinity,
after my return from the mineral springs at Göppingen.

---

1 On the publication history of "Der Herr ist mein getreuer Hirt," which is based on Ps 23, see Wackernagel, V:1, 369 (no. 582). It also appeared in the hymnal that Johann Christoph owned, Ammon's *Neuw Gesangbuch*. Johann Christoph's text closely follows Bartholomäus Ringwaldt's (1532–ca. 1599) "Herr Jhesu Christ, du höchstes gut." On its publication history, see Wackernagel, IV, 1028–29 (no. 1523). In the original German, the initial letters of the first word of each of the eight stanzas form the acrostic *ICODWAMS*. The meaning of the acrostic is unclear: Iohann Christoph Oelhafen Doctor Witwer Anna Maria Selig (Johann Christoph Oelhafen Doctor Widower Anna Maria of Blessed Memory) or, perhaps, Iohann Christoph Oelhafen Doctor Wiederkunft aus Mineral-Sauerbrunnen (Johann Christoph Oelhafen Doctor Returning from the Mineral Springs)? I have not preserved this acrostic. The rhyme structure is *ababccd*.

2 See Job 6:4; Ps 38:2; Lam 3:12.

3 The source of this pain appears to be sorrow for sin.

4 See Matt 21:44; Luke 20:18.

5 In place of the word *heart* (*Herz*), Johann Christoph here inserts a heart-shaped symbol.

6 See Matt 11:28; Luke 5:32; Acts 2:38; 3:19.

7 See Ps 51 (David); 2 Chr 33:1–20 (Manasseh).

8 In place of the word *heart* (*Herz*), Johann Christoph again inserts a heart-shaped symbol.

9 See Isa 53:5.

10 This line and the one that precedes it may indicate that Johann Christoph was in danger of dying or at least that he feared so, which may have been why Ringwaldt's hymn appealed to him.

11 Johann Christoph records in his *Diarium* that on July 25, he attended services at the St. Lorenz Church in Nürnberg and thanked God for the mineral springs in Göppingen. He also continued to drink its waters, apparently having brought some home with him.

48

To the tune of "Concerning Fortune"[1]

1.

I am driven about by Fortune,
in this world I wander and lose my way.
Lord, teach me to know
where I should turn, toward
the narrow way,
the small path,
that leads to the heavenly throne.[2]

2.

Christ, I enter into this world, into this little boat,
in your Name,
so that I learn to know
where I should turn
according to your command
and divine word,
my rudder and sail.[3]

3.

O take courage, my poor soul,
call to God, even if a storm is present
and threatens to bring you
from the right way;
look upon it as if it will
simply pass on,
no harm shall befall you.

4.

Day and night Satan grasps at my soul
with all of his cunning,
therefore, I must maneuver skillfully
and govern my heart
with God's word,
which is my refuge,
so that I not be made a mockery.

5.

Above all, I cling to this hope,
that God will give us his Holy Spirit
for the good of our souls
in our last hours
upon this earth
when it pleases Him to do so;
it is to this destination I sail.

6.

My God, since everything rests in your hands,
and because the end is approaching,[4]
turn me toward your Son
on his heavenly throne,
and make me grateful
along with the angels
in all eternity.
Amen.

August 1, 1619,
on the Tenth Sunday after Trinity.

1 "Der Fortunae." Johann Christoph's text closely follows "Von der Fortuna / und Christlicher Schiffart" in *Fünf Newe Christliche Lieder* (s.l. 1612; VD17 1:04353H). For other occurrences of the song, see VD17 12:649695B; VD17 1:670634A; and VD17 1:043287Z. These works may have been printed in Basel by Johann Schrötter. See Abrecht Classen, *Deutsche Liederbücher des 15. und 16. Jahrhunderts* (New York: Waxmann, 2001), 92–93 (no. 26); and Emil Weller, *Poetischen National-Literatur der Deutschen im XVI. und XVII. Jahrhundert* (Freiburg im Breisgau: Herder'sche Verlagshanglung, 1862), 274 (no. 427). In the original German and in my translation, the initial letters of the first word of each of the five stanzas form the acrostic *ICODAM* (Iohann Christoph Oelhafen Doctor Anna Maria). The rhyme structures are *aabbcca*, *aabbccd*, and *aabbccc*.

2 See Matt 7:13–14.

3 In the ancient world, Fortune was frequently depicted as holding the rudder (*gubernaculum*) of a ship in her hand, indicating her control over human life. The hymn here counters that God's word is this rudder, guiding the Christian's life.

4 As in the eighth stanza of the preceding entry and in the second and third stanzas of the following entry, the reference here to an approaching end may have struck a chord with Johann Christoph, who may have thought his own end was near. These references to death may be more generic, though, referring to the end of all things, which many Lutherans feared at this time. See the discussion of this feature of Lutheran religious life in the introduction. But the entries for July 26 and 27 in Johann Christoph's *Diarium* indicate that he was confined to bed, suffering from a fever, and thus there is evidence that he may have seen in these verses references to his personal situation.

49

To the tune of "May I not Withstand Misfortune."[1]

1.

Ah, Lord, do not punish me in your wrath,
otherwise I am lost
on account of my sin.
Do not discipline me in your anger,
but accept my lament and
let me find grace with you.
Save me, Lord,
from sin and death,
for this is my desire.
O Lord God,
you can conquer everything.

2.

My soul is terrified
O dear Lord,
where is your long-awaited help?
Show me your grace and goodness,
O Lord, and protect me,
for sin makes me sore afraid.
On top of this,
O Lord God,
death frightens me
so terribly,
but I hope in your goodness.

3.

Jesus Christ, graciously hear
my lamenting voice,
listen to my plea, I ask.
My strength is completely spent
in this dangerous time,
have regard for my sighing.
Great is the distress,
O Lord God,
that comes at the last hour.
Send me your help,
and I will give praise to you.

4.

Deep gratitude, I sing forth from my heart
at this hour,
and I praise God my Lord.
He is the one who rescues me from all distress,
from sin and death,
and he increases my faith
in Jesus Christ,[2]
who is my Savior.
I trust in him
and build securely on him;[3]
he will allow me to succeed in this.[4]

August 8, 1619,
on the Eleventh Sunday after Trinity.

---

1 On the publication history of the anonymous "Mag Ich Unglück nicht widerstehen," see Wackernagel, III, 118–19 (no. 156). It is also present in the hymnal that Johann Christoph owned, Ammon's *Neuw Gesangbuch*. The text appears to be original to Johann Christoph. He

draws on Ps 6:1–3 in the first two stanzas and likely also had Luke 18:9–14, the Gospel reading for the Eleventh Sunday after Trinity, in mind, especially the tax collector's penitent plea for mercy in v. 13. In the original German and in my translation, the initial letters of the first word of the first two stanzas, along with the initial letters of the first two words of the third stanza and the initial letter of the eighth line of the third stanza, coupled with the initial letter of the first word of the fourth stanza, form the acrostic *AMICOD* (Anna Maria Iohann Christoph Oelhafen Doctor). This entry provides further evidence that Johann Christoph feared his end was near. The rhyme structures are *aabccbddeeb* and *aabccbddeef*.

2 See Mark 9:24.

3 See Matt 7:24–27.

4 "Er wirdt mirs laßen gelingen."

50

To the tune of Lobwasser's "To You from the Ground of My Heart, etc."[1]

1.

Ah, God, to whom should I lament
my heartfelt suffering?
My heart is falling into despair
in this great pain.[2]
The sun used to shine,
but it will do so no more.
Misery has displaced joy,
misfortune is now my portion.

2.

I am not permitted to lament my suffering,
people ridicule me for doing so.
I must bear it alone
and find rest for my heart.
A small herb grows alone
in my widower's garden;
it is called patience,
and, unfortunately, I know it all too well.

3.

I certainly did not plant this herb,
yet daily it grows.
Still, it gives me security,[3]
for who knows what God can do?
Perhaps he will transform

my cross into a blessed end,
according to his faithful will.
Yes, God will bring this to pass.

4.

Others provide a cross for me;
ah, that God would forgive them
as they laugh at my afflictions.
I would advise them
that they should stop,
for God cannot abide it
when someone prolongs another's misery;[4]
God quickly rescues him from it.

5.

Their eyes are always full of deception,
because their hearts are far from you.
I will trust God alone,
who constantly helps me.
What they have intended for me
will befall them.
God alone is faithful;
I will rely on him.

6.

Therefore, if I were abandoned
by all of my friends,
I would simply let them go,
for the fault certainly does not lie with me.
Perhaps the summer will come soon
and drive away the wintery frost.
Joy can displace misery;
God alone is my consolation.

August 15, 2019,
on the Twelfth Sunday after Trinity.

---

1 Ambrosius Lobwasser (1515–1585) was an important German humanist who produced a collection of hymns based on the psalms entitled *Der Psalter deß Königlichen Propheten Dauids* (Leipzig, 1573). "Zu dir von hertzen grundt," Lobwasser's rendering of Ps 130, appears on fols. Aaa v r–Aaa viii r of the 1576 edition from Leipzig, available online at the Münchener DigitalisierungsZentrum (https://www.digitale-sammlungen.de). On Lobwasser, see "Lobwasser, Ambrosius" in DB. He was a Calvinist. Early modern Lutherans could make use of hymns by non-Lutherans; Johann Christoph is not unique in this practice. Aside from original incipits, Johann Christoph's text closely follows "Ein Trostlied im Creutz" (or "Ach Gott, wem soll ichs klagen") by Franz Rhode (1569–1617). See Wackernagel, III, 863–64 (no. 1016). On Rhode, see "Rhode, Franz," in the DB. In the original German, the initial letters of the first word of each of the six stanzas form the acrostic *AMICOD* (Anna Maria Iohann Christoph Oelhafen Doctor). I have not preserved the acrostic. Johann Christoph may have been drawn to this hymn because it expresses feelings he may have been experiencing at the time: increasing isolation in his widowerhood and also the sense that others were expecting him to recover from his loss more quickly than he found he could. The rhyme structure is *ababcdcd*.

2 Johann Christoph again uses the symbol of a heart instead of the word *Herz*.

3 "Treibt mich zur sichern Schantzen." Alternative translation: "It drives me to a secure place" (i.e., a fortification or a protective wall of the same, an entrenchment).

4 "das man Elend lang treibe." Alternative translations: "when someone suffers prolonged misery" or "when someone drifts in misery for long."

51

To the tune of "I thank you, dear Lord."[1]

1.

I suffer great misery now,
it has wounded my heart.[2]
From my youth onward I have been delicate[3]
and still am to this hour.
I can lament my misery to no one
but you, my faithful God.
I will not despair of your aid,
for you help me both morning and night.

2.

Crosses cannot befall us in this earthly life
apart from the will and counsel of God.
To those who honor him,
he gives help in word and deed.
On this basis, I will wager
that misfortune shall come to an end.
I will definitely not despair,
for everything rests in his hands.

3.

O God, great are your gifts to us
from your fatherly goodness,
which your Son brought forth
through his bitter death.
I will trust in him

in my fear and distress.
He will not cause me regret,
for he delivers from eternal death.

4.

Disaster increases
in this evil world;
God has taken away
what pleased me most in it.[4]
But I rejoice in what is eternal;
I pay little mind to the temporal.
I shall at all times await
the joyful final day.

5.

Ah, Lord, one more thing I ask of you,
you righteous Jesus Christ.
My request
is not hidden from you,
and I will await your help,
but, Lord, do not make it too long.[5]
Your promise consoles me,[6]
your will is pleasing to me.

6.

My God, I will praise you,
you holy Trinity.
Help me, that all my days
I might be ready to serve you.
May you give me faith
through your mercy
so that I may live according to your will
in all righteousness.

August 22, 1619,
on the Thirteenth Sunday after Trinity.

---

1 Johann Kolrose (d. 1558) provided the text for "Ich dancke dir lieber Herre." For publication history, see Wackernagel, III, 86 (no. 114). The LSB (689) lists a version attributed to Nicolaus Selnecker (1532–1592), the tune for which first appeared in the *Musika Deutsch* (Nürnberg, 1532). On the *Musika Deutsch*, see Wackernagel, IV, 294 (no. 408). Johann Christoph may have this musical setting of the hymn in mind. The text appears to be original to him. In the original German and in my translation, the initial letters of the first word of each of the six stanzas form the acrostic *ICODAM* (Iohann Christoph Oelhafen Doctor Anna Maria). The rhyme structure is *ababcdcd*.

2 Johann Christoph again inserts a heart symbol here in place of the word *Herz*.

3 "von Iugendt auf, behende." *Behende* has a wide range of meanings. Alternative translations in this context would include *agile*, *adroit*, *deft*, *competent*, and *skillful*. For "delicate," see "behende," Adjektiv, in the FB, #7. The overall impression one receives of Johann Christoph in the *Pious Meditations* is that he was a delicate or sensitive soul.

4 "Gott hatt mit [*sic*] das [*sic*] genommen, das mir am besten gfelt." Johann Christoph may have made a mistake here, writing *mit* instead of *mir*, although both *mit* and *mir* are clear in the original text, and he rarely makes such mistakes. If it is a mistake, the translation would be "God has taken away from me what pleased me most in it."

5 Johann Christoph's request in this stanza is that God not delay long in providing help.

6 Johann Christoph may have in mind Gal 3:15–22, the Epistle reading for the Thirteenth Sunday after Trinity.

52

To the tune of "Out of Deep Distress I Cry to You."[1]

1.

I have received many kindnesses
from my Lord God,
why then would I want to become
impatient in distress?
Scripture certainly tells everyone
that when misfortune assails him,
he should not despair.

2.

Crosses along with joy, God has given to us
for his good ends,
therefore, he will also preserve my life
in suffering and distress.
The Lord gives, the Lord takes away;[2]
at all times he does what is fitting in his eyes,
according to his pleasure.

3.

O Cross, the One who sent you to me
on account of my sin and misdeeds,
namely, Christ my Lord,
will turn you away from me.[3]
In this cross that has befallen me
according to the will of the Lord Jesus Christ,
he will not abandon me.

4.

At all times I believe that
in my crosses and suffering,
Jesus Christ will preserve me
and not depart from me.
For the right Man still lives,[4]
who is able to help me out of distress;
may his name be praised.

5.

Much difficulty accompanied my arrival in the world,
with much difficulty I must also wander in it.[5]
Neither goods nor riches are of any help in this task,
one counts for as little as the other.
Therefore, God should be my hope,
because only with him may help be found;
for this help I will expectantly wait.

August 24, 1619,
on St. Bartholomew's Day.

---

1 Martin Luther provided the melody for "Aus Tiefer Not," a paraphrase of Ps 130, which first appeared in *Etlich Cristlich lider* or the *Achtliederbuch* (Nürnberg, 1524) and in numerous other Lutheran hymnals. See Wackernagel, III, 7–8 (nos. 5–6). It also appeared in the hymnal that Johann Christoph owned, Ammon's *Neuw Gesangbuch*. LSB 607; ELW 600. Aside from original incipits to complete the acrostic, Johann Christoph closely follows Georg Listen's "Das Si bona suscepimus." On its publication history, see Wackernagel, IV, 590 (no. 801). In the original German and in my translation, the initial letters of the first word of each of the five stanzas form the acrostic *ICOAM* (Iohann Christoph Oelhafen Anna Maria). The rhyme structure is *ababccd*.

2 See Job 1:21.

3 "der wirdt dich von mir kehren."

4 This line, "dann Er lebt noch, der rechte Mann," is clearly an allusion to the second stanza of Luther's *Ein feste Burg*, where the Wittenberg theologian writes, speaking of Christ, "es streit' für uns der rechte Mann" (Were not the right Man were not on our side). See Wackernagel, III, 20 (no. 33); LSB 656, 657; and ELW 503–5.

5 See Job 7:1.

53

To the tune of "What my God wills, etc."[1]

1.

Arise, arise, my soul, do not despair,
God will have mercy on you.
He will give you counsel and help,
he is a source of protection for the poor.[2]
Even if the going is frequently difficult,
one cannot, after all, sit in a rose garden
all the time.[3]
The one who trusts in God,
has built well;[4]
God will protect him eternally.

2.

Consider the pious man Joseph,[5]
what did he not experience?
One can read about David and Job,
and how they knew misfortune.
But God still most graciously
protected them
in their distress.
The one who trusts in God
has built well,
even though the Enemy still rages.

3.

I see well that it appears as if
God will not protect me,
and that he has made life in this world to be wearisome
for me,
wanting to provoke me to doubt.
But I know that,
in his time,
he will still come to me.
The one who trusts in God,
has built well,
how can God then leave me?

4.

Crosses here, crosses there, my dear soul,
but you should not let this distress you at all.[6]
The world, sin, death, the devil, and hell
will not harm you eternally,
for God's Son,
the throne of grace,[7]
has overcome all of them.
Trust in God,
build securely upon him,
and he will provide help at every hour.

5.

O, God has never abandoned
those who live according to his will,
who seek grace and help from him, morning and night,
and give themselves over to him entirely.
God's grace brings with it
faith, love, and patience,
along with a good conscience.

The one who trusts in God,
has built well,
he will enjoy this grace eternally.

6.

The one who seeks help from human beings
and not from God the Lord,
the same one is godless and accursed,
never coming to honor.
For God alone wishes
to be our Helper.
The one who firmly believes
in the Name of Christ Jesus
and trusts in God
will be blessed. Amen.

August 29, 1619,
on the Fourteenth Sunday after Trinity.

---

1 On the publication history of the anonymous "Was mein Gott will, gescheh allzeit," see Wackernagel, III, 1070–71 (nos. 1240 and 1241); and LSB 758. Aside from original incipits to form his acrostic, Johann Christoph's text closely follows a hymn by Caspar Schmucker variously titled "Frisch auf, mein seel" or "Wer Gott vertraut, hat wol gebaut," which was frequently sung to the tune of "Was mein Gott will." On its publication history, see Wackernagel, V:1, 3–4 (no. 1). In the original German, the initial letters of the first word of each of the six stanzas form the acrostic *AMICOD* (Anna Maria Iohann Christoph Oelhafen Doctor). I have not preserved the acrostic. The rhyme structure is *ababccdeed*.

2 This theme is repeated throughout this hymn. See Matt 5:3.

3 Original text:

Obs offt geht hart,
Im Rosengart,

> kan man nit allzeit sitzen.

See "Rosengarten" in Grimm, #3.

4 See Matt 7:24–27 here and in the following occurrences.

5 The Old Testament saint is here in view.

6 Original text:

> Creutz hin, Creutz her, Mein Liebe Seel,
> Es soll kein Not nicht haben.

Alternative translation: "But there is / should be no need [to fret]."

7 See Rom 3:25.

54

To the tune of "May I not Withstand Misfortune."[1]

1.

My hope is in God alone;
regardless of how things go for me,
I will trust in Him.
In distress and adversity,
I will at all times and in all ways
build securely on Him.[2]
He is my source of protection;
therefore, despite the devil
and all that the world sends my way,[3]
God remains with me;
I shall dread no one.

2.

Human help is utterly in vain,
as is the favor of earthly lords,
both of which often deceive many.
For even when someone hopes for this help for a long time,
has also often earned it
and expects to receive something,
soon someone comes
who takes it away
through hypocrisy;
piety and fidelity
always lie vanquished.

3.

By way of contrast, fully blessed is the one,
who, as a Christian,
lives in fear of God,
who conducts himself in accordance with God's will,
and whose confidence
and hope are in him.
Even if misfortune
strikes him,
God delivers him from it
so that he may finally
overcome all evil.

4.

To Christ, who has nourished me up til now,
I give unceasing thanks and praise
my whole life long.
He has satisfied my needs
and given me
enough.
For many possessions
damn a person,
although many a man
depends on them
and turns his heart toward them.

5.

Even if God does not soon grant
what I wish,
I will not allow it to trouble me.
Even if he appears ungracious
and delays for a long time,
I will still trust in him as the One who is Righteous.

I will wait upon his grace
and walk uprightly,
for he never abandons
those who are devoted to him,
but helps his true servants.

6.

Therefore, I do not seek after goods and money
in this world,
for I must leave them all behind.
And no matter how rich I am,
I must travel through death
on the road common to all.
Riches, poverty—
neither is good,
for riches make one proud,
while poverty is despised.
Therefore, Lord, give all things in moderation.[4]

September 5, 1619,
on the Fifteenth Sunday after Trinity.[5]

---

1 See entry 49, where Johann Christoph refers to the same hymn. Aside from original incipits, Johann Christoph's text closely follows Ambrosius Lobwasser's "Ein schön trostlied allen fromen Christen" (or "Allein zu Gott mein hoffnung steht"). See Wackernagel, IV, 876–77 (no. 1301), vv. 1–2, 9–10, 5, 11 (in that order). In the original German, the initial letters of the first word of each of the six stanzas form the acrostic *AMICOD* (Anna Maria Iohann Christoph Oelhafen Doctor). I have not preserved the acrostic. The rhyme structure is *aabccbddeeb*.

2 See Matt 7:24–27.

3 Original text:

drumb Teufel Trotz,
Trotz aller welt.

Alternative translation:

therefore, defiance to the devil,
Defiance to the whole world.

4 See Prov 30:8.

5 In the preceding week, Johann Christoph had attended a meeting of the Protestant Union in Rothenburg ob der Tauber. It took place on September 2 (old-style calendar) or September 12 (Gregorian calendar). I am grateful to Christopher Close for confirming Johann Christoph's presence at this meeting through his work on the Unionsakten in the NStaatsA.

55

To the tune of "All Mankind Fell in Adam's Fall."[1]

1.

If it is God's will, then it is good for me,[2]
I will trust in him.
He knows what should be done,
I will build securely on him.[3]
He is the one who can give all things,
and everything rests in his hands.
He will not leave anyone in distress,
he will turn away all misfortune.

2.

Christ is the one who disciplines those who belong to him,
he keeps them under the rod,[4]
although he does not cause their misfortune to be too
difficult for them.
Therefore, bear it with a quiet soul,
place yourself under his hand,
bear your cross here on earth,
for God is faithful and allows no one
to be tempted too far.[5]

3.

O dear soul, in your misfortune,
have the heart of a lion.
Trust in God and your matter will turn out for the best,
lament your sorrows to him.

There is no person who has been born into the world,
in fact, no creature at all,
whom misfortune has not struck hard,
as experience has shown.

4.

Do not boast of your good fortune,
consider that it can easily change.
Do not despair in your misfortune,
but patiently wait for its end.
Commend your matter to the loving God,
he will not abandon you.
He holds fortune and misfortune in his hands,
he knows the proper time and measure for both.

5.

At all times fear God, love everyone,
be friendly to all people.
God will certainly not leave you,
but do not dictate time or measure to him.
Find refuge in his tower,
where he seeks you.[6]
He will reach you with his hand
in all of your sorrows.

6.[7]

"Mr. Know-it-all" ridicules you, to be sure,[8]
and despises you utterly,
as if God were not your helper;
see to it that you pay no attention to such things.
God alone is your protector;
remain eternally submitted to him.
Build securely on him,[9]

trust his word,
for he can still raise you up.

September 12, 1619,
on the Sixteenth Sunday after Trinity.

---

1 See entry 15, where Johann Christoph refers to the same hymn. Aside from original incipits to form his acrostic, vv. 1–5 of Johann Christoph's text closely follow the anonymous hymn "Ein anders" (or "Wenn mein Gott will, so geht mirs woll"), which was sung to the tune of "Durch Adams fall." See Wackernagel, V:1, 462 (no. 720). Aside from Johann Christoph's incipit, v. 6 follows v. 4 of Caspar Schmucker's hymn "Wer Gott vertraut, hat wol gebaut." See entry 53. In the original German and in my translation, the initial letters of the first word of each of the six stanzas form the acrostic *ICODAM* (Iohann Christoph Oelhafen Doctor Anna Maria). The rhyme structure is *ababcdcd*.

2 "Ists Gottes will, so geht mirs woll." Alternative translation: "If it is God's will, then I am well."

3 See Matt 7:24–27.

4 See Ps 23:4.

5 See 1 Cor 10:13.

6 Original text:

> Ergieb dich vnder seinen thurn,
> Darinn Er dich thut suchen.

Johann Christoph underlines *thurn* in red. He inserts this word in the place of *handt*, as the original hymn has it. See Prov 18:10.

7 There are nine lines in this final stanza in Johann Christoph's original text. Schmucker's hymn has ten lines in this stanza, which Johann Christoph borrows and slightly revises.

8 *Maister Klügling* was a favorite term of ridicule that Luther used for those whom he believed relied too much on human reason and not enough on God's word. See "Klügling" in Grimm, #1. It passed into usage among Lutheran theologians, including those who wrote hymns. See Wackernagel, IV, 232–33 (no. 331, note). Johann Christoph has inserted it here to complete his acrostic.

9 See Matt 7:24–27.

56[1]

Lord, my refuge, my fortress, and my God, in whom I hope, preserve me so that no evil befalls me and no plague draws near to my house. Protect me in all of my paths. Command your angels to bear me upon their hands so that I do not strike my foot against a stone.[2] You discipline me severely and humble me,[3] but, Lord, this is very dear to me and useful for me so that I learn your statutes.[4] Lord, blessed is the one whom you discipline,[5] the one whom you yourself bring low, for he shall be raised up.[6] Amen.

September 19, 1619,
on the Seventeenth Sunday after Trinity.

---

1 Johann Christoph cites, in order, Pss 91, 118, 119, and 94 in the left margin of this single-page entry. The entry is largely a composite of citations from these psalms.

2 See Ps 91:2, 10–12.

3 See Ps 118:18.

4 See Ps 119:71.

5 See Ps 94:12.

6 In addition to Ps 94:12, Johann Christoph may also have in mind here Luke 14:10–11, part of the Gospel reading for the Seventeenth Sunday after Trinity.

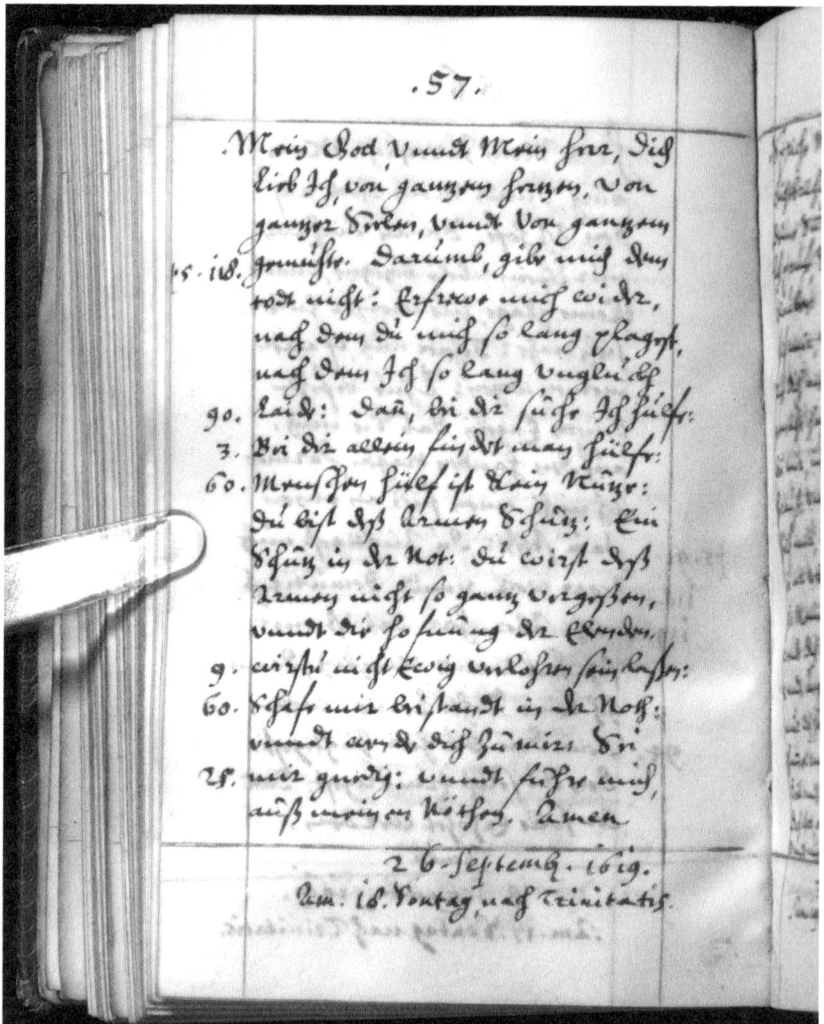

Image 8: Entry 57 of the *Pious Meditations* (*Gebetbuch des Hans Christoph Oelhafen*, GNM-HA, Familienarchiv von Oelhafen, Rep. II/80, Nr. 32)

57[1]

My God and my Lord, I love you with my whole heart, soul, and mind.[2] Therefore, do not hand me over to death.[3] Give me joy again after you have plagued me for so long, after I have suffered misfortune for so long.[4] For I seek help from you, in you alone one finds help;[5] human help is useless.[6] You are the protector of the poor, a stronghold in times of distress. You will not completely forget the cause of the poor, you will not allow the hope of the miserable to be lost forever.[7] Give me help in my distress and turn to me;[8] be gracious to me and lead me out of my distress.[9] Amen.

September 26, 1619,[10]
on the Eighteenth Sunday after Trinity.

---

1 Johann Christoph cites, in order, Pss 118, 90, 3, 60, 9, 60 (again), and 25 in the left margin of this single-page entry. The entry is largely a composite of citations from these psalms.

2 Johann Christoph almost certainly has Matt 22:37 in mind here, which was part of the Gospel reading for the Eighteenth Sunday after Trinity.

3 See Ps 118:18.

4 See Ps 90:15.

5 See Ps 3:8.

6 See Ps 60:11.

7 See Ps 9:9, 18.

8 See Ps 60:11.

9 See Ps 25:16–17.

10 The preceding day would have been Anna Maria's thirty-seventh birthday, a fact that was certainly not lost on Johann Christoph. She

was born on September 25 (old-style calendar). On September 22, Johann Christoph was in Rothenburg ob der Tauber for a meeting of the Protestant Union. I am grateful to Christopher Close for confirming Johann Christoph's presence at this meeting through his work on the Unionsakten in the NStaatsA.

58[1]

Speak to me, Lord Jesus, as you spoke to the paralytic: "Be consoled, my son, your sins are forgiven you." Ah, observe, see, and recognize my faith, for I desire your help.[2] Help me and protect me.[3] I call upon you, you who have created heaven and earth.[4] Listen to me and be with me in my distress; deliver me from it and show me your salvation.[5] Help me to be patient, because things are going badly for me.[6] Ah Lord, change my lament into a dance.[7] Turn to me, for my misery and fear are great.[8] Ah, if I only have you, I will ask for nothing in heaven or on earth. Even if my body and soul languish, yet you are God, my heart's consolation and my portion at all times.[9] Amen. Amen.

October 3, 1619,
on the Nineteenth Sunday after Trinity.

---

1 Johann Christoph cites, in order, Pss 91, 124, 91 (again), 94, 30, 25, and 73 in the right margin of this single-page entry. The entry is largely a composite of citations from these psalms, after the initial citation from Matt 9:2, part of the Gospel reading for the Nineteenth Sunday after Trinity.

2 See Matt 9:2.

3 See Ps 91:14.

4 See Ps 124:8.

5 See Ps 91:15.

6 See Ps 94:13.

7 See Ps 30:11.

8 See Ps 25:16.

9 See Ps 73:25–26.

59[1]

This is my joy, that I adhere to God.[2]
Why, then, O God, my God, do you so utterly forget me? How long will you hide your face?
Lord, how long must I seek counsel
from my own sorrowful soul?
How long will suffering afflict my heart?
Yet, Lord, I hope in your goodness,
my heart rejoices in your salvation.
I have this hope, because you are so gracious. My heart rejoices, for you are so eager to help.[3]
Do not abandon me, Lord, My God; be not far from me. Come quickly to support me.[4] Help me, Lord, and grant that I may be found not only among the called but also among the few who are chosen as true a member of your body.[5] Amen.

October 10, 1619,
on the Twentieth Sunday after Trinity.

---

1 Johann Christoph cites, in order, Pss 73, 13, and 38 in the left margin of this single-page entry. The entry is largely a composite of citations from these psalms along with a concluding reference to Matt 22:14, part of the Gospel reading for the Twentieth Sunday after Trinity.

2 See Ps 73:28.

3 See Ps 13:1–2, 5. Johann Christoph does not follow the Luther Bible in his rendering of Ps 13:2. Where Luther has "Wie lange soll ich sorgen in meiner Seele" (How long must I sorrow in my soul), Johann Christoph has "wie lang soll Ich Rathe suchen bei

meiner trawrigen Seel?" Johann Christoph's rendering emphasizes the isolation he feels along with the despair that stems from having only his own meager inward resources to draw upon in his grief. My formatting of the excerpts from Ps 13 reflects Johann Christoph's formatting, which may have been an attempt to indicate that he is here borrowing from a musical setting of the psalm. Such settings of Ps 13 were abundant in hymnals. For example, see *Geistliche Psalmen. Hymnen, Lieder und Gebett* (Nürnberg, 1611; VD17 7:683780Z—includes link to online copy), 19.

4 See Ps 38:21–22.

5 See Matt 22:14.

60

To the tune of "Lord Jesus Christ, I Know Very Well."[1]

1.

In faith the royal official cried out
to God's only Son,
"Come, help my only son."[2]
How long will you keep quiet?[3]
But I believe that you hear me,
even though you hide yourself so well from me;[4]
help me to wait on you.

2.

O my Lord, in my long suffering
I also sigh in a Christian manner
for the bright light of your grace,
or to flee the world.
But you know when you should come,
and to the one who trusts in you, you are a refuge;
yes, you will certainly still come.

3.

Although people are often deceived
as they cling to this world,
yet I know what your word says,
no one can malign it.
Even if crosses are difficult and long-lasting,
which causes the old Adam to fear,
still, long is not eternal.

4.

Daily I make my lament,
the water is almost up to my mouth,[5]
and I certainly cannot hold out
if you do not help me bear my affliction.
O Jesus Christ, my Lord and God,
help now again in distress,
otherwise, all is lost with me.

5.

I think of Paul, your faithful servant,
and say with him
that you will order all things
so that I can bear them.[6]
But, O Lord, your cup is difficult to drink,[7]
the cross is bitter and sharp;
ah, my God, help the weak.

6.

With God's grace I will now resolve
to trust in him, my Lord.
May he help me so that things do not become too much for me,
may he see my misery.
AMICO certainly also thinks of me,
even as I long to be with her;
ah, come Lord Christ. Amen.

October 17, 1619,
on the Twenty-first Sunday after Trinity.

1 Bartholomäus Ringwaldt (1530–1599) composed "Herr Jhesu Christ, Ich waiß gar woll." On its publication history, see Wackernagel, IV, 986–87 (no. 1473). The text appears to be original to Johann Christoph. In the original German, the initial letters of the first word of each of the six stanzas form the acrostic *ICODAM* (Iohann Christoph Oelhafen Doctor Anna Maria). I have not preserved the acrostic. Johann Christoph's spacing of the lines within the stanzas differs from other hymns. I have preserved this spacing. The rhyme structure is *ababccd*.

2 See John 4:46–54, the Gospel reading for the Twenty-first Sunday after Trinity. Much of this entry builds on the waiting of the royal official in this passage for Jesus to come from Cana to Capernaum to heal his sick son. Johann Christoph sees in this passage his own painful waiting for divine visitation and return.

3 See Ps 28:1; 35:22; 83:1.

4 Johann Christoph here provides additional evidence of his familiarity with Luther's theology of the cross.

5 See Ps 69:1.

6 See 1 Cor 10:13.

7 See Matt 20:22–23; 26:39.

61

Ah, you eternal God, I am the servant who owes you ten thousand talents.[1] Unfortunately, I must confess that I have merited your wrath and punishment ten thousand times over, and in my fragility and weakness, have not a single thing with which to pay you.

But, Lord, I have already given over to you my wife and a portion of my children, and everything that remains is also in your hands. Since, then, you are a Lord over all things, what is left with which I can render satisfaction to you? Ah, nothing else but my believing heart,[2] which believes that you sent your eternal and most beloved Son into the world on account of such sin as mine and allowed him to pay the ransom for my release.[3]

So, accept now such a believing heart, which at the same time has compassion on its fellow servant who owes just 100 denarii.[4] Be gracious to me, my God, have mercy on me, and have patience with me. Take pity on me, and release me from my debts that still daily increase. You are the gracious Lord, whose name is "Gracious and Merciful."[5] This is your voice: "As surely as I live, I do not desire the death of the sinner,"[6] for your grace exceeds all sin. For this reason, I appeal from your righteous wrath to your unfathomable mercy, from the judgment seat of righteousness to the throne of grace:[7] hear me, Lord, and be gracious to me.

October 24, 1619,[8]
on the Twenty-second Sunday after Trinity.

---

1 See Matt 18:24, part of the Gospel reading for the Twenty-second Sunday after Trinity.

2 See Phil 3:9, part of the Epistle reading for the Twenty-second Sunday after Trinity.

3 See Matt 20:28; 1 Tim 2:6.

4 See Matt 18:28, part of the Gospel reading for the Twenty-second Sunday after Trinity.

5 See Ex 34:6.

6 See Ezek 33:11.

7 See Ex 25:17–22; 2 Cor 5:10; Heb 4:16.

8 Johann Christoph had turned forty-five on the preceding day. His birthday was October 23.

62

Ah, you sweet Jesus Christ,[1] how has it happened that you have given your life for me, a poor and sinful person, and have adopted me as your friend?[2]

With what have I merited the freedom from servitude to the devil that you have given me,[3] along with all that you have made known to me, having heard it yourself from your Father?[4]

I did not choose you, rather, according to your own word, you chose me. So, allow me to bear fruit that lasts.[5]

Let me always feel your friendly sweetness in my heart.[6] Seal your unspeakable grace in me through your Holy Spirit,[7] who testifies to me before your heavenly Father that I am your chosen friend and through whom I am allowed to call out, sigh, and cry with true confidence, "Abba, dear Father."[8]

As you yourself have taught me in your word and thus far have allowed me to know of your friendly heart, whatever I ask your Father for in your name, he will give me.[9] Therefore, I do not doubt that you, out of loving faithfulness, will generously grant to me, as your friend, what will be useful and necessary for me at all times. Amen. Amen.

October 28, 1619,
on the feast day of Simon-Judah.[10]

---

1 This reference to divine sweetness and the one that follows a little later in this entry put one in mind of Bernard of Clairvaux (1090–1153) and Johann von Staupitz (ca. 1468–1524), both of whom had a great deal to say about spiritual sweetness in their devotional works. See Franz Posset, "The Sweetness of God," *American*

Benedictine Review 44 (1993): 143–78; and Franz Posset, "Christi Dulcedo: The 'Sweetness of Christ' in Western Christian Spirituality," *Cistercian Studies Quarterly* 30 (1995): 245–65. Closer to Johann Christoph's lifetime, Lutheran devotional writers such as Martin Moller (1547–1606) and Philipp Nicolai (1556–1608) employed the Bernardine image of the divine kiss to convey the deeply emotive aspect of Lutheran consolation. See Moller's *Mysterium Magnum* (Görlitz: Rhambaw, 1595), HAB, A:811.4 Theol., fol. 64 r; Moller, *Thesaurus Precationum* (Gorlitz: Rhambaw, 1608), HAB, A:697.87 Theol., fol. 416; and Nicolai, *Freudenspiegel des ewigen Lebens*, 80. See also the discussion of these works in Rittgers, *Reformation of Suffering*, 200–225; and Rittgers, "Mystical Union and Spiritual Desire in Late Reformation Devotion: The Case of Martin Moller's *The Great Mystery* (1595)," *Reformation and Renaissance Review: Journal of the Society for Reformation Studies* 17, no. 3 (2015): 214–29. Johann Christoph was familiar with Moller's works. He cites one directly in entry 69 and perhaps also in the present entry (see n. 6), and refers to making a gift of Moller's postils to a friend in his *Diarium* (see February 9, 1619). See the discussion of Johann Christoph as a lay representative of Protestant *Frömmigkeitstheologie* in the introduction.

2 See John 15:15, part of the Gospel reading for the feast day of Simon-Judah.

3 See Rom 8:15.

4 See John 12:49–50.

5 See John 15:16, part of the Gospel reading for the feast day of Simon-Judah.

6 "Laß mich deine freundliche süßigkeit, in meinem hertzen, allwegen, Empfinden." Johann Christoph may have been drawing on Martin Moller's *Mysterium Magnum* here. Moller prays, "Ich bitte dich / mein HERR / erzeige dich in mir lieblich vnd tro[e]stlich / durch deinen lebendigen Mahlschatz / das ich Fried vnd Frewde schmecken / vnd deine gegenwart inn mir allezeit empfinden mo[e]ge / Amen" (I ask you, O Lord, to reveal yourself in me lovingly and consolingly through your living betrothal gift [that is, the Holy Spirit], so that I may taste peace and joy and feel Your presence in me at all times). Moller also prays, "Erzeige dich in meinem Hertzten / das ich deine

gegenwart spu[e]re" (Reveal yourself in my heart that I might feel your presence). See *Mysterium Magnum*, fols. 78r and 80 r.

7 See Eph 1:13.

8 See Rom 8:15–16.

9 See John 15:16, part of the Gospel reading for the feast day of Simon-Judah.

10 October 28 was the feast day of Simon the apostle, who was sometimes also called Simon the Zealot. In his *Diarium*, Johann Christoph records that on October 26, he had a pain in his left arm, which may have been related to his earlier and nearly fatal experience with a barber surgeon in 1599 (see introduction). In the coming days, he saw a barber surgeon and also took medicine for the pain. He makes no reference to this experience in his *Pious Meditations*, but it must have been on his mind as he composed the entries for October 28 and 31.

63

O Christ, you faithful and omniscient knower of hearts,[1] you who do not regard the appearance of a person,[2] you are a true master before whom even the purest among us according to the standards of human folly are rogues. For this reason, I do not regard myself worthy to appear before your divine majesty or to lift up my eyes toward heaven.[3] But this consoles my heart, that you have also commanded us in the midst of our weakness to render to God what is God's,[4] that is, we should call upon you with appropriate reverence in our distress.[5] Therefore, on the basis of your own command, I appear before you, and because you have elsewhere richly pledged graciously to listen,[6] I thus rest myself upon such gracious pledges and promises. I call upon you, in my concern that is known to you, and ask that you would graciously hear me according to your alone wise counsel and good pleasure and, at the right time, generously give me joy. For to you I lift up my eyes, my heart, my mouth, my soul, and all my strength. O Lord, take away from me all dissolute thoughts of my mind and understanding,[7] and I shall exalt, honor, and praise your most holy Name with all that I am, and thus give to you what is yours. Amen, Lord Jesus, Amen.

October 31, 1619,
on the Twenty-third Sunday after Trinity.

---

1 See 1 Sam 16:7; Acts 1:24.

2 See Matt 22:16, part of the Gospel reading for the Twenty-third Sunday after Trinity. See also 1 Sam 16:7.

3 See Luke 18:13.

4 See Matt 22:21, part of the Gospel reading for the Twenty-third Sunday after Trinity.

5 This explanation of rendering to God what is God's closely resembles Martin Luther's explanation of the First Commandment in his Large Catechism. See BC, 386, 2.

6 Johann Christoph still appears to have John 15:16 in mind. See entry 62. See also Jer 29:12.

7 See Phil. 3:19, part of the Epistle reading for the Twenty-third Sunday after Trinity.

64

Lord Jesus, I am a sinful person; I was born into sin and death.[1] Therefore, do not depart from me; rather, come, dear Lord Jesus, come and lay your hand upon me, then I shall live.[2] Make haste to help me out of the distress of my sin, which surrounds me, so that I am not destroyed by it. For you came into this world, and were sent to it, in order to save sinners.[3] You did not come for the sake of the righteous (for, who is righteous before you?); rather, you came to call sinners to repentance.[4] Therefore, speak consolation to me, the one who appears before you,[5] that my faith has helped me,[6] that my sins have been forgiven me and shall not be remembered in eternity. Do this so that I may go forth joyfully and through the strength and help of your good Spirit, may sin no more, but may say from my heart,

> My sins greatly torment me now,
> my conscience gnaws at me,
> for my sins are as many as the sand on the seashore.
> But I will not despair.
> I think on your death;
> Lord Jesus, your red wounds,
> they will save me.

To the tune of "The Day is Surely Drawing Near."[7]

Nov. 7, 1619,
on the Twenty-fourth Sunday after Trinity.

1 "Herr Jhesu, Ich bin Ein Sundhaffter Mensch: In Sunden geboren vnndt Erstorben." Alternative translation: "I was born dead in sin."

2 See Matt 9:18, part of the Gospel reading for the Twenty-fourth Sunday after Trinity.

3 See 1 Tim 1:15.

4 See Luke 5:32.

5 Johann Christoph doubtless has in mind the woman who had been subject to bleeding for twelve years. See Matt 9:20, part of the Gospel reading for the Twenty-fourth Sunday after Trinity.

6 See Matt 9:22, part of the Gospel reading for the Twenty-fourth Sunday after Trinity.

7 Bartholomäus Ringwaldt reworked Johannes Magdeburg's text for "Es ist gewißlich an der Zeit." On its publication history, see Wackernagel, IV, 344–45 (no. 490). LSB 508. Johann Christoph's text reproduces verbatim the second stanza of Nicolas Hermann's (ca. 1480–1561) "Wenn mein stündlein vorhanden ist." See Wackernagel, III, 1211 (no. 1414). This hymn appeared in a number of hymnals, including one that Johann Christoph owned, Ammon's *Neuw Gesangbuch*. The rhyme structure is *ababccd*.

65

Ah, dear Lord, how is it that I hate what you love? How is it that I love everything that you hate? How is it that I am so weary, lazy, and lethargic when it comes to doing the good that you have commanded?[1] O God, I thus now call upon your own faithful instruction in the midst of this "abomination of desolation,"[2] looking to your unfathomable mercy. With the publican, I beat my breast;[3] grant, O God, that I do so with true earnestness.

With the prodigal son,[4] I am also ashamed of my weakness. O Christ, grant that I truly rue this weakness from my heart. Do not enter into judgment with me,[5] your poor creature. Rather, forgive me through your grace where I have sinned against your divine majesty by what I have done and left undone. And because I am by nature subject to your eternal curse, ah, Lord, receive me in grace again and, for the sake of the elect, shorten the days until your consoling promise will be fulfilled.[6] Grant that I, as part of the elect, may be and remain eternally reconciled to you through the precious rose-colored blood that you poured out on the holy cross for me and all penitent sinners.[7] Amen.

Nov. 14, 1619,
on the Twenty-fifth Sunday after Trinity.

---

1 See Rom 7:14–25.

2 See Matt 24:15, part of Gospel reading for the Twenty-fifth Sunday after Trinity. The "faithful instruction" (*Trewhertzige anweißung*) that Johann Christoph has in mind here appears to be the lesson provided by the publican in Luke 18:13, to which he refers in the next line.

3 See Luke 18:13.

4 See Luke 15:17–20.

5 See Ps 143:2.

6 See Matt 24:22, part of the Gospel reading for the Twenty-fifth Sunday after Trinity.

7 The reference here to "Rosenfarbe blut" may provide evidence for Johann Christoph's involvement in the nascent Rosicrucian movement in Germany (see the introduction).

66

Almighty and eternal God, you who have graciously called us in Christ Jesus to the great supper of your only begotten and beloved Son as to a meal for souls,[1] make this heavenly calling powerful in us through your Holy Spirit so that we, having put all else aside (as took place today in the presence of many princes and high-ranking envoys),[2] may hear and preserve your saving word in the time of grace.[3] May we also nourish our souls often with your most worthy Sacrament, as with the beloved food of divine consolation, and thus worthily prepare ourselves for the previously referenced great homecoming of your bride.[4] Grant all of this so that we, wearing holy jewelry and the proper wedding clothes, may appear before you at your right hand,[5] clothed with the righteousness of your most worthy Son's obedience, and may thus say with your chosen holy bride, from the bottom of our hearts,
"Come, yes, come, Lord Jesus."[6] Amen.

Through worry, affliction, and sorrow,
human powers gradually weaken;
but your word, beloved and good,
gives a person fresh courage.[7]

November 21, 1619,
on the Twenty-sixth Sunday after Trinity,
during the Correspondents' Meeting here in Nürnberg.[8]

---

1 See Rev 19:6–9. Johann Christoph develops the bridal themes of this passage in this entry.

2 Johann Christoph must here be referring to a Sunday-morning worship service in one of the churches in Nürnberg at which members of the Protestant Union were present. Both Lutherans and Calvinists attended this meeting of the union, but owing to ongoing tensions between the two groups on their respective theologies of the Lord's Supper, it is not clear if both groups were present at this service. Johann Christoph seems to suggest a show of unity among the members of the union, and there were joint worship services at such meetings, but it is difficult to imagine Lutherans and Calvinists taking Communion together. Johann Christoph definitely has Communion in mind, as the remainder of the entry makes clear. Perhaps he is here thinking of a service at which only Lutheran members of the union were present.

3 By "time of grace" (*in der gnadenzeit*), Johann Christoph likely means the period of time that he believed God had set for the gospel, freshly revealed through Luther, to have its sway in the German lands of the Holy Roman Empire. With a number of his fellow Lutherans, Johann Christoph may have believed that this time of grace was ending, perhaps because of biblical passages such as 2 Thess 1:3–10, the Epistle reading for the Twenty-sixth Sunday after Trinity, which speaks of Christ's return and judgment of nonbelievers (see the discussion in the introduction of a growing apocalyptic outlook in later Lutheranism, motivated in part by some Lutherans' sense that they had squandered the gospel and were therefore subject to divine wrath). Johann Christoph definitely has Rev 19:6–9 in mind throughout the entry and cites Rev 22:20, which also has to do with Christ's second coming and the judgment of nonbelievers, at its end. Additionally, since this Sunday was the last day of the liturgical year, Johann Christoph was naturally thinking of endings and new beginnings.

4 By "previously referenced" (*angedeuten*), Johann Christoph appears to have the Rev 19:6–9 passage in mind that provides the theme for this entry.

5 See Matt 25:33, 34, part of the Gospel reading for the Twenty-sixth Sunday after Trinity,

6 See Rev 22:20.

7 I have not been able to identify the source of this poem; it may be original to Johann Christoph.

> Durch Sorg, betrübnuß, Trawrigkeit,
> verlieren sich die Kräfft, bei zeit:
> Aber, dein wort, lieblich vnndt gutt,
> dem Menschen macht frischen Mut.

8 Members of the Protestant Union referred to themselves as the "Correspondierenden" and thus to their meetings or diets as a "Correspondenztag." The term was intended to indicate the inclusion in their cause of Protestants who were not part of the union, although few if any such Protestants attended the meeting in Nürnberg. It was decided at this meeting to send a delegation of the Protestant Union to Munich for further negotiations. Johann Christoph was a member of this delegation, although he makes no reference to it here or in the remainder of the *Pious Meditations*. I am grateful to Christopher Close for this information. On the Munich delegation and Johann Christoph's involvement in it, see Close, *Stated Formation*, 245–86.

67

O you, my faithful, merciful, and most loving God and Lord, you unfathomable fountain of all grace and goodness, with what utterly inexpressible generosity have you regarded me, a poor and depraved sinner, from heaven! In what a friendly manner have you received me with your great love and crowned me with grace and mercy! Ah, at the beginning of this new church year, how have I, a poor human being, come to this great grace that you, as a pledge of your fatherly love and fidelity, have given to me your Son Jesus Christ, the gentle King, along with all of his merit as my very own? O Lord, may you be thanked and praised into all eternity: "Praise be to him who comes in the name of the Lord, hosanna in the highest."[1]

For, out of pure love, grace, and mercy, you have now given your dear Son to me in such an unfathomable way.[2] Ah, I will thus never again despair of your goodness,[3] for you have cast all of my sins all at once upon the back of your Son and removed them from me, putting them to death. Give me the Holy Spirit,[4] so that he may seal such grace in my heart and enable me always to feel your fatherly fidelity in my heart, which will provide me with an enduring consolation in you against all of the bodily and spiritual trials and burdens that can torment and frighten me. Do this so that I may daily—no, hourly—cry out from my heart and say with the elect who go ahead and those who follow behind, "Praise be to him who comes in the name of the Lord, hosanna in the highest."[5]

November 28, 1619,
on the First Sunday of Advent.

---

1 See Matt 21:9, part of the Gospel reading for the First Sunday of Advent.

2 Johann Christoph may have taken Communion on this Sunday, which would account for his expression of deep gratitude for the mercy he had now (*nun*) received from God. It would also account for the language of the Holy Spirit sealing (*zusigle*) grace in his heart a few lines down.

3 This is a clear indication that Johann Christoph had in fact despaired of this goodness in the past.

4 See Eph 1:13.

5 See Matt 21:9, part of the Gospel reading for the First Sunday of Advent.

68

A Pious Dream[1]

What causes you such sadness?
   God still lives.
Only call upon him.
   He is the man
Who can help;[2]
   He will not leave
You and yours,
   For he knows those who are his.
In his hands
   Are written[3]
The names of those who trust him
   And who build firmly upon him.[4]
Therefore, hold fast to the Lord,
   For he is not far away.
Believe, do not despair;
   Only follow after him.
Console yourself with this,
   That he will finally help.
Also, be joyful,
   And exalt God.
Praise his Name
   Into eternity. Amen.

Through prayer, must one receive all things.
Through wisdom, must one make use of all things.

Through gratitude, must one preserve it,[5]
for,
the one who does not ask for it, does not receive it; to the one who does not use it with wisdom, it is not useful at all; the one who does not thank God for it, does not preserve it; and what one does not preserve is as if one had never had it, etc.[6]

November 30, 1619,
on the Feast Day of St. Andrew.

---

1 Johann Christoph does not have an actual dream in mind in this entry. The "Somnium Pium" is a pious wish for his own soul. It appears to be original to Johann Christoph. The rhyme structure is *aabbbbccddeeffgghh*. In the original German, each line begins with a capital letter. I have reflected this in my translation.

2 "Er ist der Mann, der helfen kann." For a similar formulation, see entry 52, stanza 4 (and note).

3 See Isa 49:16.

4 See Matt 7:24–27.

5 In the third line, *alles* (all things), which occurs in the first two lines, is replaced by *es* (it). The referent for *es* is not clear but it may be the word of God (see the following note). *Es* continues in the remainder of the entry.

> Durch das Gebet, muß man alles bekommen;
> Durch weißheit, muß man alles gebrauchen:
> Durch danckhbarkeit, muß man es behalten:
> Dann,
> Wer nicht darumb bittet, der bekombt
> Es nicht: wer es, mit weißheit nicht
> Gebraucht, deme ists nichts Nutz:
> Wer Gott nicht darumb danckhet,
> Der behelt es nicht: vnndt, was
> Man nicht behelt, Ist eben, alß hette
> Man es nicht gehabt.

6 These concluding lines, beginning with "Through prayer" and ending with "never had it, etc." are a direct quotation from L.V. (author unknown), *Einfaeltige Antwort vnnd Bittschreiben eines Layen doch Liebhabers der Weißheit an die Hocherleuchte Bruderschafft deß Rosencreutzes* (Frankfurt am Main: Johann Bringern, 1615), Aiiii v. Johann Christoph owned this work (see UEN, H00/HIST 403a), a fact that may provide evidence of his involvement in, or at least familiarity with, the nascent utopian brotherhood movement in Germany at the time. See the discussion of Johann Christoph's possible involvement in a proto-Rosicrucian gathering in Nürnberg in the introduction. In the *Einfaeltige Antwort*, the *es* in these lines refers to the word of God.

69[1]

Lord Jesus, my Savior, I have, yes, unfortunately, truly come into a previously prophesied time in which signs occur in the sun, moon, and stars and in which people on earth are afraid and languish because of fear and anticipation of the things that will happen on the earth.[2] Ah, protect me—"the one who awaits in his heart your redemption with upraised head"[3]—from painful illnesses and a terrifying death. Do not fall upon me suddenly in my sins nor let me die without repentance among the languishing and the cowardly. Rather, because your kingdom is near, grant me a quiet and gentle end, without great fear and pain. Do this so that I, in full possession of my faculties and with due consideration, awake and praying, may make a good end, confessing your Name until my journey home, commending my soul devoutly and sincerely into your hands, and finally, worthily standing before you, you Son of Man, after all evil has passed away. Amen.[4]

Steadfast patience
Earnest prayer } these three allow no cross to be too difficult,
Firm hope

for,

Patience does all things gladly, therefore nothing is too difficult for it; prayer always drives one to God and receives either relief or rescue; and hope prevents one from being put to shame.[5]

December 5, 1619,
on the Second Sunday of Advent.

1 Johann Christoph draws on Luke 21:25–36, the Gospel reading for the Second Sunday of Advent, throughout this entry.

2 On the fascination with such signs in late Lutheranism, see the relevant discussion in the introduction.

3 See Luke 21:28, part of the Gospel reading for the Second Sunday of Advent.

4 See the discussion of the Lutheran *ars moriendi* (art of dying) in the introduction.

5 The lines from "Steadfast patience" to "put to shame" are a nearly verbatim quotation from Martin Moller's *Manuale de praeparatione ad mortem* (Görlitz: Johann Rhambaw, 1596), 44, 45 (fols. K iiii v and K v r; VD16 M 6041—provides link to online copy). This work first appeared in 1593. See the discussion of Johann Christoph's reliance on this work in the introduction.

70

O you sweet Lord Christ,[1] in this my prolonged cross, grant to me from your holy heaven the high grace that will enable me not to take offense at you.[2] Illumine my heart with your Spirit of grace[3] so that I may be patient as I bear all such burdens, as Tobit did, that I may gladly pray, as David did, and that I may, without ceasing, hope for the best from you, as the beloved Job did. Protect me from impatience so that I do not provoke you, my God, to wrath, so that my prayers are not thereby hindered, that my hope is not destroyed—in sum, so that I do not myself make my cross more difficult to bear. Grant instead that I, with true confidence, may cast my cares upon you alone as my only savior and redeemer, and may thereby remain steadfast up to the end. May I thus appear before your judgment seat in true innocence with and next to my AMICO, whom I have already sent ahead, clothed with your merit, suffering, and resurrection. Amen, Lord Jesus Christ, Amen.

Most beloved Father, for the sake of your above mentioned only Son, do with me as you will, and lead me toward what is best for your honor and my salvation. Amen.

December 12, 1619,
on the Third Sunday of Advent.[4]

---

1 Johann Christoph also refers to "du süßer Jhesu Christe" (you sweet Jesus Christ) in entry 62. See the note there regarding the importance of spiritual sweetness in medieval and early modern Christian devotion.

2 See Matt 11:6, part of the Gospel reading for the Third Sunday of Advent.

3 See 1 Cor 4:5, part of the Epistle reading for the Third Sunday of Advent.

4 From December 11 to December 21 (December 21 to January 1, Gregorian calendar), Johann Christoph was in Munich as part of a delegation of the Protestant Union. See the discussion of Johann Christoph's involvement in the Protestant Union in the introduction and in entry 66. See also Close, *Stated Formation*, ch. 7. It is not clear why Johann Christoph neglects to indicate his temporary residence in Munich in this entry and in entries 71 and 72.

71

Ah, dearly beloved Father, you are, yes, a true lover of human beings, for you have loved the world in this way, that you have given your only Son for us so that all who believe in him will not be lost but may have eternal life.[1]

Ah, dearly beloved Son of God, Jesus Christ, you have demonstrated your love for us, poor and miserable human beings, in that you entered into our midst, died for us, and gave yourself over to death, while we were yet sinners.[2]

Therefore, from this your love that you have for me, show me also real and gracious help now. Let your love for the human race, toward which you are with all faithfulness inclined and well disposed, also be praised and revealed in me, the poor earthworm, "who is not worthy to loosen the thong of your sandal."[3]

Along with the Holy Spirit, deliver me from my current heavy burden to a blissful end and exit from this life.[4] Amen.

December 19, 1619,
on the Fourth Sunday of Advent.

---

1 See John 3:16.

2 See Rom 5:8. By "gave yourself over to death" (*dich, in Todt, gegeben hast*), Johann Christoph appears to have in mind not just Christ's death, which he has just mentioned, but also Christ's entering into the condition of death after the point of giving up his life.

3 See John 1:27, part of the Gospel reading for the Fourth Sunday of Advent.

4 It seems that Johann Christoph's inner anguish was still so great that he could wish for death, although it is possible that he here hopes for a season of life free from grief before his final end.

72

Lord Jesus Christ, my Lord and my God, grant that I may acknowledge my unbelief as Thomas did, turn myself to you with a penitent heart, and revive my languishing heart with the sweet vision of your holy and healing wounds.[1]

For if your word, your bitter suffering, and especially, your joyful resurrection, were not my consolation, I would have to die in my misery.[2] Let me experience mercy so that I may live, for I take pleasure in your word.[3] Forgive me my sins and do not cast me away on account of my weak faith.

Keep me and my descendants in the knowledge of you. Help me to place all of my confidence in you alone, my Lord and my God, and to hold fast to you with firm faith, even though I do not see you.[4] Help me also to love you from my heart, even though I do not feel your presence.[5]

Search me and know my heart, test me and know my intentions, see if I am walking in the way of evil, and lead me in the way everlasting.[6]

December 21, 1619,
on the Feast Day of Thomas.

---

1 See John 20:28, part of the Gospel reading for the Feast of Saint Thomas. See also the discussion in the introduction of the place of Christ's wounds in late Lutheran devotion, especially the mystically inflected devotion that appears to have captivated Johann Christoph. See also entries 10 and 64.

2 As Johann Christoph indicates in the left margin, this portion of his entry is based on Ps 119 (:92).

3 See Ps 119:77.

4 See John 20:29, part of the Gospel reading for the Feast of Saint Thomas.

5 In entries 62 and 67, Johann Christoph prays to have this experience of divine presence.

6 As Johann Christoph indicates in the left margin, this portion of his entry is based on Ps 139 (:23–24).

73

To the tune of "Alone to God in the Highest Be Glory, etc."[1]

1.

Ah, Christ, my most beloved Savior,
  should I languish in suffering?
I speak a definite no, based on your word,[2]
  for you can certainly provide help and consolation.
You are salvation, help, and victory
  so that no one is completely laid low;
  you yourself give strength to the weak.

2.

My suffering, therefore, now departs from me,
  my sorrow has an end;
  my consolation stands in Jesus Christ,
  my heart rests itself in him.
Help, Jesus Christ, Son of God,
  turn away from me completely
  all affliction, fear, worry, scorn, distress, and derision.

3.

I go forth from here leaping,
  with joy I now sing.[3]
For Christ is not far from me,
  he allows me to find grace with him.
And he gives sunshine after the rain,
  just when I think all help is lost;
  You yourself bind up my wounds.[4]

4.

Cross, cross, one followed after the other,
and misfortune had enveloped me.
Everyone regarded me as wretched,
in loneliness I became fearful.
Weeping stretched out its hand to wailing,
I found no help with human beings;
I had exhausted my bodily strength.[5]

5.

O, death constantly called to my heart,
"just put an end to your misery."[6]
But Christ spoke, "My son, don't do it![7]
See, my grace inclines toward you;
I enclose you in my wounds.
Keep yourself securely within them,
despite the one who seeks to lead you away from me."

6.

For this, I give thanks to you, the crown of my heart,[8]
my protector and the salvation of my life.
Ah, Lord God and Mary's Son,[9]
I remain completely surrendered to you.
Your Name truly revives me,
your body and blood give me a hero's courage;[10]
I commend my way to you.

December 25, 1619,
on Holy Christmas Day.

---

1 Nikolaus Decius (ca. 1485–after 1546) provided the initial three stanzas and melody of "Allein in der Höh sei Ehr," a vernacular Protestant version of the Gloria in the Latin Mass, which was

one of the earliest evangelical hymns (ca. 1523). Joachim Slüter (ca. 1490–1532) later added a fourth stanza. See Wackernagel, *Das deutsche Kirchenlied von Martin Luther*, 338 (no. 420); LSB 947; and ELW 410. This hymn appears to be original to Johann Christoph. In the original German, the initial letters of the first word of each of the six stanzas form the acrostic *AMICOD* (Anna Maria Iohann Christoph Oelhafen Doctor). I have not preserved the acrostic, but I have preserved the unique pattern of indentations. The rhyme structure is *ababccb*.

2 See Titus 2:12, part of the Epistle reading for Christmas Day.

3 See Ps 98:1, 4. This was the traditional introit psalm for Christmas Day. The churches in Nürnberg largely retained the traditional introits in their liturgies. See Butler, "Liturgical Music," 161, 207, 305, 374, 377.

4 Johann Christoph likely has Luke 10:34 in mind in the final line, seeing himself as the wounded man whom the Good Samaritan served.

5 "craft, saftt, Ich hatt verfangen."

6 If this hymn is original to Johann Christoph, it is the clearest evidence that he was suicidal after the death of his wife and that he believed that God rescued him from this tragic end.

7 "Mein Sohn, das soll nit sein." Alternative translation: "My son, this must not be!"

8 For the use of "meins hertzen Cron" in a hymn of Johann Christoph's time, see Martin Behm's "Dancksagung nach Empfahung des H. Sacraments" (or "Ey, wie ist dis ein selig Stund"). See Wackernagel, V:1, 222 (no. 323).

9 See Luke 2:5–7, part of the Gospel reading for Christmas Day.

10 Johann Christoph likely took Communion on this day.

74[1]

I thank you, God, my savior, that you are my protector and helper, and that you have rescued my soul from destruction at such a high price, according to your great and highly renowned mercy.

I was close to death and my life was nearly consumed by it. I sought help from people, but there was none. Then I thought about your mercy, Lord, and how you have helped your true believers each time. For, you save all who wait for you and mightily rescue them. I prayed to God and called upon the Lord, my Ruler, that he would not forsake me in my distress, and I was assured by faith of his help.

Why are you so sad, my heart, why are you so troubled and why do you bear such pain?[2] Only on account of mortal things? Trust in your Lord God. Praise his holy Name without ceasing, for he neither can nor will forsake you; he knows well what you need in this situation.

Ah, grant me steadfastness, for the sake of the salvation of my soul. Let me not be cast away eternally from your face.[3]

Amen, Lord Jesus, Amen.

December 26, 1619,
on St. Stephen's Day, etc.

---

1 As Johann Christoph indicates in the left margin, he draws on Sir 51 (:1–12) in this entry, especially in the first two paragraphs.

2 See Ps 42:5, 11; 43:5.

3 See Ps 51:11.

75

To the tune of "What My God Wills, etc."[1]

1.

As I went for a walk in my garden[2]
at the end of the year
and called to mind again the suffering
that I had nursed for a long time,[3]
especially,
where, in the last year
I have likely gone the most astray,[4]
namely, regarding the body
of my beloved wife,
which I still embraced a year ago—

2.

I considered my situation from various angles,
made plans and gave thought to
how both fortune and misfortune are definitely
subject to rounds of inconstancy.[5]
For, two years ago,
I lay with
severe bodily illness.[6]
In this very garden,
people waited,
fearing that I was in danger of dying.

3.

But I found that it was not God's will,

for I returned to health.
Instead, since then, O, Lord, I have had
to experience many sorrowful hours,
among which
I must register
the thirteenth of February,
of this
year now past,
my darling's final
adieu.

4.

Christian heart,[7] how does your persistent and great
sorrow help you now,
your worry and concern that cause your body
to be so agitated
every minute and hour?
For it is certain and true
that God himself has counted
every day and year;
therefore, I see
before me that, alas,
death's lot has fallen to you.

5.

O death, you unfriendly guest,
what indebted my honorable wife
to you that you did not allow me
to take her place?
It was within your power;
so quickly
I could have bypassed
the great pain
that my heart's beloved

caused by her departure.

6.

Is it not then abundantly clear,
attested by her own hand,[8]
how her truly loyal soul was so consistently
inclined toward me?
Her great friends,
whom I love,
recognized from what she wrote
the gratitude that
she at all times
had for me.

7.

Much acclaim, much adoration, much praise, much honor,
I could further express for her,
if only the half part were still here
to be lamented without reprieve.[9]
But I should not
think a great deal
about those times,
for when I do,
nothing happens,
except that all my suffering is increased.

8.

I lived with her honorably,
as is proper for the marital estate.
I loved and valued her from my heart,
because she was constantly obliging.[10]
In eighteen years,
she had not a

single gray hair,
although God
allowed thirteen branches
to grow from our tree.

9.

As is only right, I have now given myself,
along with all of my affairs,
over to the same God; may he do
as seems good to him,
for I certainly have
no doubts
that, assuredly and truly,
she will rise
at the Judgment Day,
free of complaint, with the believing throng.

10.

Beautiful and glorious, will she then enter
into heavenly joy,
which was prepared for her and all believers
from the beginning.[11]
Meanwhile,
in her rest,
she continues to sleep most quietly and gently,
and she is free
from all fear and pain
that are in the world.[12]

11.

Now, if my God ordains
that I am also to be led away
from this world through death

to my dear AMICO,
I will go forward
to the grave,
awaiting the voice of Christ,
"Come,
you blessed host,
into the eternal heavenly kingdom."[13]

12.

In the meantime, I must be patient
until the right time and hour come
that God has determined for me
but that no one knows.
Until he calls my journey
in this valley of tears
to an end,
may he give grace through it all,
so that I may achieve the goal
that he intends.

13.[14]

Finally, because I have spent this past year
in grievous suffering,[15]
and have found no joy in being a widower,
I have brought this song to a close.
But because of my dearest treasure,
I cannot do so at the final end
without many tears,[16]
for it is certain
that her sweet memory
will never depart From My
Heart.[17]

FINIS

AMICO: Anna Maria
Iohann Christof Ölhafin,[18]
on December 31, 1619.

---

1 See entry 53, where Johann Christoph invokes the same hymn. This song appears to be original to him. In the original German, the initial letters of the first word of each of the thirteen stanzas form the acrostic *AMICOIstVERSchIeDEn* (*AMICO ist verschieden*—AMICO has disappeared, or is gone). I have not preserved the acrostic. The rhyme structure is *ababccdeed*.

2 There is evidence that in 1624, Johann Christoph owned a garden by the Laufer Tor in Nürnberg. Whether he owned it already in 1617 (see the following stanza) and has it in mind here in 1619 is not clear. See NStadtA C 20/II Nr. 278, Darstellung des Garten Nr. 130. He could also have a garden at his main residence in mind.

3 "dem ich lang abgewartet."

4 "weß, In der Zeit, Ich wer mainstens Irr gangen." It is not entirely clear what kind of going astray Johann Christoph has in mind here. In other entries, he does not view his grief for Anna Maria as a moral error, although he does concede in a few that it only worsens his suffering (see 25 and 32, stanza 7). He also acknowledges again and again the need to commend her to God and to accept the divine will for his life, seeking to find comfort for his sorrow in God's mercy and providence. In this entry, it is possible that he has come to see his grief as a problem, since Anna Maria has now been gone almost eleven months and the normal period of mourning, one year, was quickly drawing to a close. Stanzas 4 and 7 might indicate this change and the perceived need to move on with life, something he seems resolved to do in stanza 13, albeit reluctantly. Still, Johann Christoph has defended his extended grief in other entries (see 45, stanza 3, and 50, stanza 2), and so it would be odd for him to condemn it here. He could simply be indicating that Anna Maria's bodily absence has been the greatest cause of his suffering in the past year, which has led him astray from the path he had hoped his life would take with her.

5 Original text:

> wie das glückh vnndt vnglückh doch wer,
> Rundt vndergeben dem wanckhen.

Johann Christoph likely has in mind here the traditional Wheel of Fortune (*Rota Fortunae*) and how it expresses the unpredictable nature of fate.

6 Johann Christoph records in his *Diarium* that from March 2 to 5, 1617, he was quite ill with "Ein starkher bauchfluß" (a severe diarrhea), for which he took medicine and was bled. On March 5, he records that a number of people visited him in his illness.

7 In this stanza, an unidentified person speaks to Johann Christoph. In entry 32, stanza 4, he has Anna Maria speak to him from heaven using the same address, "Christliches hertz." It is possible that Johann Christoph again has her in mind here, although he does not clearly specify so, and the stanza as a whole makes better sense if he is speaking to his own heart.

8 Johann Christoph may be referring to Anna Maria's last will and testament, which, according to his *Diarium*, she wrote with her own hand on November 13 and 14, 1617. According to the same source, on February 11, 1619, Anna Maria conveyed her final wishes to her husband. But there is no indication that she wrote anything with her own hand, so Johann Christoph likely has her earlier will and testament in mind, or perhaps a recently updated version of it.

9 Original text:

> Viel Rhumb, viel Lob, viel preiß, viel Ehr,
> hett Ich Ihr nachzusagen:
> wann nur der halbe thail noch wer,
> ohn Erfrischung, hier zuclagen.

By "the half part" (*der halbe thail*), Johann Christoph appears to be referring to Anna Maria or to the days they shared together or even possibly to her virtue. If he only had something of her still, he would gladly praise and lament her further—this is his meaning.

10 "Weil sie auch war stets willig." *Willig*, which rhymes with *billig* (proper) in line 2, here appears to connote submissiveness, something Johann Christoph would have valued as an early modern husband and patriarch. It could instead mean *willing*, in the sense of being ready and willing to do what needed to be done.

11 See Matt 25:34.

12 Johann Christoph here imagines Anna Maria resting in anticipation of the final resurrection of the dead, whereas in entry 32, he imagines her awake, conscious, and already enjoying God's presence. Both views of the afterlife are attested in Scripture.

13 See Matt 25:34.

14 Johann Christoph likely composed thirteen stanzas for this hymn because his wife died on the thirteenth day of the month.

15 Original text:

> Endlich, weil, mit Trawrigem Laid,
> Ich diß Iahr hab vmbgwendet.

Alternative translation:

> Finally, because I have turned the pages of this year
> with grievous suffering.

16 Original text:

> Meim liebsten Schatz,
> Zu gutter Letz,
> Nicht ohne threnen schwere.

Alternative translation:

> To my dearest treasure
> at the final end,
> but not without many tears.

17 Original text:

> Auß Meim Hertz kombt nimmermehre.

Johann Christoph utilizes Anna's Maria's initials—AMH (Anna Maria Harsdörffer)—in this final line, thereby emphasizing that she will never depart from his heart.

18 Johann Christoph here gives the feminine version of his surname in German, "Ölhafin" instead of "Ölhafen," because he is referring to Anna Maria.

[76a][1]

JESUS[2]

Quiet now, sad lament,
mothers, stay your tears.
May no one mourn their dear ones,
this death is a renewal of life.

What do the hollowed tombs of rock mean,
these noble monuments?
That something is entrusted to them
which is not dead but given up to sleep.

For we see that the body reposes,
empty, without the soul;
it waits a brief span of time so that
the gathered senses may return on high.[3]

The ages will come quickly, when the
companionable warmth of life will surely revisit bones,
and as these bones are animated by living blood,
it may wear again its former habitations.[4]

Corpses that long since lay inactive,
rotting in their graves,
shall be carried off in the flying winds,
accompanying their former souls.

Dry seeds thus grow green again,
now dead and buried,
they are restored from the depths of the earth,
and rehearse the harvests of old.

Now, O earth, receive him, to cherish,
take him to your soft bosom.
I surrender to you members of a human being,
I entrust to you noble fragments.

This was once the home of a soul,
created from the mouth of the Maker.
In these remains wisdom lived ardently
from Christ its source.

Cover over the body that has been entrusted to you,
not unmindful that he, the Maker and Creator,
shall require his works back,
the figurative representations of his own face.[5]

May the just times soon come
when God fulfills every hope,
and you, having been laid open, must restore
the form that I commit to you.

I.C. Ölhafen, [signed] by my own hand.

[No date.]

---

1 Johann Christoph provides no number for this entry. It appears that he intended it to be included with the following entry. Here he reproduces, with a few changes, the well-known burial hymn "Iam moesta quiesce querela," adapted from the "Hymnus circa Exequias

Defuncti" in the *Liber Cathemerinon* of the ancient Christian poet and hymn writer Aurelius Prudentius Clemens (348–ca. 410). For recent English translations of "Hymnus circa Exequias Defuncti," see Gerard O'Daly, *Days Linked by Song: Prudentius' Cathemerinon* (Oxford: Oxford University Press, 2012), 292–320; and Nicholas Richardson, ed. and trans., *Prudentius' Hymns for Hours and Seasons: Liber Cathemerinon* (Abingdon, UK: Routledge, 2016), 68–73. "Iam moesta quiesce querela" appeared in a number of Lutheran hymnals, both in Latin and German versions. See Wackernagel, I, 40 (no. 42); IV, 191–94 (nos. 278–82); and V:1, 143–44 (no. 213). See also Robin A. Leaver, *Luther's Liturgical Music: Principles and Implications* (Minneapolis: Fortress Press, 2017), 234. I have rendered my own translation.

2 I.H.S.

3 "Gathered senses" (*collegia sensus*) refers to the body (*corpus*), which returns to the soul in heaven at the resurrection of the dead.

4 Original text:

> Venient cito secula, cum iam
> Socius calor ossa revisat,
> Animataque sanguine vivo,
> Habitacula pristina gestet.

The subject of *gestet* (may wear) is unclear. It could be "warmth/blood," but, more likely, drawing from the previous and following verses, it is "the soul."

5 "prorpriusque anigmata vultus."

[76b]

I.C.O.

A.M.H.[1]

My Offering of the Same in the Form of a Heroic Song[2]

May the voices of lament and may bitter grieving be far removed from here.
May there be an end to weeping, may suffering and anxious fear be absent.
May no parent mourn her own children with perplexed sorrows, as if there were no consolations for an untimely death.
For this death is the restoration of new life.
What do these hollowed tombs of rock mean? Or what do the noble monuments teach in these days? That what is in them is not dead, but alive, in the placid slumber of those who have been set free.
For we see the body, which at the present moment is empty, without the soul, and just as if laid out to rest in a soft bed.
Moreover, it will not be long, the gathered senses will return to the lofty heights and the soul shall come back to them unharmed.[3]
The time approaches when the companionable warmth of life will surely revisit bones, the body, animated by living blood, shall rise up on winds to the heavenlies, that it may wear again its former habitations.[4]

And so, as it were, dry seeds, now dead and buried, rise up in early spring and grow green once more, rehearsing again their harvests of old.
Thus those bodies that had long since lain rotting in their graves, at that time shall suddenly be carried off in the flying winds, and will meet Christ, accompanied by their former souls.
Because I entrust this body to you, O earth, receive it now to cherish, and because I commend it to you, take it to your soft bosom.
For I surrender to you noble members of a mortal person.
This was once the dwelling place and splendid home of a soul, first created from the mouth of the Maker himself, in which wisdom was enclosed, with Christ as its source.
Cover over the body that has now only been entrusted to you for safekeeping, for when God comes to his own, be not unmindful that he, the Fashioner, shall require his works back, the figurative representations of his own face.
May the times come very soon, when the omnipotent and only true God, fulfilling what is said, surely wipes away holy tears and dries eyes.[5]
Then, at the same time, the form I commit to you will have to be restored.

I produced this on January 1, 1620.
I.C. Ölhafen, [signed] by my own hand.

"Each thing seeks its own way back,
And coming back is glad;
None is consigned to any ordered course
Save that which links the end to the beginning." Boethius[6]

January 6, 1620.

1 Iohann Christoph Oelhafen Anna Maria Harsdörffer.

2 "Idem Carmine Oblatum A Me Heroico." The title is based on the initials in the superscript of this entry—see the previous note.

3 "Gathered senses" (*collegia sensus*) again refers to the body (*corpus*), which returns to the soul in heaven at the resurrection of the dead.

4 Original text:

> Tempus exit, cum iam socius calor ossa revisens
> corpus ad aethereas animatum, sanguine vivo,
> auras consurgens, habitacula pristina gestet.

As in the original, here the subject of *gestet* (may wear) is unclear, but "the soul" is again likely to be understood.

5 See Rev 21:4.

6 The quotation from Boethius, the only direct one from a non-biblical source in the *Pious Meditations*, comes from *The Consolation of Philosophy*, III. I have followed the translation provided by H. F. Stewart and E. K. Rand, trans., *Boethius: The Theological Tractates*, Loeb Classical Library, vol. 74 (London: William Heinemann, 1918), 238–39, lines 34–37.

[77][1]

[Johann Christoph returns to "Iam moesta" again on Trinity Sunday (June 8), 1628, and composes another modified version of it with his deceased brothers and daughters in mind: Elias (d. Feb. 21, 1627), Paul (d. Jan. 18, 1628), Anna Maria (d. 1626), Susanna Maria (d. 1627).[2] This ancient hymn thus continued to provide an important framework for him as he lamented the loss of loved ones. He records this version of "Iam moesta" in the final pages of his *Pious Meditations*. Because it does not shed light on Johann Christoph's experience as a widower, I have not translated this Latin entry.]

1 Johann Christoph provides no number for this entry.

2 See Biedermann, CCCLVII (Elias), CCCXLV B (Paul), CCCLVII (Anna Maria), and CCCLVIII (Susanna Maria). Biedermann does not provide the month and day for the deaths of Johann Christoph's daughters.

Epilogue[1]

Even as Johann Christoph was putting the finishing touches on the *Pious Meditations*, he was preparing for his second wedding to Catharina Pfinzing (1585–1637).[2] There was nothing unusual about this in early modern Europe, and it should not be seen as evidence of his lack of love for Anna Maria. Johann Christoph's father and grandfather had done the same, and most widowers of the time remarried within one year of their wives' deaths.[3] He needed help raising his eight children, and facing the vicissitudes of early modern existence with a companion made better sense than seeking to face them alone. His soon-to-be new wife had already been twice widowed and so was likely no stranger to the grief that had so occupied Johann Christoph in the preceding year (and perhaps beyond). Additionally, Catharina was a family friend who, along with others, had visited him when he lay ill in March of 1617.[4] She was also the godmother of Johann Christoph and Anna Maria's final child, Catharina; Johann Christoph records in his *Diarium* that Catharina (his future wife) visited Anna Maria on her sickbed on January 8, 1619, presenting her with a beautiful necklace.[5]

Like Johann Christoph, Catharina was from a prominent Nürnberg family. As with Anna Maria, her father had been a member of the Smaller Council.[6] Her first and second husbands, Jacob Imhoff (1572–1609) and Sebastian Imhoff (1589–1612), who were from different branches of the Imhoff family,[7] were also among the imperial city's elite. On January 3, 1620, Johann Christoph's brother Paul (1573–1628) invited Catharina and him to dinner, and by January 6, Johann Christoph had proposed to her; she immediately accepted.[8]

The date of this proposal and acceptance are important, as it is the same date that accompanies the Boethius quotation in the penultimate Latin entry from 1620 in the *Pious Meditations*. The quotation takes on special significance in this context:

> Each thing seeks its own way back
> And coming back is glad;
> None is consigned to any ordered course
> Save that which links the end to the beginning.[9]

In the *Pious Meditations*, Johann Christoph was seeking his way back to some kind of normal and good life. Even as he sought various purgatives to restore balance to his body, likely with limited success, he engaged in a sustained act of emotional purgation in the *Pious Meditations* to restore emotional and spiritual health, seemingly with more success. His wonderfully creative meditations, informed by Scripture, prayer, and song, along with his participation in private confession and the Lord's Supper and also conversation with friends, all appear to have acted as salutary medicines for him. Johann Christoph's year-long lament was his remedy for his grief, an aid to help him become fit again for all that life would hold in the future, including a new marriage, which he no doubt assumed would eventually take place. He must have finished work on the *Pious Meditations*—save the final Latin entry from 1628—before his second wedding, which took place on February 21, 1620.[10]

Had Johann Christoph lived a couple of centuries earlier, he likely would have sought to recover his emotional and spiritual health in a different way. He would have been allowed and even expected to express his grief for Anna Maria publicly and demonstrably, beginning at her funeral. As a sign of his love for her and of his own honor, he would have wept and wailed loudly, perhaps even ripping at his beard, and others would have joined him. Embodied lament would have been integral to his healing. By way of contrast, there is no reference to such bodily displays of grief in public in the *Pious Meditations*, perhaps aside from some of the illnesses that Johann Christoph records, which may have been caused, in part, by his inner turmoil and depression. We do not know how Johann Christoph conducted himself at Anna Maria's funeral. In keeping with a trend that began in the later Middle Ages, especially among men of Johann Christoph's class in his day, grief was to be internalized as a means of protecting the social and political order from perceived threats to it by strong emotional displays.[11]

Still, as we have seen, despite the quotation from Boethius, Johann Christoph was no Stoic, certainly not in the majority of the entries in the *Pious Meditations*.[12] In fact, the *Pious Meditations* may be seen as an attempt to oppose the growing Stoicism of his day, for while the work was a largely private and interior affair, it rejects a central assumption of stoic grief management: that a human being can control his emotional life through recourse to rational remedies. With Job and David, Johann Christoph turns instead to lament before the Almighty, a very different form of self-management. He also weeps and wails, both on his own and privately with his children. Additionally, one may see this anti-Stoicism in some of the hymns that he reproduces that have a grief-stricken person complain of being ridiculed by others for lingering too long in lament.[13] Along with others, especially hymn writers, Johann Christoph was seeking, even if haltingly, to rewrite the emotional script of his day to include a greater role for lament and the human agency it assumes.[14] The kind of lament one encounters in his *Pious Meditations* is difficult to find in the devotional literature of his day.[15] Perhaps he would have welcomed the opportunity to lament in a more public and bodily way, quite apart from the cultural expectations of his day. But this is something we cannot know.

Johann Christoph's second wedding was a magnificent event with dignitaries in attendance from far and wide.[16] We know very little about his marriage with Catharina, other than that they had one surviving child, Hans Paul (1621–1645).[17] We also know that he referred to her as his CICO—Catharina Iohann Christoph Oelhafen, another mark of a new beginning.[18] Johann Christoph's *Diarium* ends in 1622, and I am aware of no further extant ego-documents from his quill that document the remaining years of his life.[19]

We do know that his professional life continued to prosper during his marriage to Catharina. In addition to his existing honors and duties, and all the travel that they entailed,[20] Emperor Ferdinand II (1578–1637, r. 1619–1637) appointed Johann Christoph as a legal advisor to his court (*Hofrath*). In 1623, Nürnberg's Smaller Council chose him to give a formal speech on its behalf at a ceremony in which he also presented imperial privileges to the Altdorf Academy, thus recognizing its status as a university. In the speech, his great learning was on full display, as he cited Latin, Greek, and even Hebrew sources, including the Bible and the Church Fathers, while also referencing more contemporary sources.[21] (The privileges he bestowed on the new university included a golden scepter and new seal.) In 1626, he was appointed prochancellor (*Prokanzler*) of the University of Altdorf,[22] and two years later, he became the elder (*Senior*) of his family line,[23] an honor he enjoyed for only three years. In April of 1631, while at an imperial diet in Regensburg, Johann Christoph was stricken with an unknown illness that claimed his life a month later in Nürnberg. Shortly before he passed away on May 12, a person at his side asked him if he was dying with sure faith in the merit of Jesus Christ. Johann Christoph replied, "Well of course, how else!" (*Ei freilich, wie anders!*)[24] His famous nephew, Tobias Oelhafen (1601–1666), delivered a Latin eulogy in Altdorf that celebrated Johann Christoph's many accomplishments; Saubert also provided an epicedium.[25]

Johann Christoph was buried in the famous St. Johannisfriedhof in Nürnberg,[26] where the likes of Albrecht Dürer, Willibald Pirckheimer, Lazarus Spengler, Hans Sachs, Veit Dietrich, and his grandfather Sixtus had also been laid to rest. The remains of Anna Maria and, later, Catharina are in the same tomb, a practice that was typical for the time. The epitaph that covers the tomb (see image 9) is an updated version of the one that he had prepared in 1599 and that appeared in revised form in his *Pious Meditations* (see image 6).[27] Created in 1625, after which the couple must have had no further children,[28] in comparison with the version in the *Pious Meditations*, the resurrected Christ figure is much larger and now occupies the central frame, with frightened Roman guards on either side (Matt 28:4). Meanwhile, the Grim Reaper figure has been diminished in size and seeming importance. Perhaps this difference can be seen as a testimony to Johann Christoph's growing faith in the Restorer's meritorious suffering and victory over death, a faith that had been tested and proved throughout his life's journey, especially during his year of lament, 1619.

Image 9: Johann Christoph's epitaph in the St. Johannisfriedhof in Nürnberg (copyrighted by Belschner, St. Johannisfriedhof, Nürnberg)

Notes to the Introduction

1 On the presence of lament-as-grief and lament-as-protest in the Bible, see Todd J. Billings, *Rejoicing in Lament: Wrestling with Incurable Cancer and Life in Christ* (Grand Rapids, MI: Brazos, 2015), 19; and Sally A. Brown and Patrick D. Miller, eds., *Lament: Reclaiming Practices in Pulpit, Pew and Public Square* (Louisville, KY: Westminster John Knox, 2005), xv–xvi.

2 See Oswald Bayer, "Toward a Theology of Lament," in *Caritas et Reformatio: Essays on Church and Society in Honor of Carter Lindberg*, edited by David M. Whitford (St. Louis, MO: Concordia, 2002), 211–20; and Ronald K. Rittgers, *The Reformation of Suffering: Pastoral Theology and Lay Piety in Late Medieval and Early Modern Germany* (Oxford: Oxford University Press, 2012), 257–63.

3 My own previous engagements with this work are the only ones in print: "Grief and Consolation in Early Modern Lutheran Devotion: The Case of Johannes Christoph Oelhafen's *Pious Meditations on the Most Sorrowful Bereavement* (1619)," *Church History: Studies in Christianity and Culture* 81, no. 3 (September 2012): 601–30; *Reformation of Suffering*, 249–56; and "A Widower's Lament out of the Reformation Past," *Lutheran Forum* 52, no. 4 (Winter 2018): 58–62. Portions of this introduction are reprinted with permission from "Grief and Consolation in Early Modern Lutheran Devotion" (© American Society of Church History, 2012).

4 For biographical information on Johann Christoph, see "Oelhafen von Schöllenbach, Johann Christoph" in DB (follow the links to the relevant articles in the ADB and the NDB). See also Georg Andreas Will, *Nürnbergisches Gelehrten-Lexicon*, vol. 3 (Neustadt an der Aisch: C. Schmidt, 1997–1998 [originally published in Altdorf, 1802–1808]), 60–63; *Deutsches biographisches Archiv: Eine Kumulation aus 254 der wichtigsten biographischen Nachschlagwerke für den deutschen Bereich bis zum Ausgang des neunzehnten Jahrhunderts*, vol. 1, microfiche ed. (Munich: K. G. Saur, 1982), 911: 218–24; Sigismundus Jacobus Apinus, *Vitae et Effigies Procancellariorum Academiae Altorfinae* (Nürnberg: Tauber,

1721), 10–19; *Oratio Panegyrica In piam memoriam Viri* [. . .] *Dn. Johannis Christophori Ölhafen* [. . .] (Altdorf, 1631; VD17 23:246104M; available online via Google Books); Sigmund Christoph von Oelhafen, ed. and trans., *Zwei Reden zum Gedächtnis an die Prokanzler der Universität Altdorf: Dr. Johann Christoph und Dr. Tobias Oelhafen von Schölnbach* (Nürnberg, 1891), GNM-HA, Familienarchiv von Oelhafen, Rep. II/80, Nr. 120; *Familienbuch, welches z. Zt. noch fortgesetzt wird*, GNM-HA, Familienarchiv von Oelhafen, Rep. II/80, Nr. 22, fols. 313–30; and Biedermann, CCCLVII.

5 See entry 51, stanza 1, in the *Pious Meditations*.

6 See Biedermann, CXLIX. No further information is available about Anna Maria aside from the brief family history provided later in this introduction and the references to her in her husband's *Diarium* and *Pious Meditations* noted in this volume. (On Johann Christoph's *Diarium*, see the following n. 15.) For their epithalamium, see VD17 125:031161Y.

7 *Familienbuch*, fol. 327. According to Apinus, Johann Christoph lived with Anne Maria "octodecim annos suavissime" (most sweetly for eighteen years). See *Vitae et Effigies*, 16.

8 Biedermann, CCCLVII.

9 Johann Christoph repeatedly expresses this concern in his *Pious Meditations*.

10 On the evangelical house church and its piety, see the following works by Patrice Veit: "Das Gesangbuch in der Praxis Pietatis der Lutheraner," in *Die lutherische Konfessionalisierung in Deutschland: Wissenschaftliches Symposium des Vereins für Reformationsgeschichte*, edited by Hans-Christoph Rublack (Gütersloh: Gerd Mohn, 1992), 435–59; "Private Frömmigkeit, Lektüre und Gesang im protestantischen Deutschland der frühen Neuzeit: Das Modell der Leichenpredigten," in *Frühe Neuzeit—Frühe Moderne? Forschungen zur Vielschichtigkeit von Übergangsprozessen*, Rudolf Vierhaus and coworkers of the Max Planck Institute for the History of Science (Göttingen: Vandenhoeck & Ruprecht, 1992), 271–95; "Die Hausandacht im deutschen Lutherthum. Anweisungen und Praktiken," in *Gebetsliteratur der frühen Neuzeit als Hausfrömmigkeit. Funktionen und Formen in Deutschland und den Niederlanden*, edited by Ferdinand van Ingen and Cornelia Niekus Moore (Wiesbaden: Harrassowitz, 2001), 193–206; and "Die evangelische 'Hauskirche':

Ein Zwischenraum?," in *Die Erschliessung des Raumes. Konstruktion, Imagination und Darstellung von Räumen und Grenzen im Barockzeitalter*, edited by Karin Friedrich (Wiesbaden: Harrassowitz, 2014), 195–206. On the respective roles of the *Hausvatter* and *Hausmutter* in the domestic church, see "Private Frömmigkeit," 276 (*Hausvatter*), 281–90 (*Hausmutter*); and "Die evangelische 'Hauskirche,'" 195 (*Hausvatter*), 200 (*Hausmutter*). On the *Hauskirche* as complement to the local church, see "Private Frömmigkeit," 271–72; and "Die evangelische 'Hauskirche,'" 206.

11 On the importance of hymnals and singing in the *Hauskirche*, see Veit, "Private Frömmigkeit," 276. Veit also notes that hymnals became increasingly designed for home use in the early modern period, in some cases being dedicated to house fathers. See "Das Gesangbuch als Quelle lutherischer Frömmigkeit," *Archiv für Reformationsgeschichte* 79 (1988): 206–23 (here 208); and "Das Gesangbuch in der Praxis Pietatis der Lutheraner," 440.

12 See *Oratio Panegyrica*, D r; and Oelhafen, *Zwei Reden*, 12.

13 See entry 32 in the *Pious Meditations*. Johann Christoph learned to play the lute in France during his seven-year tour of Europe (mentioned later in this introduction). See *Oratio Panegyrica*, B4 v; and Oelhafen, *Zwei Reden*, 8. Johann Christoph was by no means alone among Nürnberg's patricians in his love for music. Many of his standing, including his brother Maximilian (1569–1618), shared this affection. See Bartlett Russell Butler, "Liturgical Music in Sixteenth-Century Nürnberg: A Socio-Musical Study" (PhD diss., University of Illinois Urbana-Champaign, 1970), 509–24 (on Maximilian, see 513). On Maximilian Oelhafen, see Biedermann, CCCXLIV and CCCXLVI; and "Oelhafen von Schöllenbach, Maximilian" in DB.

14 See *Oratio Panegyrica*, D r; and Oelhafen, *Zwei Reden*, 12.

15 In Johann Christoph's *Diarium*, he records when he and members of his household would participate in confession and Communion. For examples, see the entries for June 8, 1605; November 2, 1617; January 10, 1619; March 24 and 25, 1619; and January 15 and 16, 1620. The diary begins from Johann Christoph's birth in 1574 and runs to 1622. However, it is not organized like a typical diary, going day by day and year by year. It is organized around each day of each of the twelve months of the year. That is, it begins with January 1

and lists everything of significance that happened on this day in each of the years under consideration in the diary (1574–1622), and then proceeds to January 2, and so on. On the Lutheran practice of private confession, see Ronald K. Rittgers, *The Reformation of the Keys: Confession, Conscience, and Authority in Sixteenth-Century Germany* (Cambridge, MA: Harvard University Press, 2004).

16 The *Pious Meditations* is full of such praise.

17 Mary Lindemann has argued that early modern people were not constantly ill but constantly in danger of falling ill and felt this vulnerability keenly. See *Medicine and Society in Early Modern Europe* (Cambridge: Cambridge University Press, 1999), 157.

18 For the names of the children, see Biedermann, CCCLVII–CCCLVIII.

19 *Diarium*, entries for October 25 and 26 and November 2, 10, 12, 13, and 14, 1617.

20 Lindemann, *Medicine and Society*, 10.

21 *Diarium*, entries for January 30 and February 1 and 10, 1619.

22 "Ach lieber hertz, wie wolte ich es so gerne sagen: Aber Gott waiß: Ich werde je lenger je schwächer." *Diarium*, entry for February 11, 1619.

23 "Also, sehe Ich Euch auch noch ein mahl, vor meinem Endt, uf diese welt. Eheu! Eheu!" *Diarium*, entry for February 12, 1619.

24 "Ach schatz, hilf mir noch Einmal, auß dieser qual!" *Diarium*, entry for February 13, 1619.

25 *Diarium*, entry for February 13, 1619. See also entry 32 in the *Pious Meditations*.

26 On the history of Nürnberg, see Gerhard Pfeiffer, ed., *Nürnberg—Geschichte einer europäischen Stadt* (Munich: C. H. Beck, 1971). For a brief overview of this history to the early sixteenth century, see Rittgers, *Reformation of the Keys*, 9–22.

27 On this school and its relationship to the Altdorf Academy, see Wolfgang Mährle, *Academica Norica. Wissenschaft und Bildung an der Nürnberger Hohen Schule in Altdorf (1575–1623)* (Stuttgart: Franz Steiner, 2000), 51–70.

28 On the Oelhafen family, see Peter Fleischmann, *Rat und Patriziat in Nürnberg. Die Herrschaft der Ratsgeschlechter vom 13. bis zum 18. Jahrhundert*, 3 vols. (Nürnberg: Verein für Geschichte der Stadt Nürnberg, 2008), here vol. 2: 1173–74; and NDB 19: 437–39. See also "Oelhafen von Schöllenbach, Patrizierfamilie" in the SN. For bibliographical information on the Harsdörffer and Oelhafen families, see Gunther Friedrich, *Bibliographie zum Patriziat der Reichsstadt Nürnberg* (Nürnberg: Selbstverlag des Vereins für Geschichte der Stadt Nürnberg, 1994), 106–9 and 62–67.

29 See Christoph von Imhoff, ed., *Berühmte Nürnberger aus neun Jahrhunderten* (Nürnberg: Albert Hofmann, 1984), 66.

30 Other members of the Oelhafen family settled in Leipzig and Breslau. See "Oelhafen von Schöllenbach, Patrizierfamilie" in the SN.

31 On Sixtus Oelhafen, see ADB 24: 292–96; Imhoff, *Berühmte Nürnberger*, 65–66; and Friedrich, *Bibliographie*, 107–8 (items 1000, 1003, 1006, 1007, 1008, and 1009).

32 On the history and structure of Nürnberg's civic government, see Fleischmann, *Rat und Patriziat in Nürnberg*, vol. 1; and Rittgers, *Reformation of the Keys*, 14–18.

33 See Imhoff, *Berühmte Nürnberger*, 66. The coat of arms was improved after Sixtus's first marriage. See image 4.

34 ADB 24: 295.

35 Sixtus married Anna Pfinzing in 1501 (d. 1506) and Barbara Rieter in 1508.

36 ADB 24: 295–96.

37 On the Reformation in Nürnberg, see Ronald K. Rittgers, "Nuremberg," in *Encyclopedia of Martin Luther and the Reformation*, edited by Mark Lamport (Lanham, MD: Rowman & Littlefield, 2017), 565–67; and Rittgers, "Nuremberg," in *Dictionary of Luther and the Lutheran Traditions*, edited by Timothy J. Wengert (Grand Rapids, MI: Baker Academic, 2017), 544–55. The following two paragraphs draw on these two articles.

38 For a critical edition of this work, see Lazarus Spengler, *Schutzrede und christliche Antwort* [. . .] *warum Dr. Martin Luthers Lehre* [. . .] *als christlich gehalten werden soll* (1519), in *Lazarus Spengler Schriften*, edited by Berndt Hamm and Wolfgang Huber, vol. 1: *Schriften der Jahre 1509–1525* (Gütersloh: Gütersloher, 1995), 75–102. For an older English treatment of Spengler, see Harold J. Grimm, *Lazarus Spengler: A Lay Leader of the Reformation* (Columbus: Ohio State University Press, 1978).

39 See Johannes Kamann, "Aus Hans Ölhafens Reisetagebuch (1541–1580)," *Mitteilungen des Vereins für Geschichte der Stadt Nürnberg* 5

(1884): 224–25. Hans Oelhafen's diary is in the GNM-HA: Rst. Nürnberg, Oelhafen/6, Nr. 18, Reise- und Tagebuch des Johann Oelhafen, 1541–1580.

40 The Oelhafens were granted the ability to serve as judges (*Gerichtsfähigkeit*) in Nürnberg in 1546. See Imhoff, *Berühmte Nürnberger*, 66; and "Oelhafen von Schöllenbach, Patrizierfamilie" in the SN. In 1512, Sixtus I purchased Ober- and Unterschöllenbach from the family Rech von Rechenberg. In 1538, he bequeathed the villages to Hans and two of his brothers. In 1557/58, Hans completed work on a residence there, and some time later, the family became known as the Oelhafens von Schöllenbach. See Fleischmann, *Rat und Patriziat in Nürnberg*, vol. 2, 1173; and Imhoff, *Berühmte Nürnberger*, 66. Johann Christoph must have spent at least some time living there, although he also resided in Nürnberg. See the following discussion.

41 On the marriage of Hans and Sybilla, see Hans Bösch, "Verlobung und Verehelichung in Nürnberg im 16. Jahrhundert," *Mitteilungen des Germanischen Museums*, 1893, 41–53.

42 Biedermann, CCCXLIV. On Susanna, see Biedermann, CLVI.

43 This summary of Johann Christoph's life is based on the sources listed in the previous n. 4 and also on what he reveals about his family life in his *Diarium* and the *Pious Meditations*. Where a specific fact or aspect of his life is based on a single source, I list the source along with any additional relevant ones. Johann Christoph may have begun his studies at the St. Lorenz School in Nürnberg. See *Familienbuch*, fol. 313. For plague as the cause of Johann Christoph's transfer to the Altdorf Academy, see *Familienbuch*, fol. 314. The plague of 1585 claimed some five thousand lives in Nürnberg. See Joel F. Harrington, *The Faithful Executioner: Life and Death, Honor and Shame in the Turbulent Sixteenth Century* (New York: Farrar, Straus and Giroux, 2013), 134.

On the history of the Altdorf Academy, which would evolve into the University of Altdorf (discussed later), see Mährle, *Academica Norica*, 43–107; Georg Andreas Will, *Geschichte und Beschreibung der Nürnbergischen Universität Altdorf* (Altdorf: in Commission der akademischen Monath-Kusslerischen Buchhandlung, 1795 [reprint, Aalen: Scientia Verlag, 1975]); Heinrich Kunstmann, *Die Nürnberger Universität Altdorf und Böhmen: Beitrage zur Erforschung der Ostbeziehungen deutscher Universitäten* (Cologne: Böhlau, 1963), 1–19; Hanns Christof Brennecke,

Dirk Niefanger, and Werner Wilhelm Schnabel, eds., *Akademie und Universität Altdorf. Studien zur Hochschulgeschichte Nürnbergs* (Cologne: Böhlau, 2011); and Hanspeter Marti and Karin Marti-Weissenbach, eds., *Nürnbergs Hochschule in Altdorf. Beiträge zur frühneuzeitlichen Wissenschafts- und Bildungsgeschichte* (Cologne: Böhlau, 2014).

44 See ADB 24: 296. See also Frederick John Stopp, *The Emblems of the Altdorf Academy: Medal and Medal Orations* (London: Modern Humanities Research Association, 1974), 132–33.

45 ADB 24: 296.

46 *Oratio Panegyrica*, C2 r–C3 r; Oelhafen, *Zwei Reden*, 9–10; Will, *Nürnbergisches Gelehrten-Lexicon*, vol. 3, 61. Johann Christoph may have given thought to his epitaph before this event. It was common for the devout in the upper classes to prepare for their death long before it occurred, especially by indicating in their personal Bibles and devotional literature the verses and hymns they wanted at their funerals. See Veit, "Die Hausandacht im deutschen Lutherthum," 205. Otto Steensen Brahe was related to Tycho Brahe: the famous astronomer was his uncle on his father's side of the family.

47 See entry 29.

48 On the duties of a *Ratskonsulent* in early modern Nürnberg, see Kunstmann, *Die Nürnberger Universität Altdorf und Böhmen*, 87; and the entry on "Ratskonsulenten" in the SN. On the history of jurists in Nürnberg, see Wolfgang Friedrich Ellinger, "Die Juristen der Reichsstadt Nürnberg vom 15.-17. Jahrhundert," in *Genealogica, Heraldica, Juridica. Reichsstadt Nürnberg, Altdorf und Hersbruck* (Nürnberg: Kommissionsverlag Verlag Die Egge, 1954), 130–222. In brief, the task of the *Ratskonsulent* was to prepare legal opinions (both written and oral) for the Smaller Council to consider on various matters, to engage in diplomatic missions now and again on behalf of the Smaller Council, and also to prepare legal opinions for other cities. The *Ratskonsulent* was not a member of the Smaller Council, something that was forbidden in Nürnberg, but his opinions typically exercised great influence over its policies. On the legal history of Nürnberg, see Wolfgang Leiser, "Nürnbergs Rechtsleben," in Pfeiffer, *Nürnberg—Geschichte einer europäischen Stadt*, 171–76. On the unprecedented nature of Johann Christoph's appointment as *Ratskonsulent* before finishing the doctoral degree, see *Oratio Panegyrica*, C4 r; and Oelhafen, *Zwei Reden*, 11.

49 Anna Maria's paternal grandfather, Wolff I Harsdörffer (1502–1572), was the brother of Johann Christoph's maternal grandfather, Christoph I Harsdörffer (1505–1578). See Biedermann, CXLIX, CLVI. On the Protestant effort to allow such a marriage, which was forbidden by the Catholic Church's traditional teaching on consanguinity, see Steven Ozment, *When Fathers Ruled: Family Life in Reformation Europe* (Cambridge, MA: Harvard University Press, 1983), 44–48. Anna Maria had five siblings, at least three of whom survived her. See Biedermann, CXLIX. Both of her parents predeceased her.

50 ADB 24: 298.

51 See ADB 24: 298; NDB 19: 437–39.

52 See NDB 19: 437–39. See also the entry for "Hofpfalzgraf" in *Deutsches Rechtswörterbuch* (Weimar: H. Böhlaus Nachfolger, 1914–), vol. 5, sp. 1308 (available online at http://drw-www.adw.uni-heidelberg.de/drw/). On Johann Christoph's authority to create poet laureates, see John Flood, *Poets Laureate in the Holy Roman Empire: A Bio-Bibliographical Handbook*, vol. 4 (Berlin: De Gruyter, 2006), 2406.

53 On the *Reichsschultheißhof* as Johann Christoph's place of residence, see NStadtA, GSI 175 Nr. 346.574, Stand 23.11.2020. The structure no longer exists. This residence was located at 24/26 Burgstraße. See "Burgstraße" in the SN. On the duties of the *Reichsschultheiß* in Nürnberg, see the relevant entry in the same source.

54 The entry on Johann Christoph in the Oelhafen *Familienbuch* mentions his many "hinderlassene Volumina und Diaria" (left-behind volumes and diaries), in which he made numerous annotations, some juridical, others theological and philosophical, and still others quotidian. See fol. 327. This entry does not mention the *Pious Meditations* by name, but it is possible that the writer was aware of its existence, for he or she refers to *diaria*—diaries. The *Pious Meditations* is a sort of diary. It is more likely, however, that this reference is to diaries of the more typical variety—that is, recordings of daily activities and reflections. We know Johann Christoph produced many such diaries, although, aside from the lone *Diarium* in the GNM-HA, they do not appear to be extant. For evidence of these many diaries, see *Oratio Panegyrica*, E r; and Oelhafen, *Zwei Reden*, 14. See n. 19 in the Notes to the Epilogue.

55 The relevant entries in the ADB and Will, *Nürnbergisches Gelehrten-Lexicon*, set the number of volumes at 1,040, while more recent work shows that Johann Christoph had amassed 1,900 works bound in 1,400 volumes or more. See Gunda Werner and Eleonore Schmidt-Herrling, *Die Bibliotheken der Universität Altdorf* (Leipzig: Otto Harrassowitz, 1937), 34–35. The most recent source sets the number of volumes at "1500 Bde Rechtsliteratur." See Eberhard Dünninger, ed., *Handbuch der historischen Buchbestände in Deutschland*, vol. 11 (Hildesheim: Olms-Weidmann, 1997), 263, section 1.19. It is clear, however, that Johann Christoph's library contained more than works of jurisprudence.

56 Today this university is the Friedrich-Alexander-University Erlangen-Nürnberg. The University of Altdorf closed in 1809.

57 See UEN, Handschriftenabteilung, ms. 2436, fols. 60 r–v, 127 r–131 v. I am grateful to Frau Sigrid Kohlmann for providing me with a copy of the inventory of Johann Christoph's nonjuridical books housed in this library.

58 On the ancient and medieval consolation tradition in the West, see Rittgers, *Reformation of Suffering*, 37–62. Johann Christoph cites Boethius at one point in the *Pious Meditations* (see entry 76b), but there are no other direct references to the Christian consolation tradition.

59 On this practice, see Veit, "Private Frömmigkeit," 295.

60 The Oelhafen coat of arms may still be seen on the wall of one of the rooms in Melanchthon's home in Wittenberg. Hans Oelhafen likely had it painted there.

61 See Kunstmann, *Die Nürnberger Universität Altdorf und Böhmen*, 134. On the place of Nürnberg in the Thirty Years' War, see Rudolf Endres, "Vom Religionsfrieden zur protestantischen Union"; Endres, "Politische Haltung bis zum Entritt Gustav Adolfs in den Dreißigjährigen Krieg"; and Endres, "Endzeit des Dreißigjährigen Krieges," all in Pfeiffer, *Nürnberg—Geschichte einer europäischen Stadt*, 265–79.

62 See entry 35 in the *Pious Meditations*.

63 See Endres, "Endzeit des Dreißigjährigen Krieges," 275–76. On Nürnberg and the Thirty Years' War, see also Ernst Mummenhoff, *Altnürnberg in Krieg und Kriegsnot*, vol. 2, *Aus den schlimmsten Tagen des dreißigjährigen Kriegs* (Nürnberg: J. L. Schrag, 1917).

64 See Christopher Close, *Stated Formation and Shared Sovereignty: The Holy Roman Empire and the Dutch Republic, 1488–1696* (Cambridge: Cambridge University Press, 2021), ch. 7, "Religious Alliance and the Thirty Years War (1610–1632)," 245–86. I am grateful to the author for sharing this chapter with me in draft form. It deals extensively with Johann Christoph's involvement in the Protestant Union. On Nürnberg's role in the union, see Endres, "Politische Haltung," 269–71.

65 See entries 34–40, 55, 66, and 72–76 in the *Pious Meditations*. The quotation is from entry 35. As contemporary funeral sermons make clear, for the devout like Johann Christoph, travel was a special time for devotional reading and singing. In the case of Johann Christoph, it was also a time for devotional writing. See Veit, "Private Frömmigkeit," 281.

66 See entry 35 in the *Pious Meditations*.

67 See entry 37 in the *Pious Meditations*.

68 On the presence of Calvinism in the officially Lutheran Nürnberg, along with a resurgent Catholicism and various forms of Spiritualism, see Klaus Leder, "Die religiöse Entwicklung Nürnbergs nach dem Augsburger Religionsfrieden," in Pfeiffer, *Nürnberg—Geschichte einer europäischen Stadt*, 279–83. See also Richard van Dülmen, "Schwärmer und Separatisten in Nürnberg (1618–1648). Ein Beitrag zum Problem des 'Weigelianismus,'" *Archiv für Kulturgeschichte* 55 (1973): 107–37; and Wolfgang Mährle, "Eine Hochburg des Kryptocalvinismus und des Kryptosozinianismus? Heterodoxie an der Nürnberger Hochschule in Altdorf um 1600," *Mitteilungen des Vereins für Geschichte der Stadt Nürnberg* 97 (2010): 195–234.

69 Mährle, *Academica Norica*, 483; Mährle, "Eine Hochburg des Kryptocalvinismus."

70 *Familienbuch*, fol. 313.

71 On Saubert, see Richard van Dülmen, *Orthodoxie und Kirchenreform: Der Nürnberger Prediger Johannes Saubert (1592–1646)* (Munich: Beck, 1970). See also "Saubert, Johannes" in DB.

72 On Schopper, see "Schopper, Jakob" in DB; and Mährle, *Academica Norica*, 491–99.

73 On Soner, see "Soner, Ernst" in DB; and Mährle, *Academica Norica*, 405–7.

74 There is an expansive literature on Socinianism at the Altdorf Academy. The following are among the most important treatments: Mährle, *Academica Norica*, 501–14; Mährle, "Eine Hochburg des Kryptocalvinismus"; Martin Schmeisser and Klaus Birnstill, "Gelehrtenkultur und antitrinitarische Häresie an der Nürnberger Akademie zu Altdorf," *Daphnis* 39 (2010): 221–85; Hanns Christoph Brennecke, "Heterodoxie und sozinianische Häresie in Altdorf," in Brennecke, Niefanger, and Schnabel, *Akademie und Universität Altdorf*, 151–66; Cornelia Rémi, "Möglichkeiten heterodoxe Verständigung im Umfeld der Atldorfer Akademie," in Brennecke, Niefanger, and Schnabel, *Akademie und Universität Altdorf*, 167–91; and Günter Frank, "Ernst Soners Kritik am Trinitätsdogma. Strategien zur Legitimierung trinitätstheologischer Heterodoxie in Soners Traktat 'An Doctrina Trinitatis sit Mysterium?,'" in *Religiöser Nonkonformismus und frühneuzeitliche Gelehrtenkultur*, edited by Friedrich Vollhardt (Berlin: De Gruyter, 2014), 161–78. On Saubert's opposition to Socinianism during his days as a student in Altdorf, see Mährle, *Academica Norica*, 511.

75 On the close friendship between Gerhard and Saubert, see van Dülmen, *Orthodoxie und Kirchenreform*, 646. See also Wolfgang Sommer, "Johann Sauberts Eintreten für Johann Arndt im Dienst einer Erneuerung der Frömmigkeit," in *Politik, Theologie und Frömmigkeit im Luthertum der Frühen Neuzeit. Ausgewählte Aufsätze von Wolfgang Sommer* (Göttingen: Vandenhoeck & Ruprecht, 1999), 243. For a treatment of Gerhard and mysticism in the late Reformation, see Johann Anselm Steiger, *Johann Gerhard (1582–1637): Studien zu Theologie und Frömmigkeit des Kirchenvaters der lutherischen Orthodoxie* (Stuttgart-Bad Cannstatt: Frommann-Holzboog, 1997), 54–89.

76 On Arndt, see Thomas Illg, "Johann Arndt," in *Protestants and Mysticism in Reformation Europe*, edited by Ronald K. Rittgers and Vincent Evener (Leiden: Brill, 2019), 309–27.

77 For a facsimile edition of Arndt's famous work, see Johann Anselm Steiger, ed., *Johann Arndt: Vier Bücher von wahrem Christenthumb, Die erste Gesamtausgabe (1610)*, 3 vols. (Hildesheim: Georg Olms, 2007).

78 See van Dülmen, *Orthodoxie und Kirchenreform*, 718; and Sommer, "Johann Sauberts Eintreten für Johann Arndt."

79 Rémi, "Möglichkeiten heterodoxe Verständigung," 177–78.

80 A translation of Saubert's note appears later.

81 Saubert wrote a work of devotion in 1619 that might have influenced Johann Christoph, but it does not appear to be extant: *Schola crucis oder christliche kreutzschule*. On Saubert's later importance in the production of devotional literature (and images) for lay ministry to the sick and dying, see Jill Bepler, "Practicing Piety: Representations of Women's Dying in German Funeral Sermons of the Early Modern Period," in *Women and Death 3: Women's Representations of Death in German Culture Since 1500*, edited by Clare Bielby and Anna Richards (Rochester, NY: Camden House, 2010), 21.

82 On this literature, see Rittgers, *Reformation of Suffering*, 200–225.

83 See entry 69. Johann Christoph may have owned the *Manuale de praeparatione ad mortem*, but a copy held by the UEN, which houses his collection, does not appear to have belonged to him. Johann Christoph may also quote Moller's *Mysterium Magnum*. See entry 62.

84 See the entry for February 9, 1619, in the *Diarium*. The original-language title of the work is *Praxis Evangeliorum*. On Moller, see Eric Lund, "Martin Moller and Philipp Kegel," in Rittgers and Evener, *Protestants and Mysticism in Reformation Europe*, 224–42; Elke Axmacher, *Praxis Evangeliorum: Theologie und Frömmigkeit bei Martin Moller (1547–1606)* (Göttingen: Vandenhoeck & Ruprecht, 1989); and Ronald K. Rittgers, "Mystical Union and Spiritual Desire in Late Reformation Devotion: The Case of Martin Moller's *The Great Mystery* (1595)," *Reformation and Renaissance Review: Journal of the Society for Reformation Studies* 17, no. 3 (2015): 214–29.

85 See Rittgers, *Reformation of Suffering*, 6. There I use the term *Reformation Frömmigkeitstheologie*.

86 See Robert J. Bast, *The Reformation of Faith in the Context of Late Medieval Theology and Piety: Essays by Berndt Hamm* (Leiden: Brill, 2004), xv. For Hamm's own (translated) description of *Frömmigkeitstheologie*, see 18–24. See also Berndt Hamm, "Was ist Frömmigkeitstheologie? Überlegungen zum 14. bis 16. Jahrhundert," in *Praxis Pietatis: Beiträge zu Theologie und Frömmigkeit in der frühen Neuzeit. Wolfgang Sommer zum 60. Geburtstag*, edited by Hans-Jörg Nieden and Marcel Nieden (Stuttgart: Kohlhammer, 1999), 9–46.

87 Bast, *Essays by Berndt Hamm*, 18–19.

88 Johann Christoph owned at least one hymnal: Wolfgang Ammon's *Neuw Gesangbuch Teutsch und Lateinisch* (Frankfurt a. M., 1591). See UEN, H00/THL-XVII 792. Some of the hymns he reproduces appear in this hymnal. (See notes to the relevant entries in the *Pious Meditations*.)

89 Strauch produced portraits of many Nürnberg patricians and also completed paintings of important buildings and locations within the imperial city itself. On Strauch, see "Strauch, Lorenz" in DB; Hannshubert Mahn, *Lorenz und Georg Strauch. Beiträge zur Kunstgeschichte Nürnbergs im 16. und 17. Jahrhundert* (Reutlingen: Gryphius, 1927); and Wilhelm Schwemmer, "Lorenz Strauch," in *Fränkische Lebensbilder*, edited by Gerhard Pfeiffer, vol. 4 (Neustadt an der Aisch: Verlagsdruckerei Schmidt, 1971), 186–95. Strauch produced at least one other portrait of Johann Christoph in 1625. It is housed in the National Museum in Warsaw. In 1630, Lucas Kilian (1579–1637) would prepare a copper engraving of Johann Christoph's bust. Years later, Wolfgang Philipp Kilian (1654–1732) would do the same. See "Oelhafen von Schöllenbach, Johann Christoph" in DB (see the links under "Porträt [nachweise]").

90 See the epilogue for further discussion of this proposed date.

91 Veit refers to the "Verhäuslichung" of religious life in "Private Frömmigkeit," 271–72; "Die Hausandacht im deutschen Lutherthum," 195; and "Die evangelische 'Hauskirche,'" 195. He writes about "eine Sakraliesierung des Alltags" in "Die Hausandacht im deutschen Lutherthum," 204.

92 On this literature, see Anna Linton, *Poetry and Parental Bereavement in Early Modern Lutheran Germany* (Oxford: Oxford University Press, 2008); Anna Carrdus, *Classical Rhetoric and the German Poet 1620 to the Present: A Study of Opitz, Bürger and Eichendorff* (Oxford: European Humanities Research Centre, 1996); Carrdus, "'*Thränen=Tüchlein für Christliche Eltern*': Consolation Books for Bereaved Parents in Sixteenth- und Seventeenth-Century Germany," *German Life and Letters* 49, no. 1 (January 1996): 1–17; Carrdus, "Consolatory Dialogue in Devotional Writings by Men and Women of Early Modern Protestant Germany," *Modern Language Review* 93 (1998): 411–27; and Rittgers, *Reformation of Suffering*.

93 On the consolation literature dealing with grief, see Carrdus, "Consolatory Dialogue," 414.

94 See Carrdus, 414.

95 See Carrdus, 414; and Linton, *Poetry and Parental Bereavement*, 98.

96 For a discussion of these and other rhetorical figures and their use in early modern Lutheran consolation literature, see Carrdus, "Consolatory Dialogue," 415.

97 See entry 32. For parallels in other sources, see Carrdus, "*Thränen=Tüchlein für Christliche Eltern*," 12–14; Carrdus, "Consolatory Dialogue," 420–21; and Jill Bepler, "Practicing Piety," 23.

98 For other examples, see Carrdus, "Consolatory Dialogue," 417 and 419; and Linton, *Poetry and Parental Bereavement*, 79–85.

99 See Carrdus, "*Thränen=Tüchlein für Christliche Eltern*," 11.

100 Carrdus, 15.

101 Carrdus, "Consolatory Dialogue," 414.

102 See entries 3, 31, and especially 73 (stanza 5).

103 Rittgers, *Reformation of Suffering*, 211–12.

104 Luther's candor was influenced in part by his reading of German mystics such as Johann Tauler and the anonymous *Theologia Deutsch*. See Rittgers, 98. Johann Anselm Steiger has linked such candor in the Lutheran consolation literature to Luther's unique Christology and the way it allegedly allowed for divine suffering. See Johann Anselm Steiger, "Zorn Gottes, Leiden Christi und die Affekte der Passionbetrachtung bei Luther und im Luthertum des 17. Jahrhunderts," in *Passion, Affekt und Leidenschaft in der Frühenneuzeit*, edited by Johann Anselm Steiger (Wiesbaden: Harrassowitz, 2005), vol. 1, 179–201.

105 Georg W. McClure, *Sorrow and Consolation in Italian Humanism* (Princeton, NJ: Princeton University Press, 1991), 46.

106 Conrad H. Rawski, trans. and comm., *Petrarch's Remedies for Fortune Fair and Foul: A Modern English Translation of De remediis utriusque Fortunae*, vol. 3 (Bloomington: Indiana University Press, 1991), 63–64.

107 Johann Christoph did not own Lipsius's *On Constancy*. For the place of this work in the Lutheran consolation tradition, see Carrdus, *Classical Rhetoric*, 47; and Linton, *Poetry and Parental Bereavement*, 187. For a discussion of the work's general influence in the late sixteenth and early seventeenth centuries, see John Sellars, ed. and intro., *Justus Lipsius, On Constancy: De Constantia*, trans. Sir John Stradling (1595) (Exeter: Bristol Phoenix, 2006), 1–19.

108 See Rittgers, *Reformation of Suffering*, 62, 153, 244–56; and Rittgers, "Protestants and Plague: The Case of the 1562/3 *Pest* in Nürnberg," in *Piety and Plague: From Byzantium to the Baroque*, edited by Franco Mormando and Thomas Worcester (Kirksville, MO: Truman State University Press, 2007), 132–55 (esp. 143, 144, 146, and 150).

109 See Charles Taylor, *Sources of the Self: The Making of the Modern Identity* (Cambridge, MA: Harvard University Press, 1989), 115–19, 155.

110 In addition to *Sui Ignorantia* (On his own ignorance), Johann Christoph also owned a collection of Petrarch's works (*Opuscula*), which may have included *Remedies*.

111 See entries 25 and 33.

112 See the discussion of the *Pious Meditations* as an anti-Stoic remedy for grief in the epilogue. On the importance of anti-Stoicism in the Renaissance and Reformation, including in the works of Luther, see Richard Strier, "Against the Rule of Reason: Praise of Passion from Petrarch to Luther to Shakespeare to Herbert," in *Reading the Early Modern Passions: Essays in the Cultural History of Emotion*, edited by Gail Kern Paster, Katherine Rowe, and Mary Floyd-Wilson (Philadelphia: University of Pennsylvania Press, 2004), 23–42.

113 Georg Walther, *Trostbüchlein aus der heiligen Schrift und D. Martini Lutheri Bücher*, fol. Q6 v. Cited in Linton, *Poetry and Parental Bereavement*, 29 (Linton cites from the 1573 edition). For the Nürnberg editions, see VD16 W 982, VD16 W 983, VD16 W 981, and VD16 ZV 24136. (The 1560 and 1600 editions provide access to the full text online.)

114 See Michael Parsons, *Luther and Calvin on Grief and Lament* (Lewiston, NY: Edwin Mellon, 2013).

115 See Johann Anselm Steiger, "Die Gesichts- und Theologie-Vergessenheit der heutigen Seelsorgelehre: Anlaß für einen Rückblick in den Schatz reformatorischer und orthodoxer Seelsorgeliteratur," *Kerygma und Dogma* 39 no. 1 (January/March 1993): 64–87, here 75–76.

116 For the Nürnberg editions of Huberinus's work, *Vom Christlichen Ritter*, see VD16 H 5457 and H 5461 (both provide access to the full text online). For an edition that includes the original German with English translations of Spangenberg's works, *Trostbüchlein für die Kranken* and *Vom Christlichen Ritter*, see Robert Kolb, *A Booklet of Comfort for the Sick, & On the Christian Knight by Johann Spangenberg (1548)*

(Milwaukee, WI: Marquette University Press, 2007). For the Nürnberg editions of Spangenberg's work, see (1565) VD16 S 7882 (see also VD16 S 8074 and VD16 S 8092); (1577) VD16 S 7885 (see also VD16 S 8077); (1580) VD16 S 8078 (see also VD16 S 8095); and (1598) VD16 ZV 14614.

117 For the Nürnberg editions of Spangenberg's work, see (1565) VD16 S 7882 (see also VD16 S 8074 and VD16 S 8092); (1577) VD16 S 7885 (see also VD16 S 8077); and (1598) VD16 ZV 14614.

118 Kolb, *A Booklet of Comfort for the Sick*, 60 (German), 61 (English).

119 See entries 11, 30, and 33.

120 On Lutheran funeral sermons, see the online Forschungstelle für Personalschriften at http://www.personalschriften.de; Rudolf Lenz (vols. 1–4) and Eva-Maria Dickhaut (vol. 5), eds., *Leichenpredigten als Quelle historischer Wissenschaften*, 5 vols. (Cologne: Böhlau, 1975, 1979, 1984 [vols. 1–3]; Stuttgart: Franz Steiner, 2004, 2015 [vols. 4–5]); Irene Dingel, "'True Faith, Christian Living, and a Blessed Death.' Sixteenth Century Funeral Sermons as Evangelical Proclamation," *Lutheran Quarterly* 27 (2013): 399–420; Cornelia Niekus Moore, *Patterned Lives: The Lutheran Funeral Biography in Early Modern Germany* (Wiesbaden: Harrassowitz, 2006); and Bepler, "Practicing Piety." The scholarship of Patrice Veit noted earlier is similarly based largely on the investigation of funeral sermons.

121 Johann Will, *Eine Christliche Leichpredigt / Vber den Abschied ond [sic] Begra[e]gnuß* [. . .] *Carl Tetzels* (Nürnberg: Georg Leopold Furhmann, 1611), HAB A: 190.22 Theol (3), fols. Aii v–Aiii r. (This sermon does not appear in the VD16.) Will would later serve at Nürnberg's St. Sebald Church.

122 Johann Anselm Steiger, *Medizinische Theologie. Christus Medicus und Theologia Medicinalis bei Martin Luther und im Luthertum der Barockzeit* (Leiden: Brill, 2005), 106.

123 See Claudia Resch, *Trost im Angesicht des Todes. Frühe reformatorische Anleitungen zur Seelsorge an Kranken und Sterbenden* (Tübingen: A. Francke, 2006), 114. The Latin title of Erasmus's famous work is *Enchiridion militis Christiani*.

124 On the importance of Lutheran laypeople becoming their own confessors, see Rittgers, *Reformation of the Keys*, 205–6.

125 Veit notes that Lutheran hymnals placed an increasing emphasis on consolation in the face of various afflictions. See "Das Gesangbuch als Quelle lutherischer Frömmigkeit," 208–9, 223; and "Das Gesangbuch in der Praxis Pietatis der Lutheraner," 440–41.

126 Susan Karant-Nunn, *The Reformation of Feeling: Shaping the Religious Emotions in Early Modern Germany* (Oxford: Oxford University Press, 2010), 96, 97, 105, 178, 201, 226, 251–52.

127 See later discussion of self-narratives.

128 See later discussion of Johann Christoph's intended audience.

129 On this goal, see Thomas Kaufmann, *Geschichte der Reformation* (Frankfurt am Main: Verlag der Weltreligionen, 2009), 630. On early modern confessionalization, see Thomas A. Brady Jr., "Confessionalization: The Career of a Concept," in *Confessionalization in Europe, 1555–1700: Essays in Honor and Memory of Bodo Nischan*, edited by John M. Headley, Hans J. Hillerbrand, and Anthony J. Papalas (Aldershot, UK: Ashgate, 2004), 1–20; and Ute Lotz-Heumann, "Confessionalization," in *Reformation and Early Modern Europe: A Guide to Research*, edited by David M. Whitford (Kirksville, MO: Truman State University Press, 2008), 136–57.

130 See, for example, Hans Medick and David Sabean, eds., *Emotionen und materielle Interessen. Sozialanthropologische und historische Beiträge zur Familienforschung* (Göttingen: Vandenhoeck & Ruprecht, 1984; English version: *Interest and Emotion: Essays on the Study of Family and Kinship* [Cambridge: Cambridge University Press, 1984]); Paster et al., *Reading the Early Modern Passions*; Steiger, *Passion*, 2 vols.; Karant-Nunn, *Reformation of Feeling*; Freya Sierhuis and Brian Cummings, eds., *Passions and Subjectivity in Early Modern Culture* (Farnham, UK: Ashgate, 2013); Barbara Rosenwein, "Worrying about Emotions in History," *American Historical Review* 107, no. 3 (June 2002): 821–45; and Rosenwein, *Generations of Feelings: A History of Emotions, 600–1700* (Cambridge: Cambridge University Press, 2015).

131 See Carol Lansing, *Passion and Order: Restraint of Grief in the Medieval Italian Communes* (Ithaca, NY: Cornell University Press, 2008); and Lynne Tatlock, ed., *Enduring Loss in Early Modern Germany: Cross Disciplinary Perspectives* (Leiden: Brill, 2010).

132 On "emotional communities," see Rosenwein, "Worrying about Emotions in History," 842–45; and Rosenwein, *Generations of Feeling*, 3–10. Rosenwein refers to "systems of feeling" in "Worrying about Emotions in History," 842.

133 See entry 50 (stanza 2). See also entry 45 (stanza 3).

134 See Resch, *Trost im Angesicht des Todes*; Austra Reinis, *Reforming the Art of Dying: The ars moriendi in the German Reformation (1519–1528)* (Aldershot, UK: Ashgate, 2007); and Elizabeth C. Tingle and Jonathan Willis, *Dying, Death, Burial and Commemoration in Reformation Europe* (Farnham, UK: Ashgate, 2015).

135 The classic work on the great divide between elites and commoners with respect to religious belief and practice in this period remains Gerald Strauss's *Luther's House of Learning: Indoctrination of the Young in the German Reformation* (Baltimore: Johns Hopkins University Press, 1978). For a study that is sympathetic to Strauss's argument and applies it to the largely rural area surrounding Nürnberg, see C. Scott Dixon, *The Reformation and Rural Society: The Parishes of Brandenburg-Ansbach-Kulmbach, 1528–1603* (Cambridge: Cambridge University Press, 1996). For critiques of Strauss's thesis, see Scott H. Hendrix, "Luther's Impact on the Sixteenth Century," *Sixteenth Century Journal* 16 (1985): 3–14; and James M. Kittelson, "Successes and Failures in the German Reformation," *Archiv für Reformationsgeschichte* 73 (1982): 153–75.

136 See the following works by Steven Ozment: *When Fathers Ruled*; *Magdalena and Balthasar: An Intimate Portrait of Life in 16th-Century Europe Revealed in the Letters of a Nuremberg Husband and Wife* (New Haven, CT: Yale University Press, 1989); *Three Behaim Boys: Growing Up in Early Modern Germany* (New Haven, CT: Yale University Press, 1990); *Flesh and Spirit: Private life in Early Modern Germany* (New York: Viking, 1999); and *Ancestors: The Loving Family in Old Europe* (Cambridge, MA: Harvard University Press, 2001).

137 There is very little scholarship on widowers in the early modern period. This may be because many widowers remarried, thus making widowerhood a temporary and transitional station in life. By way of contrast, widowhood could be a more permanent and rather vulnerable station. There was also a long and venerable tradition of supporting and honoring widows in Christian piety. Additionally, the late medieval clergy wrote works of consolation for widows, a practice that continued into the early modern period. See Britta-Juliane Kruse, *Witwen. Kulturgeschichte eines Standes in Spätmittelalter und Frühen Neuzeit* (Berlin: Walter de Gruyter, 2007). Relevant searches of the VD16 and VD17 reveal comparatively few works of consolation written for widowers. On early modern widowhood, see also Jill

Bepler, "Enduring Loss and Memorializing Women: The Cultural Role of Dynastic Widows in Early Modern Germany," in Tatlock, *Enduring Loss in Early Modern Germany*, 131–60.

138 See Ronald K. Rittgers, "The Age of Reform as an Age of Consolation," American Society of Church History Presidential Address, *Church History: Studies in Christianity and Culture* 86, no. 3 (September 2017): 607–42.

139 See Harrington, *Faithful Executioner*, 26–27.

140 This drive certainly existed in late medieval and early modern Nürnberg, something made clear by an older study of the city's sumptuary laws. These laws, which were created by the governing patricians, became more numerous, detailed, and socially stratified from the fourteenth to the seventeenth centuries. See Kent Roberts Greenfield, *Sumptuary Law in Nürnberg: A Study in Paternal Government* (Baltimore: Johns Hopkins University Press, 1918).

141 I develop this argument further in "The Age of Reform as an Age of Consolation."

142 For a recent helpful overview of self-narratives (also called ego-documents) research, see the introduction to Claudia Ulbrich, Kaspar von Greyerz, and Lorenz Heiligensetzer, eds., *Mapping the "I": Research on Self-Narratives in Germany and Switzerland* (Leiden: Brill, 2015), 1–12. For studies of self-narratives from early modern Nürnberg, see the following: Ozment, *Magdalena and Balthasar*; Ozment, *Three Behaim Boys*; Ozment, *Flesh and Spirit*; Matthias Beer, *Eltern und Kinder des späten Mittelalters in ihren Briefen: Familienleben in der Stadt des Spätmittelalters und der frühen Neuzeit mit besonderer Berücksichtigung Nürnbergs (1400–1550)* (Nürnberg: Stadtarchiv Nürnberg, 1990); Albrecht Keller, ed. and intro., *A Hangman's Diary; Being the Journal of Master Franz Schmidt, Public Executioner of Nuremberg, 1573–1617*, trans. C. V. Calvert and A. W. Gruner (Montclair, NJ: Patterson Smith, 1973); and Harrington, *Faithful Executioner*.

143 See Gabriele Jancke and Claudia Ulbrich, "From the Individual to the Person: Challenging Autobiography Theory," in Ulbrich, von Greyerz, and Heiligensetzer, *Mapping the "I,"* 20, 33; Medick and Sabean, *Emotionen und materielle Interessen*, especially p. 17 (*Interest and Emotion*, 3); Bengina von Krusenstjern, "Die Tränen des Jungen über ein vertrunkenes Pferd: Ausdrucksformen von Emotionalität

in Selbstzeugnissen des späten 16. und 17. Jahrhunderts," in *Von der dargestellten Person zum erinnerten Ich. Europäische Selbstzeugnisse als historische Quellen (1500–1800)*, edited by Kaspar von Greyerz, Hans Medick, and Patrice Veit (Cologne: Böhlau, 2001), 157; and Linton, *Poetry and Parental Bereavement*, 225–26. For more confident expressions of the access historians have to the inner lives of human beings in the past via self-narratives, see Ozment, *Three Behaim Boys*, ix–xiv; Beer, *Eltern und Kinder*, 32; and, especially, James S. Amelang, "Saving the Self from Autobiography," in *Selbstzeugnisse in der Frühen Neuzeit: Individualisierungsweisen in interdisziplinärer Perspektive*, edited by Kaspar von Greyerz (Munich: R. Oldenbourg, 2007), 129–40.

144 See Jacob Burckhardt, *Die Kultur der Renaissance in Italien* (1860; *The Civilization of the Renaissance in Italy*) and *Die Geschichte der Renaissance in Italien* (1867; *The History of the Renaissance in Italy*). Both works were translated into English and are available in numerous editions.

145 On the distinction between having a self versus simply having a sense of having a self, see Galen Strawson, "The Sense of Self," in *From Soul to Self*, edited by M. James Crabbe (London: Routledge, 1999), especially 127 and 131. See also Lynn Hunt, "The Self and Its History," *American Historical Review* 119, no. 5 (December 2014): 1576–86.

146 There is an expansive scholarly literature on the origins of the self and the historical quest for the same. See the summary of this literature in Rittgers, "Age of Reform as an Age of Consolation," 633–39. Most of the literature on self-narratives also deals directly with notions of the self in autobiographical sources.

147 Here the classic work remains Hebert Butterfield, *The Whig Interpretation of History* (London: George Bell & Sons, 1931).

148 *Chastened realism* is American historian Mark Noll's term for an epistemology that is based on a consideration of older scientific (i.e., realist) and newer postmodern (i.e., nominalist) approaches to historical knowledge in light of the Christian doctrines of creation, the fall, and incarnation. See Mark Noll's four-part series on the "History Wars" in *Books and Culture: A Christian Review* 5, no. 3 (May/June 1999), no. 4 (July/August 1999), no. 5 (September/October 1999), and no. 6 (November/December 1999). Noll discusses chastened realism in no. 6. See also two book chapters by Noll: "Traditional

Christianity and the Possibility of Historical Knowledge," in *Religious Advocacy and American History*, edited by Bruce Kucklick and D. G. Hart (Grand Rapids, MI: Eerdmans, 1997), 28–53; and "The Potential of Missiology for the Crises of History," in *History and the Christian Historian*, edited by Ronald A. Wells (Grand Rapids, MI: Eerdmans, 1998), 106–23.

149 Taylor, *Sources of the Self*, 176. For criticism of Taylor's work, see Rittgers, "Age of Reform as an Age of Consolation," 635n153, 635n155.

150 Here I borrow the concepts of a "porous self" and a "buffered self" from Charles Taylor. See *A Secular Age* (Cambridge, MA: Belknap Press of Harvard University Press, 2007), 37–38.

151 Eva Kormann has emphasized that early modern male and female autobiographers as a group had a relational sense of self. They understood themselves in relation to God, the world, and other groups of human beings. Their self-understanding or self-concept was "heterolog," or relationally oriented. See *Ich, Welt, Gott. Autobiographik im 17. Jahrhundert* (Cologne: Böhlau, 2004), quotation on p. 6. See also Gabriele Jancke, "Autobiographical Texts: Acting within a Network. Observations on Genre and Power Relations in the German-Speaking Regions from 1400–120," in Ulbrich, von Greyerz, and Heiligensetzer, *Mapping the "I,"* 119, 160, 164–65. Jancke argues that scholars must interpret the authorial "I" in autobiographical texts as "anchored in a network of social relations" (119).

152 In different ways, Zizioulas, Grenz, and Kelsey have each sought to ground understandings of human personhood in Trinitarian theology—a salutary project, in my view. See John. D. Zizioulas, *Being as Communion: Studies in Personhood and the Church* (Crestwood, NY: St. Vladimir's Seminary, 1985); Stanley J. Grenz, *The Social God and the Relational Self: A Trinitarian Theology of the Imago Dei* (Louisville, KY: Westminster John Knox, 2001); Grenz, "The Social God and the Relational Self: Toward a Theology of the *Imago Dei* in the Postmodern Context," in *Personal Identity in Theological Perspective*, edited by Richard Lints, Michael S. Horton, and Mark Talbot (Grand Rapids, MI: Eerdmans, 2006), 70–92; and David H. Kelsey, *Eccentric Existence: A Theological Anthropology* (Louisville, KY: Westminster John Knox, 2009).

153 I develop this argument further in "The Age of Reform as an Age of Consolation."

154 On the presence of multiple understandings of the self in the early modern period, see David Sabean and Malina Stefanovska, eds., *Space and Self in Early Modern European Cultures* (Toronto: University of Toronto Press, 2012), 3–4; and Thomas Robisheaux, "Penance, Confession, and the Self in Early Modern Lutheranism," in *Ideas and Cultural Margins in Early Modern Germany: Essays in Honor of H.C. Erik Midelfort*, edited by Majorie Elizabeth Plummer and Robin Barnes (Farnham, UK: Ashgate, 2009), 117–30.

155 See entry 15 (stanza 1).

156 See entry 49 (stanza 3).

157 See entry 51 (stanza 1).

158 See entry 60 (stanza 4). It should be noted that Johann Christoph also questions the utility of his laments. See entry 25.

159 See entry 59.

160 See entry 40.

161 For a brief survey of the recent recovery of lament, along with discussion of the important contributions of Daniel Migliore and Kathleen Billman, Claus Westermann, and Walter Brueggemann, see Brown and Miller, *Lament*, xiv–xvi. For additional recent treatments and examples of lament, see Bayer, "Toward a Theology of Lament"; Bruce Waltke, James M. Houston, and Erika Moore, *The Psalms as Christian Lament: A Historical Commentary* (Grand Rapids, MI: Eerdmans, 2014); Parsons, *Luther and Calvin on Grief and Lament*; Dennis Ngien, *Fruit for the Soul: Luther on the Lament Psalms* (Minneapolis: Fortress Press, 2015); C. S. Lewis, *A Grief Observed* (Toronto: Bantam Books, 1961); Nicholas Wolterstorff, *Lament for a Son* (Grand Rapids, MI: Eerdmans, 1987); and Billings, *Rejoicing in Lament*.

162 Dennis Ngien has argued that Luther is an exception to this rule. See *Luther on the Lament Psalms*, xxvii (but see xxvi and 176 for qualifications of this argument). Michael Parsons has made a similar case for both Luther and Calvin. See *Luther and Calvin on Grief and Lament*. Ngien and Parsons take issue with Richard A. Hughes, who has argued for a decline of lament in the Reformation. See *Lament, Death, and Destiny* (New York: Peter Lang, 2004), 101–17. While Ngien and Parsons have shown that Hughes overstates his case, at least on my reading of Luther in light of the relevant biblical passages, the Wittenberg reformer still seems to stop short of allowing for the strong protests that one finds in Scripture, especially those in which human beings seek to hold God to accounts (see Ps 44; 80; 88). Luther does, however, allow for what Mary Jane Haemig has called "authentic communication" between Christians and God that involves genuine give-and-take and real honesty about the pain of suffering. See "Luther on Prayer on Authentic Communication," *Lutheran Quarterly* 30 (2016): 307–28 (especially 312–13); and "Prayer as Talking Back to God in Luther's Genesis Lectures," *Lutheran Quarterly* 23 (2009): 270–95 (especially 286 and 289).

163 See Rittgers, *Reformation of Suffering*, 261–62.

164 Johann Christoph would have learned from the Small Catechism that each day, his sinful nature needed to be drowned through repentance and his new nature raised anew with Christ. See "The Sacrament of Holy Baptism, Fourth [Question]," BC, 360.11–12.

165 See especially entry 8.

166 See entries 3, 10, 66, 67, and 70.

167 See entries 12 and 62. On recent debates concerning forensic and effective justification along with the role that union with Christ plays in Luther's soteriology, see Risto Saarinen, "Justification by Faith: The View of the Mannermaa School," and Mark Mattes, "Luther on Justification as Forensic and Effective," in *The Oxford Handbook of Martin Luther's Theology*, edited by Robert Kolb, Irene Dingel, and L'ubomír Batka (Oxford: Oxford University Press, 2015), 254–63 and 264–73, respectively.

168 Luther refers to "der froelich wechßel" in the German version of *The Freedom of a Christian*. See WA 7: 25.34.

169 See entries 14, 26, and 27.

170 See entry 65. On the Lutheran belief in the possibility of losing salvation, see Ronald K. Rittgers, "Early Modern Protestants and the 'Hard Knots' of the Epistle to the Hebrews: A Study of Reformation Certainty," in *Reading Certainty: Exegesis and Epistemology on the Threshold of Modernity. Essays Honoring the Scholarship of Susan E. Schreiner*, edited by Ralph Keen, Elizabeth Palmer, and Daniel Owings (Leiden: Brill, forthcoming).

171 See entries 49 and 69. On prophecy and apocalypticism in late Reformation Lutheranism, see Robin Bruce Barnes, *Prophecy and Gnosis: Apocalypticism in the Wake of the Lutheran Reformation* (Stanford: Stanford University Press, 1988); Philip M. Soergel, *Miracles and the Protestant Imagination: The Evangelical Wonder Book in Reformation Germany* (Oxford: Oxford University Press, 2012); Ken Kurihara, *Celestial Wonders in Reformation Germany* (London: Pickering and Chatto, 2014); and Jürgen Beyer, *Lay Prophets in Lutheran Europe (c. 1550–1700)* (Leiden: Brill, 2017).

172 See entries 71, 73, and 75.

173 See entry 1.

174 On Luther's theology of the cross, see Robert Kolb, "Luther on the Theology of the Cross," *Lutheran Quarterly* 16 (2002): 443–66.

175 See entry 33. See also entry 21 (stanza 6).

176 See entries 14, 16, 31, and 67.

177 See entry 67.

178 See Rittgers, *Reformation of Suffering*.

179 On the place of *Herzensfrömmigkeit* (heart-piety) in the increasingly mystically inflected hymnody of the late sixteenth and seventeenth centuries, a likely source for Johann Christoph's own heart-piety, see Veit, "Das Gesangbuch als Quelle lutherischer Frömmigkeit," 218.

180 See entries 47, 50, and 51.

181 For treatments of Luther's understanding of the "heart," see Bengt Hofmann, *Theology of the Heart: The Role of Mysticism in the Theology of Martin Luther* (Minneapolis: Kirk House, 1998); Birgit Stolt, *Martin Luthers Rhetorik des Herzens* (Tübingen: Mohr Siebeck, 2000), 48–56; and Susan C. Karant-Nunn, *The Personal Luther: Essays on the Reformer from a Cultural Historical Perspective* (Leiden: Brill, 2018), 155–73.

182 See entry 62.

183 See entry 9 and relevant note. This reference to the wounds of Christ is also evidence for Johann Christoph's preference for the mystically inflected Protestant piety theology discussed earlier. On the place of Christ's wounds in this piety, especially as it appears in hymnals of the time, see Veit, "Das Gesangbuch als Quelle lutherischer Frömmigkeit," 218.

184 See especially image 7 and entry 46.

185 For a child's baptism, see the entry for July 10, 1605. For Johann Christoph and his family participating in confession and

Communion, see the entries for June 8, 1605; November 2, 1617; January 10, 1619; March 24 and 25, 1619; and January 15 and 16, 1620. For Anna Maria taking Communion at home while ill, see the entry for June 8, 1605. Johann Christoph records on February 11, 1619, that he called for a pastor to attend to Anna Maria before her death. He does not say if Anna Maria confessed and took Communion, although it is likely that she did, for this was standard Lutheran practice. See Rittgers, *Reformation of Suffering*, 165, 169–70.

186 See entry 10.

187 See entries 9 and 11.

188 See entries 12, 13, and 14.

189 See entries 20 and 33 (legal counsel), along with entries 1, 14, 18, 32 (stanza 7), and 44 (father).

190 See entry 2.

191 See entries 1, 8, 22, and 44. It is interesting to note that Luther included widowhood in his "Household Chart" or "Table of Duties" in the Small Catechism, seeing it as a Christian calling. He did not include widowerhood, though, even though it was a common, if usually shorter lived, experience in his day. See BC, 367.12.

192 See entry 75 (stanza 13).

193 See entry 75 (stanza 8).

194 See entry 1.

195 By way of contrast, in his *Breviate* (1681), Richard Baxter reproduces a number of documents written by his deceased wife, Margaret, choosing to honor her memory and manage his grief by writing a short spiritual biography of her rather than an introspective meditation on his own grief, although the *Breviate* also contains some of the latter. See J. I. Packer, ed., *A Grief Sanctified (Including Richard Baxter's Timeless Memoir of His Wife's Life and Death): Through Sorrow to Eternal Hope* (Wheaton, IL: Crossway, 2002), 66–86.

196 See entry 33.

197 See Theodore G. Tappert, trans. and ed., *Luther: Letters of Spiritual Counsel* (Vancouver, BC: Regent College, 2003 [first published 1960 by Westminster Press, Philadelphia]), 91. For a rhetorical examination of Luther's consolation literature, see Neil Leroux, *Martin Luther as Comforter: Writings on Death* (Leiden: Brill, 2007).

198 See entry 50 (stanza 2). See also entry 45 (stanza 3)

199 It is tempting to seek to relate Johann Christoph's extended lament to modern theories of grief management. While it is possible to see certain points of contact between his experience and, say, Kübler-Ross's classic five stages (denial, anger, bargaining, depression, and acceptance), I have resisted the temptation to develop this comparison. In the first place, I lack the expertise to do so. Beyond this, theories such as Kübler-Ross's are time-bound and do not apply to all human beings in all cultures in all times. For example, early modern Europeans did not live in denial of death as many modern Westerners do—Kübler-Ross's first stage simply does not seem apply to someone like Johann Christoph, who set to contending with his wife's death the very day she passed away. Finally, there is considerable debate today about the appropriateness of any stage theory of grief, and thus it seems unwise to seek to apply a theory that is contested in modern times to the early modern period. See E. Kübler-Ross, *On Death and Dying* (New York: Scribner, 1969); and E. Kübler-Ross and D. Kessler, *On Grief and Grieving: Finding the Meanings of Grief through the Five Stages of Loss* (New York: Scribner, 2005 and 2014). For a critique, see Margaret Stroebe, Henk Schut, and Kathrin Boerner, "Cautioning Health-Care Professionals: Bereaved Persons Are Misguided through the Stages of Grief," *OMEGA—Journal of Death and Dying* 74, no. 4 (2017): 455–73. On the importance of not setting predetermined bounds to grief, see also Dorothy P. Holinger, *The Anatomy of Grief* (New Haven, CT: Yale University Press, 2020).

200 For an example of an early modern Lutheran layman who also turned to the Bible for comfort in the midst of tribulation, see Kaspar von Greyerz, Kim Siebenhüner, and Roberto Zaugg, eds., *Joseph Furttenbach. Lebenslauff 1652–1664* (Cologne: Böhlau, 2013). As his only son lay languishing, Furttenbach, the chief architect in Ulm, read the whole Bible to him over the course of nine months and also copied down myriad consoling verses into multiple notebooks, returning to them for his own solace during his son's illness and again after his death. See pages 22, 173–75, and 240–41.

201 The churches in early modern Nürnberg followed both the traditional lectionary and a *lectio continua* approach to the public reading of Scripture, and Johann Christoph must have experienced both. See the helpful table regarding the shape of the liturgy in Nürnberg's churches in Butler, "Liturgical Music," 374–82. See also Edward T. Hord, "The Reformation of Worship in the City of Nürnberg," *Lutheran Church Review* 11, no. 2 (April 1892): 123–45 (especially 142–43); and Max Herold, *Alt-Nürnberg in seinen Gottesdiensten. Ein Beitrag zur Geschichte der Sitte und des Kultus* (Gütersloh: Bertelsmann, 1890), especially 132–33, 224–26. In the following notes, I have identified places where Johann Christoph draws on the traditional Epistle and Gospel pericopes for Sundays and feast days and also where he references traditional readings for other days of the liturgical year. I have also noted his references to Scripture, both direct and indirect, that do not follow the traditional lectionary and that appear to be more spontaneous. Because the extant sources do not include specific daily or weekly schedules of *lectio continua* readings—they only list the passages without indicating when they should be read—I have not been able to identify biblical references that may be based on this practice in Nürnberg churches. It is also possible that Johann Christoph had developed his own lectionary and was drawing on it in the *Pious Meditations*. On this practice among the nobility, see Jill Bepler, "The Use of Prayer Books at Court: The Example of Wolfenbüttel," in *Gebetsliteratur der frühen Neuzeit als Hausfrömmigkeit. Funktionen und Formen in Deutschland und den Niederlanden*, edited by Ferdinand van Ingen and Cornelia Niekus Moore (Wiesbaden: Harrassowitz, 2001), 50, 52.

202 Luther included most of the Apocrypha in his translation of the Bible but specified that it was not on par with Scripture. On the place of the Apocrypha in Luther's thought, see "Apocrypha," in Denis R. Janz, *The Westminster Handbook to Martin Luther* (Louisville, KY: Westminster John Knox, 2010), 6–7; and Christopher M. Croghan, "Grist for the Mill: Luther on the Apocrypha," *Word & World* 29, no. 4 (Fall 2009): 389–96.

203 On Luther and a life conformed to the stories of Scripture, see Robert Kolb, *Luther and the Stories of God: Biblical Narratives as a Foundation for Christian Living* (Grand Rapids, MI: Baker Academic, 2012).

204 See entries 60 and 61, respectively.

205 See entry 20. On the interpretation of Job in early modern Lutheranism, see Ronald K. Rittgers, "Job in the German Reformation," in *A Companion to Job in the Middle Ages*, edited by Franklin T. Harkins and Aaron Canty (Leiden: Brill, 2017), 254–86.

206 On Lutheran hymnody in the Reformation period, see Rebecca Wagner Oettinger, *Music as Propaganda in the German Reformation* (Aldershot, UK: Ashgate, 2001); Christopher Boyd Brown, *Singing the Gospel: Lutheran Hymns and the Success of the Reformation* (Cambridge, MA: Harvard University Press, 2005); Robin A. Leaver, *Luther's Liturgical Music: Principles and Implications* (Minneapolis: Fortress Press, 2017); and Joseph Herl, *Worship Wars in Early Lutheranism: Choir, Congregation, and Three Centuries of Conflict* (Oxford: Oxford University Press, 2004). Nürnberg was an important center of hymnal publishing in the early modern period. See Lukas Lorbeer, *Die Sterbe- und Ewigkeitslieder in deutschen lutherischen Gesangbüchern des 17. Jahrhunderts* (Göttingen: Vandenhoeck & Ruprecht, 2012), 128–40. Interestingly, none of the many hymnals published there were for official use in the city's churches; congregants sang mostly from memory (see 128).

207 See entries 47–55.

208 WA 35: 483 (no line numbers).

209 See Martin Scheutz and Harald Tersch, eds., *Trauer und Gedächtnis. Zwei österreichische Frauentagebücher des konfessioellen Zeitalters (1597–1611, 1647–1653)* (Vienna: Verlag der österreichischen Akademie der Wissenschaften, 2003), 83–84 (and relevant notes). This volume contains a diary, the "Geraschen Gedächtnisbuch" of the noblewoman Esther von Gera, in which cross- and consolation-songs appear frequently. But unlike Johann Christoph's *Pious Meditations*, the "Geraschen Gedächtnisbuch" takes the form of a traditional diary that is full of entries about quotidian events, occasionally including prayers and hymns. Johann Christoph's work belongs to a different genre (see later discussion).

210 See the earlier discussion of these sources and also the one that follows.

211 Although see n. 54.

212 See the list of Johann Christoph's writings on jurisprudence in ADB 24: 298.

213 Biedermann, CCCLVII, refers to "Hans Christoph Oelhafen," while the Oelhafen *Familienbuch* (313) has "Hans Christoff Oelhafen," but in both the *Pious Meditations* and his *Diarium*, Johann Christoph refers to himself either as "Iohann" or "Johann," and all the acrostics in the former work use *I* for his first name, not *H*. When Johann Christoph has Anna Maria address him in entry 32 (stanza 2) of the *Pious Meditations*, she refers to him as "ICO" (Iohann Christoph Oelhafen), not as Hans. It is possible that he occasionally went by Hans, but there is no evidence for this practice in the extant works from his own quill.

214 For example, see *Ein new Betbüchlein des seligen und teuren Mann Gottes Doctoris Martini Lutheri* (Leipzig, 1577; VD16 L 3544—includes link to online copy.)

215 On Reformation / early modern *Gebetbücher*, see Frieder Schulz, "Gebetbücher III—Reformations- und Neuzeit," TRE 12: 109–19.

216 See the following works by Bepler: "Practicing Piety," 16–17; and "Enduring Loss and Memorializing Women," 142–43. See also the following works by Veit: "Das Gesangbuch in der Praxis Pietatis der Lutheraner," 448; "Die Hausandacht im deutschen Lutherthum," 205; and "Die evangelische 'Hauskirche,'" 204–5.

217 On the intensive reading of devotional works among early modern Protestants along with the subsequent memorization of their contents, see Veit, "Die evangelische 'Hauskirche,'" 201, 202, 205; and Veit, "Die Hausandacht im deutschen Lutherthum," 204.

218 The term *Piae Meditationes* was by no means original to Johann Christoph. It occurs in the titles of a number of early modern printed works of devotion. In the VD16, see B 7429, L 2157, P 2816, R 3294, T 663, and W 1928. In the VD17, see 1:080028G, 3:309785F, 3:604879V, 7:670538A, 12:100170L, 12:100174R, 12:104659L, 12:105981Q, and 23:677689B. Perhaps the most famous example of a work with a similar title is Johann Gerhard's *Meditationes Sacrae*. Johann Christoph may well have been familiar with this work. For a critical edition of Gerhard's work, see Johann Anselm Steiger, ed., *Johann Gerhard: Meditationes Sacrae (1606/7), Lateinisch-Deutsch*, 2 vols. (Stuttgart-Bad Cannstatt: Friedrich Froman, 2000).

219 See Bepler, "Use of Prayer Books at Court," 51, 57–58.

220 For an additional example of an early modern autobiographical source in which hymns, both borrowed and original, appear frequently, see n. 209.

221 I am grateful to Jill Bepler for confirming via email these important differences between Johann Christoph's *Pious Meditations* and the meditational diaries of the Wolfenbüttel nobility.

222 For an autobiographical account from the later Middle Ages of a widower bitterly lamenting his loss, see the *Chronik und Selbstbiographie* of Ludwig von Diesbach (1452–1527) in Horst Wenzel, ed., *Die Autobiographie des späten Mittelalters und der frühen Neuzeit*, vol. 1, *Die Selbstdeutung des Adels* (Munich: Wilhelm Fink, 1980), 92–152 (here, 35–42). Still, in comparison to Johann Christoph's *Pious Meditations*, Diesbach's account of his wife's passing and his subsequent grief is greatly truncated and entirely devoid of artistry. Diesbach's work is a chronicle, after all, not an extended meditation.

223 For a roughly contemporary printed work of consolation that was written under circumstances similar to Johann Christoph's, see Johann Gerhard's *Enchiridion Consolatorium* (1611), which he created after the death of his wife and son (VD17, 12:101598L, 23:245883Q, and 23:332322B). Gerhard provided a German translation in 1626: *Handbüchlein Krefftigen Trostes* (VD17 14:670681L). Unlike the *Pious Meditations*, this work is not a personal lament—rather, it is a lengthy theological and pastoral treatment of how one may face death and the fear it causes. For an earlier example of clerical consolation literature written by a pastor-widower, see Johannes Mathesius, *Leychpredigten Auß dem Fünfftzehenden Capitel der I. Epistel S. Pauli zun Corinthiern* (Nürnberg, 1559; VD16 M 1520; contains links to online copies). In this work, Mathesius describes his grief as a recent widower and also includes a poem he wrote for his deceased wife and sermons he preached to his children at home after their mother's death. See the discussion of this work in Stefan Michel, "Doctrina et consolatio. Zur katechetischen Funktion der Trost- und Leichenpredigt bei Johannes Mathesius (1504–1565)," *Zeitschrift für Kirchengeschichte* 121, no. 2 (2010): 205–22; and Rittgers, *Reformation of Suffering*, 238–40.

224 The vast majority of devotional works, including the most popular ones, appeared in the vernacular in the early modern period.

225 See entry 32 (stanza 10).

226 Carrdus, "*Thränen=Tüchlein für Christliche Eltern*," 11.

227 Throughout the Small Catechism, Luther calls upon the "head of a house"—that is, the father (*Hausvatter*)—to rehearse its contents with the members of the household. See the edition in BC, 345–75.

228 Von Greyerz maintains that early modern self-narratives generally had the authors' posterity in view as the primary audience. See "Observations on the Historiographical Status of Research on Self-Writing," in Ulbrich, von Greyerz, and Heiligensetzer, *Mapping the "I,"* 34. Von Greyerz has also argued that a dominant concern in early modern German and Swiss self-writing was providing evidence of one's religious conformity. See Kaspar von Greyerz, "Religion in the Life of German and Swiss Autobiographers (Sixteenth and Early Seventeenth Centuries)," in *Religion and Society in Early Modern Europe, 1500–1800* (London: George Allen and Unwin, 1984), 223–41.

229 See Stephen Greenblatt, *Renaissance Self-Fashioning: From More to Shakespeare* (Chicago: University of Chicago Press, 1980).

230 *Familienreliquie* is Patrice Veit's term. See "Die Hausandacht im deutschen Lutherthum," 206. See also Veit, "Das Gesangbuch als Quelle lutherischer Frömmigkeit," 218; and Bepler, "Use of Prayer Books at Court," 52.

231 On Andreae, who was the nephew of the famous Jakob Andreae, see TRE 2: 680–83.

232 On the influence of Arndt on Andreae, see Donald R. Dickson, *The Tessera of Antilla: Utopian Brotherhoods and Secret Societies in the Early Seventeenth Century* (Boston: Brill, 1998), 105–6.

233 Dickson, 106. On Rosicrucianism, see TRE 29: 407–13.

234 Dickson, *Tessera of Antilla*, 101.

235 Dickson, 106.

236 See the entries for February 11 and March 24, 1619, in the *Diarium*. See also entry 10 in the *Pious Meditations*.

237 Leibnitz had studied at the Altdorf Academy, earning his master's degree in 1603. On Leibnitz, see Will, *Nürnbergisches Gelehrten-Lexicon*, vol. 2, 416–18; and "Leibnitz, Christoph" in DB.

238 Dickson, *Tessera of Antilla*, 108.

239 *Einfaeltige Antwort vnnd Bittschreiben eines Layen doch Liebhabers der Weißheit an die Hocherleuchte Bruderschafft deß Rosencreutzes* (VD17 23:275405R). See UEN, H00/HIST 403a. The work's author is identified simply as

"L.V." Johann Christoph does not cite this source but clearly quotes from it. See entry 68.

240 *Fama Fraternitatis oder Entdeckung der Bruderschafft deß löblichen Ordens deß Rosen Creutzes*, 1615 (VD17 39:138845M, contains link to online copy). See UEN, H00/HIST 403a.

241 *Sendbrieff oder Bericht an alle, welche von der newen Brüderschafft deß Ordens vom Rosen-Creutz genant, etwas gelesen oder von andern per modum discursus der sachen beschaffenheit vernommen*, 1615 (VD17 14:050875A). See UEN, H00/HIST 403a.

242 *Epistola Ad Illustrem ac Reverendam Fraternitatem Rosae Crucis*, 1615 (VD17 23:286960B, contains link to online copy.) See UEN, H00/HIST 403a.

243 See entry 65.

244 See entry 33, where Johann Christoph refers to "visible angels"—that is, his good friends who have ministered to him. Perhaps these friends were part of the proto-Rosicrucian group proposed here.

245 Johann Christoph had journeyed to England and owned at least one English book, which means he could likely read and understand at least something of the language. Whether he could speak it is unknown. He owned Christopher Marlowe's *The Troublesome Raigne and Lamentable Death of Edward the Second, King of England* (London, 1594), UEN, H00/THL-XVIII 96.

Notes to the Epilogue

1 Portions of this epilogue are reprinted with permission from Rittgers, "Grief and Consolation in Early Modern Lutheran Devotion" (© American Society of Church History, 2012).

2 On Catharina, see Biedermann, CCCCXII.

3 See Harrington, *Faithful Executioner*, 140.

4 See *Diarium*, March 5, 1617. See also entry 75 (stanza 2 and the relevant note) in the *Pious Meditations*.

5 See *Diarium*, January 8, 1619. Johann Christoph refers to Catharina as "meine Fr. Gevatter," which could indicate that she was a relative or even that she was a friend or neighbor, although the primary meaning is "godparent." See "Gevatter" in the FWB. Given that Johann Christoph and Anna Maria named their child Catharina and that Catharina Pfinzing presented Anna Maria with an expensive gift, it is more likely that Catharina Pfinzing was the deceased child's godmother than that she was a relative, friend, or neighbor. Johann Christoph's famous grandfather, Sixtus I Oelhafen, had married into the Pfinzing family—his first wife was Anna Pfinzing (1480–1506; see Biedermann, CCCXXXVIII, CCCXXXIX, CCCCV). But according to Biedermann, there do not appear to have been other marriages between Oelhafens and Pfinzings, at least not in Johann Christoph's father's line. None of Johann Christoph's siblings married a Pfinzing. Thus it does not seem that Johann Christoph and Catharina were related.

6 See Biedermann, CCCCXII.

7 Catharina had married Jacob Imhoff II on May 11, 1605, and Sebastian Imhoff on November 16, 1612. Biedermann (CCCCXII) says that she had no children from either marriage. However, she did have four stepchildren from her first marriage to Jacob by his first wife. Johann Christoph refers to Catharina's stepson in his *Diarium*, almost certainly Jacob III (1600–1649). See the entry for March 7, 1619. On Jacob II and Jacob III, see Biedermann, CCXLV; on Sebastian, see Biedermann, CCXLVIII. Johann Christoph's sometime

traveling companion, Enders Imhoff (see *Pious Meditations*, entry 22 and relevant note), was from yet a different branch of the family. See Biedermann, CCLV.

8 Johann Christoph documents these events in his *Diarium*. See the entries for January 3, 4, 5, and 6, 1620.

9 See entry 76b.

10 Johann Christoph was likely in formal mourning for one year after Anna Maria's death, probably wearing distinctive black clothes during this time. Such was the case with Joseph Furttenbach after the death of his son. See von Greyerz, Siebenhüner, and Zaugg, *Joseph Furttenbach*, 215.

11 See Lansing, *Passion and Order*, 6–7, 76, 154, 187, 220–21; and Karant-Nunn, *Reformation of Feeling*, 65, 193–202.

12 See the discussion of this point in the introduction.

13 See entry 50 (stanza 2). See also entry 45 (stanza 3).

14 For another example of such rewriting of the emotional script, see the discussion of lament in the hymns of Johann Hermann Schein (1586–1630), Johann Christoph's contemporary, in Lorbeer, *Die Sterbe- und Ewigkeitslieder*, 441–47, 481. On the importance of such agency in the human-divine relationship as it concerns lament, see Walter Brueggemann, "The Costly Loss of Lament," *Journal for the Study of the Old Testament* 36 (1986): 57–71 (here 60).

15 See Rittgers, *Reformation of Suffering*, 257–63. See also n. 162 in the Notes to the Introduction.

16 Johann Christoph details the plans for the wedding along with the many gifts the couple received in his *Diarium*. See the entries from January 6 to February 21, 1620. On the wedding, see also Biedermann, CCCCXII; and ADB 24: 298. For the epithalamium, see VD17 39:121666N. For the many wedding songs/poems (*Hochzeitscarmina*) performed or recited in the couple's honor, see NStadtA A 31 Nr. 568 / 1.

17 Biedermann (CCCLVIII) lists only Hans Paul, but on Johann Christoph's final epitaph (see image 9), there are three additional daughters next to Catharina, all with crosses over their heads, indicating that they predeceased him. Judging by their size on the epitaph, it seems that they died young.

18 "CICO" appears above the image of Catharina on Johann Christoph's final epitaph. See image 9.

19 The funeral oration for Johann Christoph, given by his nephew, Tobias Oelhafen (see the following discussion), mentions numerous diaries from the Nürnberg lawyer. See *Oratio Panegyrica*, E r; and Oelhafen, *Zwei Reden*, 14. Aside from his *Diarium* and *Pious Meditations*, there is also his *Stammbuch* in the GNM-HA (Familien: Oelhafen mit Nachlasse Heerwegen, Signatur 24), but it only covers the years 1596–1601 and simply contains signatures and salutations from Johann Christoph's various friends, acquaintances, and traveling companions. Otherwise, I am aware of no additional diary-like sources connected to his name in this or other Nürnberg archives. See also n. 54 in the Notes to the Introduction.

20 From 1602 to 1631, Johann Christoph's various professional obligations took him on over fifty missions throughout the German lands and other parts of Europe. ADB 24: 297; *Deutsches biographisches Archiv*, 221.

21 See Hans Liermann, "Geistiges und gelehrtes Leben im Zeitalter des Barocks und der Aufklärung," in Pfeiffer, *Nürnberg—Geschichte einer europäischen Stadt*, 335; and ADB 24: 297. Johann Christoph's speech was published. See *Actus Publicationis Privilegiorum Doctoralium Universit. Altorph. Norimbergens* (Altdorf, 1624; VD17 23:246845H).

22 On the duties of the *Prokanzler*, see Mährle, *Academica Norica*, 128–29; and Mährle, "Bildungspolitik im Zeichen Melanchthons. Die Familie Camerarius und das höhere Schulwesen in Nürnberg 1526–1624," in *Nürnbergs Hochschule in Altdorf*, edited by Marti and Marti (Cologne: Böhlau, 2014), 34–36.

23 *Deutsches biographisches Archiv*, 221.

24 See *Oratio Panegyrica*, F2 v; and Oelhafen, *Zwei Reden*, 18. Johann Christoph must have spoken his last words in German, as the Latin oration given after his death records the words in both Latin and German, a rarity in this oration.

25 *Oratio Panegyrica*. For an abridged German version, see Oelhafen, *Zwei Reden*. On Tobias, see "Oelhafen von Schöllenbach, Tobias" in the DB; Friedrich, *Bibliographie*, 1013, 1017–20; and Imhoff, *Berühmte*

Nürnberger, 180. For Saubert's epicedium for Johann Christoph, see *Oratio Panegyrica*, G 4 v.

26 The grave number is 2125. See Peter Zahn, *Die Inschriften der Friedhöfe St. Johannis, St. Rochus und Wöhrd zu Nürnberg [Teilband III, I: 1609–1650]* (Wiesbaden: Dr. Ludwig Reichert, 2013), 382–84.

27 The artist for the epitaph was Jakob Weinmann. On him, see Manfred H. Grieb, *Nürnberger Künstlerlexikon. Bildende Künstler, Kunsthandwerker, Gelehrte, Sammler, Kulturschaffende und Mäzene vom 12. bis zur Mitte des 20. Jahrhunderts*, vol. 3 (Munich: Saur, 2011), 1641–42.

28 It is interesting that Johan Christoph did not have a final version of the epitaph prepared that included some of his later honors, especially his pro-chancellorship of the University of Altdorf. There is a plate on the epitaph after "ANNOS" that was intentionally left blank at its creation. His years of service as legal counsel to emperors, the Duke of Saxony, members of the imperial nobility, and Nürnberg were to have been supplied but, curiously, never were.

Person Index

Page numbers in *italics* refer to figures.

Scripture Index

Old Testament

Apocrypha

New Testament

Subject Index

Page numbers in *italics* refer to figures.